HEALING MEDICARE

HEALING MEDICARE
Managing Health System Change the Canadian Way

Michael B. Decter

CANADIAN CATALOGUING IN PUBLICATION DATA
Decter, Michael B.
Healing medicare: managing health system change the Canadian way
Includes bibliographical references and index.
ISBN 0-9698064-1-8 (bound) ISBN 0-9698064-0-X (pbk.)

1. Medical care - Canada 2. Public health - Canada 3. Medical policy - Canada
4. Health planning - Canada I. Title

RA449.D43 1994   362.1'0971   C94-931685-7

Excerpts from the *Living Will* copyright Centre for Bioethics, University of
Toronto, used with permission.
Excerpts from the work of Brendan Kearney copyright Brendan Kearney, used
with permission.
Excerpts from the *KF News*, vol. 26, No. 2, copyright the King's Fund, U.K.

Excerpts from "The Economics of Self-Medication," *Social Policy and
Administration*, vol. 19, No. 3, copyright Professor Michael Cooper

Editor: Ann Decter
Copy editor: Angela Hryniuk
Cover design: Denise Maxwell
Layout: Heather Guylar

Dedication

For Una and Percy Decter, my parents, one a socialist politician and the other an orthopaedic surgeon, both of whom struggled for Medicare's creation during their lives.

And for my children, Geneviève and Riel, and my wife, Lucille, for whom I continue the struggle.

Contents

Preface

Medicare is among the most cherished of Canadian achievements. After twenty-five years, the elimination of finance as a barrier between individual citizens and health care services remains a true Canadian success story. Our pride in Medicare is vitally important. It is a national achievement that compares well with all other industrialized countries. It is as good or better than the others. It is home-grown, made the Canadian way, modelled on our values and not on the importation of a British or American system.

Yet, change is underway in Canadian Medicare; reform which alarms many and sparks emotional debate. Assumptions about what determines our health, and how we organize our health care delivery system, are undergoing profound, necessary rethinking and re-engineering. These changes are crucial to the future of health care in Canada, and on-going evaluation of this reform process is essential. We must monitor whether reforms are eroding or improving our health care system. Are we healing Medicare or harming it?

This book is about managing change. It is a journey, a search for the outlines of Canada's next health care system as it emerges from the struggles of healing professionals, managers, government leaders, researchers and teachers. No lofty utopian goal is intended and no precise description of the future shape of health care is offered. This is not a book about theory. Practical advice and advocacy for constructive and necessary reform are the objectives. Concrete examples of successful modifications illustrate the effectiveness of innovation and an open quest for a better way of doing things.

This book outlines two fundamental shifts — different but interwoven — happening in Canada. The first is a revolution in how we assess the real determinants of our health. Is it the formal health care delivery system or the broader way we live and organize our society that allows us to live longer, healthier lives? Do more doctors and hospitals make us healthier or just treat us more extensively when we are ill? The second revolution is in how we view health care services. There is a dramatic shift from an unquestioning provision of inputs, to a mounting and sustained questioning of outcomes. A debate rages about appropriateness of care, about what works, and how well it works. Consumers no longer take a backseat to providers in the struggle for resource allocation. Re-engineering the supply side of health services is underway. Managing the demand for health services is the next key challenge.

This is not a sterile book of policy concepts. It is a chronicle of the efforts of tens of thousands of Canadians — from Ministers of Health to ward nurses — to keep our health care system affordable and of high quality through constructive change. If I have one clear hope in writing these ideas and experiences it is that we may learn from each other how to succeed in saving our Medicare. We need to accelerate our learning. Providing health care to all Canadians on the basis of needs is a proud, national accomplishment, but sustaining it into the twenty-first century will be hard, hard work.

Complacency and self-congratulation will not serve us well in a difficult financial and policy environment. Resting on our laurels will not maintain public confidence. Openness to change and to learning is essential. The preservation of Medicare is not a task for museum curators who can capture a glorious past like a fossil in amber. Medicare was born out of a struggle for a better way. Healthy Medicare means waging a continuing struggle to serve the larger purpose of the nation. We need the advice and determination of all those who have invested their working lives in health care. We need the nurses as well as the doctors, the workers as well as the managers, the orderlies as well as the researchers. We need leaders in business and labour, as well as those in government and in our universities. We need to care and struggle to succeed. Leadership and vision, not curatorship and hindsight, will enable Medicare to continue.

Quality and Affordability

Many commentators — Canadians and non-Canadians — have fallen into the trap of believing that affordable cost and quality are mutually exclusive objectives. Quality is quite wrongly seen by some as something added on at extra cost. This is not my view. Quality flows from how well the system is organized, from how both consumers and providers are educated, and how individual decisions about care are implemented. The United States spends 35% more of its GNP on health care than Canada, yet this additional spending does not result in better quality medical care or improved health outcomes. Reforms across Canada provide clear evidence that others quality and affordability can be improved *simultaneously*. Day by day quality and affordability are joining the five statutory principles of the *Canada Health Act* as practical foundations of our approach to health care. The right question is not whether we can afford Medicare, it is how can we better allocate resources within health.

Health Economic Development

In Canada, we have a high standard of living. We are no longer able to sustain our living standard by selling wheat or nickel or other natural resources. Canada has developed valuable expertise in various aspects of health care, including health care products, expertise we can export. We can concurrently help the rest of the world to be healthier and boost our economy.

Health care systems are rooted in the culture and values of the society they serve. In 1969, my parents drove me to Boston to begin studies at Harvard College. As we crossed the border I saw a New Hampshire license plate with its very American motto "Live Free or Die," our's read "Friendly Manitoba." I knew I had arrived in another country. The American Declaration of Independence premise of "life, liberty and the pursuit of happiness" contrasts drastically with the Canadian constitutional tradition of "peace, order and good government." The values of Canadians are as deeply entrenched in our health care system as they are in our constitution. The transformation we are undergoing must continue to respect those values.

Healing Medicare is a hopeful book, because I am an optimist about the prospects for our health as individuals and for the health of a reformed Medicare. I draw my confidence from my encounters with the thousands of individual Canadians who work in health care, whether as part-time volunteer hospital trustees, Ministers of Health, ambulance attendants, nurses or doctors. Each contact has left me filled with respect and hope.

We are managing change in Canadian Medicare in our own very distinct classically Canadian fashion. Change is taking place at a different pace with a slightly different approach in each province. Quebec is unique in how it's implementing change in health care.

We invest vast energy debating these changes in each provincial legislatures and in the media. The Government of Canada is somewhat uncertain of its role. There is great, loud political debate. All of this is very Canadian and quite healthy.

There is much to be done. Canadians have the will and the talent to succeed in reforming, healing and sustaining Canadian Medicare. We also have an obligation and an opportunity to use our expertise in the larger world beyond our borders to improve the health of the other five billion people with whom we share this planet. There is urgency to both challenges.

Introduction:
Our Health as a Nation

Over the past forty years life expectancy has improved more than during the entire previous span of human history.... Smallpox which killed more than five million annually in the 1950's, has been eradicated entirely.... Vaccines have dramatically reduced the occurrence of polio and measles.... Despite these improvements enormous health problems remain.... By 2000 the growing toll from (AIDS) in developing countries could easily rise to more than 1.8 million deaths annually.... Tobacco related deaths from heart disease and cancers alone are likely to double by the first decade of the next century, to two million a year, and, if present smoking patterns continue, they will grow to more than twelve million a year in developing countries in the second quarter of the next century.[1]

The story of the first era of Medicare belongs to Tommy Douglas in his role as Premier of Saskatchewan from 1944 to 1961. As a child, the charity of a doctor enabled Tommy Douglas to avoid permanent damage to his leg. Later in life, the political leader created Medicare amidst the relative poverty of Saskatchewan. Driven by the dream of saving others, not from the charity of physicians, but from the necessity of that charity, Premier Douglas introduced universal hospital insurance in Saskatchewan in 1948. The Government of Canada followed in 1957 with the *Hospital and Diagnostic Services Act*, which provided 50/50 cost-sharing to the provinces. By 1961, the entire country had this coverage. When the Co-operative Commonwealth Federation (CCF) — later the New Democratic Party (NDP) — Government of Saskatchewan endured a doctors' strike in 1962

---

1   *Investing In Health, The 16th Annual Development Report of The World Bank*, 1993, Overview, p.1.

to introduce government insurance of physician services, the federal government felt the pressure. The Royal Commission on Health Services, headed by Justice Emmett Hall, prepared the blueprint, and, by 1968, Canada had the Medical Care Act and 50/50 cost-sharing. By 1972, all provinces were in. Canadian Medicare, as we know it, was born.

But, there was a flaw in Medicare. The design, with government as the sole insurer, did not solve the leadership question. Nor did it ensure the dynamism to change and evolve. In 1982, Tommy Douglas reflected on Medicare's progress: "When we began to plan Medicare, we pointed out that it would be in two phases. The first phase would be to remove the financial barrier between those giving the service and those receiving it. The second phase would be to reorganize and revamp the delivery system — and of course, that's the big item. It's the big thing we haven't done yet." [2]

In 1994, Canada has already entered the second era of reorganizing and revamping Medicare. A rational starting point for this second phase of Canadian Medicare is to examine health goals as individuals, and as a nation. Once they are established, we can discuss how to behave and what to invest to achieve these goals. It is also instructive to look beyond the borders of Canada. Which of our goals are shared by other nations, and which are uniquely Canadian?

The key story of the second era may already have taken place in Saskatchewan. In that province, Health Minister Louise Simard converted fifty small, rural hospitals to health centres and transferred the budgets to regional boards, in order to invest in health services. Saskatchewan galvanized other provinces to question what promotes good health and whether health services need to be hospital-based. [3]

Some Canadians doubt that Medicare, stable as it has been, can be made to change fast enough to survive. Their sense of the impossibility of this task often derives from earlier, failed attempts to lead change before it was seen as absolutely necessary. They will

---

2 T.C. (Tommy) Douglas, Interview, 1982, as quoted in *Alberta Roundtable Report*, Government of Alberta, August, 1993, p. 17.
3 Saskatchewan's hospital situation, it should be noted, was more extreme than that of other provinces. For a population of under one million people, Saskatchewan was operating 137 separate hospitals prior to reform or about one hospital for every 7000 residents compared to Ontario with 10.8 million people and 223 hospitals for a ratio of one hospital for every 50,000 residents. Hospital consolidation is an active issue in Ontario, Saskatchewan and virtually every other province.

not be the last reformers to become casualties of the status quo in Canadian health care. My considered view is that necessary chan￼es are already underway in every Canadian jurisdiction and they are *essential. It is not reform that will bring about the demise of Medicare but the absence of it.*

This book follows four broad themes in the healing of Canadian Medicare and its evolution into a dynamic - and therefore sustainable — system for the next century:

- Re-engineering care delivery
- Restructuring health work, re-skilling and redeploying health workers
- Taking control of individual health and health care
- Health economic development

This agenda for action can achieve the affordability and quality improvements our nation needs from Medicare. The road ahead is not easy or smooth, but the map has been planned and charted by the ideas, advocacy and actions of thinkers and leaders at every level in Canadian health. We only need to look carefully at the evidence and learn from our experiences.

The road ahead cannot be travelled simply by health ministers and their officials. No one group has the legal, intellectual or moral authority to affect the needed reforms alone. We need a much broader base of understanding and popular acceptance. We need requisite political will, leadership and citizen support. Changes require local decisions about how health services are to be delivered, by whom, to whom and where, in the future. Upward delegation to the political level will, in most instances, delay change, making it more abrupt and painful when it finally occurs. Health ministers and premiers have an obligation to provide leadership. But leadership alone will not be enough. The tens of thousands of Canadians who serve as hospital trustees, members of health boards and directors of health organizations must understand and support change. So must the hundreds of thousands of workers who deliver health care services. Without their active support, our elected leaders will have no one to lead.

In a period of change, leaders are among the first casualties. The accelerated turnover of Canadian health ministers, both provincially and federally, reflects the anxiety and political turmoil which accompanies altering our view of health. New methods of leading and consulting are evolving as governments seek to share the difficult burden of public policy choices. We must understand our health care history and learn from it.

Health and health care are different concepts, requiring different goals. For health, a broader agenda is crucial. Our population needs positive action on the issues that pose the greatest threat to life expectancy and health status: unemployment, cigarette smoking, substance abuse, Aboriginal impoverishment and social disintegration, obesity, adolescent suicide and AIDS. As social issues, not illnesses, these cannot be cured by doctors in hospitals. They must, however, be the core of our approach to investing in our health as a nation. Through determined efforts in our communities and workplaces, redirected spending and new laws, we can *improve health where it is really decided.*

In Canada, we invest in health in a myriad of different ways. As individuals when we join a fitness club, buy a bicycle, our weekly groceries or a car, we invest in our health. Some of our investments are subtle. The purchase of a desk chair may have a long-term impact on our back, qualifying it as yet another health investment.

At the community level, housing bylaws, fire regulations and public health initiatives are all health investments. At the provincial government level, investing in health occurs not only when the health ministry budget is shaped but also when decisions are made about housing programmes, environmental regulations and road safety. How should we make these investments? Should we be guided by history and politics or by health evidence? Should we please the crowd by doing what is immediately popular or is there a better way? Governments not only expend financial capital raised by taxation or borrowing, they also expend their "political capital" or credibility, by leading change in society. Narrow interests, hostile to change, are always noisier and more disruptive than the broad public at large. Seat belt legislation was very unpopular with some segments of society when it was introduced. Toughening restrictions on smoking is a continuing challenge. For governments, these are investments, not of tax dollars, but of even scarcer political capital. They are also key investments in determining our future health.

We have success stories to learn from in this field. Automobiles, long a source of pollution, death and injury, have been redesigned and vastly improved. Product safety changes, forced by law and consumers, are only part of this story. Safer roads and greater success in regulating dangerous drivers are also important levers. Non-coercive sanctions, such as altered societal attitudes, are essential tools.

Much remains to be done in restoring the health of our environment, through combatting tobacco use and improving the health of our most impoverished citizens. Investing in health must rank as the most important of our societal goals.

For nearly forty years, our attention has been focused on building an excellent, modern care delivery system. In that period, about half the lifetime of the average person born in our country, life expectancy has grown more than in the previous 5,000 years. Are these two realities connected? Is it really the health care system which has given us greater health status and longer lives? Credit belongs mainly to improvements in income, diet, housing, sanitation and other public policy and social factors. The state of our health is a social issue. And the state of our health determines, to a significant degree, the demands placed upon our health care system.

Re-Engineering Care Delivery

Rapid progress in technology, strained public finances and shifting public expectations are all strong drivers of re-engineering in the care delivery system. Frustrated consumers want a health care system that meets their needs in a high quality, timely fashion. Weary taxpayers want an affordable, cost-efficient system. Technology can help with both tasks, but significant changes in how we do business will be necessary. Simply automating current practices is not evolution. We need to re-engineer care delivery, starting with the basic questions: what are we trying to achieve and how can we achieve it? It means starting over and rethinking the system, using technology as a powerful tool.

Re-structuring/Re-skilling/Re-deploying

How we make change is as important as the change we make. Our humanity demands we pay careful attention to Canadian health care workers, providing opportunities for them to gain the skills to flourish in the new Medicare. Forcing thousands of skilled health workers into unemployment will damage individuals and the nation. Yet any attempt to resist financial and technological pressures, in support of an employment status quo, is doomed to failure. There is a better way, which will require greater cooperation among workers, managers, bargaining agents and governments.

Mechanisms and solid workable approaches are emerging to

create a more skilled *and* flexible workforce in health care. We need to learn from the early successes emerging in hospitals and communities across Canada. We need to ensure that people who work in health care are able to gain the skills to cope with changes in where and how health care is delivered.

Taking Control

Assuming greater personal responsibility for our health and health care is a necessary ingredient in healing Medicare. By taking control of our own health we can live longer in good health. The simple steps are well-known. Stop smoking (or don't start), eat a healthy diet, exercise, and you are well along the road to maintaining health. We can also take more responsibility as consumers of care services by becoming informed decision-makers. We need to ask more questions of health care providers and insist on more and better answers. Effectiveness of treatment depends not only on the skill of the provider, but, also, on the fit between patient circumstance and outcome. Just as we have learned to conserve energy, we must now learn to access health care services, when needed and with full knowledge of consequences. We have an obligation to become *informed* consumers.

Health Economic Development

Health care is one of the major activities in every nation on earth. Although Canadian Medicare should not be slavishly copied from elsewhere, we can learn from experiences in the United States, in Europe and even in the less developed nations of the south.

We also need to heal the Canadian economy. Unemployed Canadians, particularly 1.5 million unemployed Canadians, are a large health problem. Developing a greater capacity to export our excellence in health, by making more health products in Canada and by expanding research, can be a strong contributor to enhanced Canadian economic renewal. Health economic development can improve our economic performance and create jobs in Canada. Jobs and wealth are major determinants of health.

Why Less of the Same Will Not Work

In *The Learning Organization*, Peter Senge points out that sawing a large elephant in two does not give you two smaller elephants.[4] I would add that starving a large elephant will not leave you with a smaller but healthy one, either.

We need to change *how* we do things in Canadian health care, not simply reduce what we do. Less of the same will not work. We need to focus on how we define health and pursue it and how we deliver care and measure its outcome. Simply doing a little less of everything would give us a very expensive and wholly unsatisfactory outcome.

Bad Ideas Which Will Do Harm

There are a few very dangerous ideas loose in the health debate, ideas with surface appeal that camouflage potentially damaging impact. The most seductive and dangerous is the thought that more money will solve the problem. If government can't afford to pay *all* the costs, the refrain runs, why not let consumers pay some of the cost? We already have the second most expensive health care system on the planet. We don't need more money, but better value for the existing spending. Adding more money works to postpone, however briefly, needed reforms.

User fees, often proposed as a funding mechanism, would cause a fundamental and negative shift in the basis of our health care system. There are two foundations on which nations have constructed health and health care delivery systems: ability-to-pay and ability-to-benefit. The American system, which the Clinton administration is trying to reform, is based on ability-to-pay. Our Canadian system is based on ability-to-benefit. In the United States, the care you receive — even the decision about whether you receive care or not — is based upon whether you, or someone else can pay for it. In Canada, the decision about care is based on need. There is no way to "co-mingle" these principles successfully. Once user fees are introduced, there is an inevitable shift towards a mixed or two-tier system. Ability-to-pay takes precedence. How ironic it would be for the Canadian health care system to mirror the American system at the very point when the Americans have decided to shift toward the Canadian ability-to-benefit or, in President Clinton's terms, health

4   Peter Senge, *The Fifth Discipline, The Art & Practice of the Learning Organization* (New York: Doubleday, 1990) p. 66.

security, model. Adam Smith's invisible hand works less well when it is wearing a surgical glove. It is neither invisible nor efficient.

Another idea given currency is the Oregon Plan.[5] While the Oregon Plan may constitute progress for Oregon, it offers an old direction for Canada. Concerned about citizens with no coverage, the State of Oregon decided to rank necessary medical procedures. Through a massive public consultation process it created a list of services for which all residents of Oregon would be insured. Oregon chose to draw the line on the list of procedures, rather than on the list of those eligible for coverage. This is accurately viewed as the introduction of the ability-to-benefit principle into the American health care system. Canada may have problems with providing each and every Canadian in our vast territory with access to the same quality of services, but we do not have any groups without coverage. Coverage for all medically necessary services is a basic principle of Medicare. That the definition of medically necessary is undergoing debate and examination in Canada should not cause us to confuse our situation with that of Oregon.

Oregon-style consultation has lessons for Canada, but our situation is fundamentally different. Adopting their approach would be a huge step backward. Canada can go backward and reinstate financial barriers to access or forward and reform the health care system. It is an easy choice.

Technology is often offered as a possible panacea. Like other tools, it depends on how it is applied. Technology without compassion is a bad idea; technology with compassion is a good one. For example, we need to examine whether the technology of respirators and heart pumps is being used to restore life or to prolong death in an intrusive and undesired way. What is the impact of a new information system? Does it assist better patient care? Technology itself, neither possesses or lacks compassion. How we use it determines its outcome. It's not wise to greet each new technology as a universal good and embrace it unquestioningly. A thorough assessment of new technology and thoughtful consideration of the ethics of applying it, is.

5   *Prioritization of Health Services,* A Report to the Governor and Legislature, Oregon. Health Services Commission 1993.

Health Goals

Focus on health goals is emerging as the new religion of international development on health. Among international development issues, health has gained prominence with the World Bank. It has agreed to lend money for health purposes and devoted its entire sixteenth annual *World Development Report* (1993) to considerations of health. Closer to home, health goals and visions of health have had prominence in the provinces pursuing health care reforms.

Advocacy for broader health goals and a wider view of health has been with us for two decades. The *Lalonde Report* in 1974 and the *Alma-Ato Conference on Health for All* in 1978 set a framework. The *Alma-Ato Conference* concluded with the goal of:

> The attainment of all of the peoples of the world by the year 2000 of a level of health that will permit them to lead a socially and economically productive life.

An array of Canadian royal commissions, task forces and advisory councils have each made a persuasive case for a vision of health based on broad population health, rather than a narrow treatment of illness. We are gradually embracing these views and acting upon them. Seat belt and tobacco control legislation have their roots in this fertile soil.

Population Health and Health Care Delivery

In Canada, debate about health is generally framed in the terms population health or determinants of health. Depending on provincial jurisdiction and analysis, the argument runs that, while the health delivery system is a contributor to the health status and life expectancy of a population, far larger contributions are made by socioeconomic factors. Some of these are: income and its distribution, healthy public policy, the safety of the environment, quality of air, water, and lifestyle choices about consumption of alcohol, tobacco and other substances, as well as diet.

The determinants of health view points to the significant allocation — generally over 90% — of financial resources to the delivery system, and argues that Canada is over-invested in health care delivery at the expense of progress on the other determinants of health. We spend our health dollars treating illness, not developing health. However, Canadian governments do spend significant dollars in housing, education, transportation. Ministries of Health are not the sole players when it comes to investments in health. Advocates of a broad determinants of health approach cite significant differences in health outcomes based on socio-economic status.

At an historic 1992 meeting of all of Canada's Federal, Provincial and Territorial Health and Finance Ministers, a presentation made by the Government of Manitoba indicated that the poorest 20% of Canadians would gain thirteen years of disability-free life if their socio-economic status was the same as the top 40% of income earners in the population. This contrasted with gains of three to five years which could be achieved by the complete eradication of all forms of cancer or heart disease. Evidence of this sort has been available for a number of years. A focus on broader socio-economic factors is now gaining currency, as fiscal pressures force politicians to restrict investment in the health care delivery system.

Public health advocates have suggested that the population health view is simply a rediscovery of the basic principles of public health in Canada. A recent Government of Manitoba document,[6] sets out the argument in this fashion:

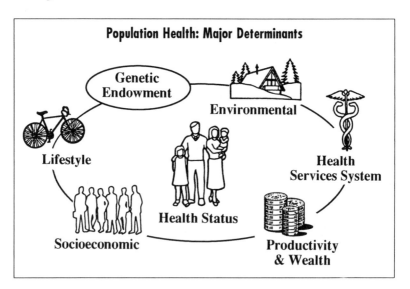

Population Health: Major Determinants

Genetic Endowment

Environmental

Lifestyle

Health Services System

Health Status

Socioeconomic

Productivity & Wealth

Ontario captured the same basic concepts in a vision statement and related health goals.

6   *Quality Health for Manitobans: The Action Plan*, published by the Government of Manitoba, May, 1992, p.9.

A Vision of Health

We see an Ontario in which people live longer in good health, and disease and disability are progressively reduced. We see people empowered to realize their full health potential through a safe non-violent environment, adequate income, housing, food and education, and a valued role to play in family, work, and the community. We see people having equitable access to affordable and appropriate health care regardless of geography, income, age, gender or cultural background. Finally, we see everyone working together to achieve better health for all.

Health Goals for Ontario

Goal 1   Shift the emphasis to health promotion and disease prevention.

Goal 2   Foster strong and supportive families and communities.

Goal 3   Ensure a safe, high-quality physical environment.

Goal 4   Increase the number of years of good health for the citizens of Ontario by reducing illness, disability and premature death.

Goal 5   Provide accessible, affordable, appropriate health services for all.[7]

In Canada, there has been an increased emphasis on *healthy* public policy, following previously explored roads such as compulsory seat belt laws and the much harsher penalties for drinking and driving. New initiatives likely to proceed in some provinces include compulsory use of bicycle helmets, further emphasis on reduction of access to tobacco for young people and diminishing second-hand smoke in various environments. Most Canadian public transportation modes — airplanes, buses, trains — are now largely smoke-free.

Generally, these intrusions by government are met with initial public resistance and become accepted social values. Most governments have newly-appointed senior officials responsible for healthy public policy or population health. In most Canadian jurisdictions, there is a strong emphasis on shifting from investment in the delivery system to a greater focus on population health. Investments in health

7   Health goals adopted by the Government of Ontario in 1992 on the advice of the Premier's Council on Health Well Being and Social Justice.

promotion, prevention and healthy public policy are being pursued at both the national and provincial level.

Over the past twenty years a series of commissions, task forces, studies and reports have concluded that:

- The formal health care system is only one factor that affects the health of the population. More important factors are our wealth as a society and how we distribute it, our physical environment, lifestyle choices, educational opportunities, housing, social supports and employment.
- The existing health system concentrates too much on treatment, and the necessary investments in population health are not being made.

What Health Goals Are Not — Eternal Life and Medical Myth-Making

We have been convinced by miracle technology dreams and endless television portrayals of valiant surgeons restoring life that immortality is a goal just beyond the grasp of modern medicine. It is not. Our expectations, and the burdens we place on health goals, must take reality into account. For our species, at this evolutionary point, a life span of seventy to eighty years in reasonable health is achievable. The factors which deprive billions of our fellow human beings of the reasonable expectation of a healthy life are rooted in economic disparities. Poverty is our most damaging global epidemic. Within Canada, our poor are disproportionately our sick.

Our health goals must focus our resources on the greatest good to the greatest number while respecting extraordinary cases. If we are true to our fundamental principle of directing health and health care resources on ability-to-benefit, then our goals must reflect that core value. We must rank comprehensive immunization, safer automobiles, a less violent society and other health goals that can benefit our children and their children, ahead of vastly expensive technologies that prolong dying without gains to quality of life. How to establish, and, more importantly, how to gain acceptance of such broad goals is a challenge faced by each health minister in Canada.

Goals in Health Care Delivery Reform

What should be our health *reform* goal in Canada? What will determine whether we are able to look back on this period, from the vantage point of the late 1990s, and say we made change that led us back to a stable, efficient health and health care? What will cause us to say we are proud of our work in managing change, that it reinforced our core values and principles? It really turns on being able to simultaneously improve both quality and affordability.

The turbulence you see in every provincial jurisdiction as governments, the medical profession and hospitals, try different approaches, is a process of change that will lead us to health care services that are affordable and of better quality. That statement clearly puts me in the category of optimists. I would probably have had trouble getting up in the morning and going to work as Ontario's Deputy Minister of Health if I were not an optimist, because the obstacles to change are formidable.

There are several themes to this shift, all of them essential. There has been a tendency to think we are going to find one answer. That total quality management or clinical epidemiology or determinants of health is *the* answer. We like to think some magic equation or formula is going to get us out of our difficulties. I am not optimistic about magic. We are going to have to work very hard to bring about transformation or improvements that will let us look back at this period as one of constructive reform. There is not likely to be an end to reform. Continuous improvements of quality and a continuous pressure for affordability are most probably permanent features.

Population health requires a revitalized public health system. One of the less-featured aspects of Canada is that we have had historically a very high quality public health system. That system is seen by many as a building block in an approach to healthy communities. Seeing health as an environmental issue, and environment as a health issue, we move forward. It is crucial for communities and individuals, to have a sense of responsibility. Health is not simply a repair business after the fact. Health has a lot to do with individual lifestyle choices: how safe our communities are; how well-designed our roads and cars are; and other aspects of our broader public policy. Within government, it means that the health ministry must advocate in other ministries for change in policies that go to the root causes.

Another theme is clinical epidemiology. Across Canada, in virtually every province, governments are finding ways of establishing, whether it is through commissions or institutes, benchmarking or quality processes, clinical guidelines (essentially applied clinical epidemiology) for the practice of medicine. This cannot be achieved through government dictates that have no credibility with the medical profession. It can be accomplished, rather, by having the best available talent that we have (and we have a good deal of it in this country) communicate with both providers and consumers. This will certainly impact on the knowledge and practice of medicine.

Our health goals underwent a great historic narrowing from the early broad goals of public health to a focus on health care. We are now in the second long wave, a return to comprehensive health goals.

Risk-Taking

Getting to a sustainable future will be neither easy nor smooth. Quality leadership is essential. Professional risks are real for those who lead change and those who support it. Improvements can stall, and those in favour will be discredited and hurt. Risks must not be taken carelessly or recklessly, but they must be taken. Without Tommy Douglas taking a risk, without Emmett Hall and Claude Castonguay possessing courage and vision, we could not have built Medicare.

Stop Blaming

There are no bad guys in the Canadian health care dilemma. We are here with the best of intentions. To quote the famous medical ethicist and philosopher, Pogo:

We have met the enemy
And he is us.

We need to reach beyond the search for villains and into the healing process.

Optimism in a Time of Transition

Change is stressful. One good definition of health is the ability of the organism — be it a person, an organization or a nation — to cope with change. Optimism is an important ingredient in dealing with change and a key ingredient in health. Thankfully, it is also somewhat contagious.

Confidence is part of the necessary optimism for this transition. Confidence to venture along the road of change, without a detailed map, without knowing every twist and turn in advance. Our leaders will be from among us, not delivered from on high. As Peter Senge notes:

> Most of the outstanding leaders I have worked with are neither tall, nor especially handsome; they are often mediocre public speakers; they do not stand out in a crowd; and they do not mesmerize an attending audience with their brilliance or eloquence. Rather, what distinguishes them is the clarity and persuasiveness of their ideas, the depth of their commitment and their openness to continually learning more. They do not have the answer. [8]

Confidence, optimism and openness to learning new ways of working are required attributes to heal Medicare. There are more intelligent questions to be asked than there are answers offered. We will learn by doing, by making mistakes and learning from them. And it is not beyond reason that we might enjoy the challenge of change, rather than facing it with grim determination to survive. Greater mastery over our work should be both a source of pride and joy to each of us.

We have started to build some of the necessary machinery, but it is far from finished. Change might bruise some of the people involved: elected officials and those who serve them; those that deliver care; and those that receive it. It will take some very broad support in our Canadian society to get the job done. I remain an optimist because I see the beginnings of the kind of change that we need.

Good Stuff To Read

World Development Report — 1993 Investing in Health-World Development Indicators published for the World Bank by Oxford University Press, New York, June 1993, is rich in data and analysis. Offering an overview of health and health systems on a worldwide base, it is required reading for those serious about understanding health and health care policy in both the developed and developing worlds. The decision as to which health investments to make is aided by the analytical tools provided. The report advocates sensible investments in public health and essential clinical services.

---

8   Op. cit., Senge p. 359.

The advocacy of a greater private sector role in clinical services is the sole bit of dubious advice which may reflect the World Bank's private enterprise roots and the current American fascination with managed competition. There is certainly no evidence to support this particular advocacy. The notion that a competitive health insurer model will produce more money for health care is debunked by every serious comparison of Canada and the United States whether conducted by the U.S. General Accounting Office or others. Single payer systems are efficient in administrative terms and should not be discarded as an option by the developing world simply because the United States has moved past the point where vested interests can be overcome in favour of a single payer approach.

Report of the Ontario Premier's Council on Health Strategy. This report and the related reports of the Premier's Council which have evolved to the Premier's Council on Health, Well-Being and Social Justice are solid approaches to broader population health goals. The advice of the Premier's Council was adopted as policy by the Government of Ontario.

Restructuring Canada's Health Services System — How Do We Get from Here to There? Proceedings of The Fourth Canadian Conference on Health Economics, edited by Raisa B. Deber and Gail G. Thompson, University of Toronto Press, 1992, is a rich, well-edited collection of interesting insights and powerful data. It captures valuable drivers of change and a variety of perspectives in a series of readable presentations. A solid, one-stop-shop on Canadian health care issues.

Part 1

Re-Engineering the Care Delivery System

Whatever the grand scheme of things, I hope many people in health services will recognize that small scale change, personal involvement and acceptance of responsibility, some creativity, imagination and friendliness are likely to make things better, and unlikely to make things worse. So far, a better idea eludes us. [1]

Fiona Hastings
Beyond Provider Dominance

Of our twin challenges — investing in health and re-engineering our current health care delivery systems — re-engineering is the more difficult task. Achieving affordability and quality at the same time requires significant change in the way we do business. We may like the results of reform but no one really likes the process. Change means uncertainty, unease and even fear. Exceptional leaders who enjoy change, often have the courage to accept its necessity and decide to have some fun along the way. We will meet a few of these remarkable people, Canadians who are leading reform in health care.

Conceptually, re-engineering the system requires more dramatic reconstruction than simple marginal improvements. As Michael Hammer and James Champy note in *Re-engineering the Corporation,* "When someone asks us for a quick definition of business re-engineering, we say that it means 'starting over.'" Re-engineering doesn't mean tinkering with what already exists or making incremental changes that leave basic structures intact.[2] Instead, Champy and Hammer define it as "the fundamental rethinking and radical redesign of business processes to achieve dramatic improvements in critical, contemporary measures of performance, such as cost, quality, service and speed."[3]

Let there be no doubt about the urgency of the re-engineering challenge in our health care delivery system. Without improvements it will drift rapidly into unaffordable crisis. Fortunately, the urgency of the situation is motivating boards, managers, providers and gov-

1   Fiona Hastings, *Beyond Provider Dominance*, King's Fund, 1993, p.169.
2   Michael Hammer and James Champy, *Re-engineering the Corporation* (New York: Harper Collins Publishers Inc., 1993), p.31.
3   Ibid., 32.

ernments from coast to coast to act quickly. What follows is an effort to capture the direction of constructive reform as well as many of the worthwhile stories about those leading it. Few successes are transportable holus-bolus from one province to another or from one hospital to another. Circumstances are always unique due to differing histories. Nevertheless, we can learn and successfully adapt experiences and ideas to our own situation.

We must keep in mind that we are not starting with a blank canvas. Re-engineering occurs while we continue to deliver care. We need to balance history and values against imperatives for change. The next health care system must arise in an evolutionary way from current realities and cannot be designed or implemented in a vacuum. There are few 'eurekas' in health reform.

Our objective in re-engineering must be to achieve the highest quality health care service possible, in the most appropriate setting, in response to patient needs. This has several implications. We must take a more consumer-centred view, shift to a continuum of care model and detach health care from the hospital bed to which it has been yoked in the past. As services and institutions are unlinked, the basis for previously-defined roles shifts. What was once done by a physician in a hospital might be accomplished, with equal effectiveness, by a nurse in a home. We are headed toward more holistic, integrated health systems planning. Parts of Canada have implemented these approaches, but the shift from a hospital-physician image of health care to a wider, broader view of services and providers is still difficult for many people. New Brunswick's Extra-mural Hospital[4] — literally, a hospital without walls — is a powerful example of where we must move.

From Insured Services to Managed Delivery Systems

Movement to greater management of the present system is concur-

4   The New Brunswick Extra-Mural Hospital was established by the New Brunswick Government in 1981. The role of the Extra-Mural Hospital is to provide health services in the home setting. With fourteen service delivery units the emphasis has been on long-term care. Caseloads in the range of 3400 patients and a spectrum of active, palliative and chronic care characterize the activities. In 1992, when New Brunswick announced the regionalization and consolidation of the hospital system it also announced an expansion of the Extra-Mural Hospital. The most striking aspect of the Extra-Mural Hospital is how long it has been a success without drawing many imitators across the country. A non-bricks and mortar hospital is still too distant a concept for most of us.

rent with the shift to population health. Restructuring, in many parts of Canada, means rapid consolidation. The era of the largely independent hospital, operated by a volunteer board of directors, with a loose relationship to an overall delivery system, is ending. Hospital mergers, regionalization and measurements of outcomes are all themes in recent reforms. Movement towards shared services, regional or district needs-based planning and regional systems is underway.

Five provinces — New Brunswick, British Columbia, Alberta, Nova Scotia and Saskatchewan — have introduced legislation to bring hospitals within regional systems. This follows Quebec. Other jurisdictions are proceeding on a more evolutionary, less legislative path, but are still consolidating hospitals, particularly in multi-hospital centres. Religious owners, largely Catholic, are also examining and undertaking movement towards systems.

In other provinces, major shifts in bed usage and bed allocation is underway. Manitoba has mandated a transfer in bed use of shift patients to community hospital and community care settings. This has been accomplished by significant bed reductions in the two teaching hospitals — the Health Sciences Centre and St. Boniface General Hospital — as well a movement of patients to community hospitals. The opening of additional beds in chronic care hospitals and increased home care are the necessary investments which have enabled the restructuring to proceed.

Restructuring the System to Achieve Effective Patient Care[5]

Re-engineering is not confined to the hospital sector. Major change is also occurring in long-term care, in public health and in how drugs are prescribed, dispensed and managed. In fact, there are few areas of health care which are not undergoing questioning and reworking. The pressures driving these changes are not limited to the financial problems of governments in Canada. Other impetuses, which may be more powerful over the medium term, are changing consumer expectations and the dramatic impact of technology, particularly information technology. It may be that the silicon chip, with its incredible capacity to make information an inexpensive commodity,

5 *Quality Health for Manitobans: The Action Plan*, Government of Manitoba, May, 1992, p.28.

Restructuring the System to Achieve Effective Patient Care: An Example

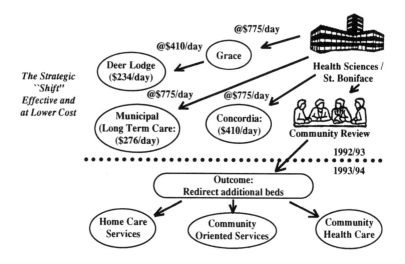

becomes one of our greatest allies in re-engineering health care services.

Where does the responsibility for re-engineering lie? Is it the job of ministries of health? Of hospital managers? Of trustees? Of all those who represent the public interest on District Health Councils in Ontario or on health services boards in Saskatchewan? *All of the above* is the best answer. The task is so large and diverse that all parties will need to be involved and share responsibility. There is no single right answer or pat, cookie-cutter solution.

Ministers and departments of health will need to show leadership through clear direction and policies. They may decide to restructure health governance in order to provide a broader investment in health and health services. This process has gone through several phases in Quebec. Government should not, however, try to micro-manage change and usurp the role of hospital and community health govern-ances. Rather, the citizen governors who serve as board members of hospitals, health councils, community health centres and the like should shoulder the governance role in times of change, as well as in times of preserving services. It is not enough for a board to meekly accept the advice of management. Board members must ensure that the advice conforms to changing and evolving community expectations. It is no longer enough to know that physicians, nurses and other providers support new directions. Consumers must also have a voice. Boards must carefully balance the views of providers and management but they must *act* in the interests of those with health care needs. Service to the consumer hasn't often received the central role in health care delivery discussions. Boards have a vital role in shifting this aspect of decisionmaking. Archimedes once commented that with a long enough lever he could move the earth. The consumer is a lever long and powerful enough to move the health care system, but only with the active support of informed board members.

Hospital management teams need to lead change and ensure more active participation from staff at all levels. Advisory groups established at the community, district or regional level must balance their advice. The need for evolutionary, not revolutionary, reform of service delivery must be accompanied by tough-minded questioning of old solutions and conventional wisdom. As advisors on health as well as health care delivery, these groups must be open to new investments that assist health status. Each group playing its appropriate role will combine to create successful change.

New partnerships are being created to bring together the necessary participants in managing change. Partnerships evolving between providers of health services and payers (largely governments) is one essential element. However, broader partnerships must involve representatives of an array of community and institutional governances, the boards that direct managers in the system. In most provinces, reforms are consolidating governances and agencies. Consumers must occupy more seats at more decision-making tables. Partnerships need to share risks and rewards to succeed. They also require clarity as to roles, not a naive assumption of common interests.

Successful policy making is tough in health care delivery, implementation is far more difficult. Making change at the field level will be a major, continuing theme. Some parts of the medical profession have long since adopted clinical practice guidelines, and others are contemplating them. Clinical guidelines will only work if they are seen to be developed independent of government, scientifically credible and based on the evidence. If we apply more of what we know about outcomes and evidence to the practice, we will simultaneously improve both quality and affordability in the system. Physicians will change their behaviour when confronted with evidence, not exhortation.

Better Management

Better management at all levels, improved application of technology and more feedback loops for information, are some areas of significant success. Better management will require new tools and new incentives. Managers are rewarded for maintaining the status quo, not for administrating change. In fact, the stability of Canadian Medicare supports the skill of managers in resisting change. There must be a shift in the incentive structure to reward managers for implementing change.

In comparison with the Americans, we are often complimented for our leanness on the management side. In fact, recent studies published by both the *New England Journal of Medicine*[6] and the General Accounting Office in the United States,[7] concluded that if the Americans could reduce their administrative costs to the Canadian level they could provide coverage for those thirty-five million Americans currently without it. Though this may be heresy, I would suggest that we may be a little too lean on the management side. I know many readers will say that "My hospital management doesn't feel very lean. It has been adding layers of management for as long as I can remember," and that may well be true. However, at the central or government level we have largely been an insurance agency, a collection of bill payers, rather than having analytical capacity to ask real outcome questions. We have not been asking tough enough questions about results as we pay for the inputs. We have lacked management in managing the outcomes rather than inputs. This additional management should not be translated as more managers' jobs but rather as more managerial responsibility for everyone who works in health care delivery.

This situation is changing. In Canada, there has been a dramatic movement in the last few years to more day and outpatient surgery

6   Redelmeier et al., "Hospital Expenditures in the United States and Canada," *New England Journal of Medicine*, March 18, 1993.
7   General Accounting Office, *Canadian Health Insurance Lessons for the United States: Report to the Chairman, Committee on Government Operations, House of Representatives*. GAO Publication No. GAO/HRD-91-90, B-244081. U.S. Government Printing Office, Washington, 1991.

resulting in profound impact on the system of enhanced affordability and quality. Rethinking how hospitals look at themselves — from essentially a collection of beds that are managed, to being a collection of services that may or may not be linked to a bed — has begun.

In Windsor, Calgary, Edmonton and Vancouver and in many other communities, the more difficult task of the inter-hospital rationalization is underway. Across the country, governments are putting significant funding into information systems. In the Ontario Drug Benefit Program, as a result of automation, the government will be able to not pay for the dispensing of the same prescription multiple times to a senior who has visited multiple doctors. Ontario, like Saskatchewan, will have a real time, on-line drug information system and will catch fraudulent transactions. The pharmacist filling the prescription will know whether that prescription has been filled recently and whether the prescription they are filling will interact in a negative way with other medication the patient is on. Eventually, all hospital emergency rooms will be linked into the system. Patients presenting for treatment will have their drugs identified rapidly whether they are conscious or unconscious. Physicians offices will eventually be linked up, but that is a longer term proposition.

These are a few examples. The point is that there are real gains in better management at all levels. This is not advocacy for more managers, rather, for acquiring the tools to really manage. Information systems and outcomes research are part of getting management information to providers to make decisions about health care. We must not add layers of management, instead we should be removing layers. We should increase accountability — whether with physicians or nurses — at the front line, for managers and workers. The purpose is not to put anyone in conflict with their professional responsibilities to the patient by imposing additional work, but to enlist the help of those who know what actually goes on. The possibility of improvement depends on the active support and participation of all health workers in change.

Technology Assessment

Finding the right place for technology, and harnessing it to care and compassion, is a priority in many areas of health care reform. Technology includes not only medical devices and equipment, but also drugs, techniques and procedures, plus the systems that support the delivery of care. Decision-making through technology assessment is about balancing cost containment and the desire to provide the latest technology.

The image of new technology as always driving up costs is simplistic and inaccurate. For example, laparoscopic surgery has been receiving coverage in the journals as a minimally-invasive alternative to traditional surgery. Laparoscopic or "keyhole" surgery involves small incisions rather than large ones and use of new techniques like fibre-optics. Laparascopic cholecystectomy or "lap-choly" is the removal of the gall bladder utilizing the techniques of laparoscopic surgery. Patients can expect a one-night stay in hospital and a return to work within seven to ten days, rather than five to seven days in hospital and six weeks recovering at home from conventional gall bladder removal surgery.[8] In fact, in the U.S. today 30% of patients undergo the operation on a day-surgery basis.

From the patient's point of view, this surgical option also means less pain and probably lower risk of complications. For the hospital, the significant reduction in length of stay produces major savings in acute service costs. The capital costs of setting up the service can be quickly recovered, after which the hospital is ahead financially. Laparoscopic surgery is a technology that has potential to cut costs and improve quality. However recent evidence suggests that cholecystectomy rates are rising due to the convenience and speed of the laparoscopic procedure.[9]

To continue to afford the latest technology, we need better assessment and better planning. Technology assessment is the basis for information-based decision-making and it is an integral part of the move toward more accountable, quality-assured, outcome-oriented health care.

Through more rigorous analysis the bane of medical technology, the fact that in health care the new rarely drives out the old, might be overcome. Every new development tends to become an add-on, creating new demands rather than replacing existing services. Better comparisons between technologies can tell us exactly which old

8   Dr. John V. White, "Laparoscopic Cholecystectomy: The Evolution of General Surgery," Dr. John V. White, *Annals of Internal Medicine*, October 15, 1991, Volume 115, Number 8, p. 651-653.
9   Private correspondence June 2, 1994 with Dr. David Naylor in which he references work by the Epstein Group at Harvard as published in the *New England Journal of Medicine*, 1994 and unpublished work by Marsha Cohen of Institute for Clinical Evaluative Sciences (ICES). Rising number of procedures with lower rates of death and complication per procedure. This underscores the complexity of any technology change in health care.

devices and services should be replaced when new options come on stream.

The essential first step in assessing a technology is randomised clinical trials to demonstrate clinical effectiveness. Such trials are routinely performed on drug therapies but, are used much less for other therapeutic and diagnostic technologies. It is clear from the literature that uncontrolled studies often produce wrong answers. There is no substitute for rigorous scientific controls. More and more, those who pay for new technologies are going to insist on proof that they work. This will challenge medical device manufacturers to conduct clinical trials and produce credible research results.

But clinical effectiveness is not the end of the issue. We also need to weigh cost effectiveness. We need to ask how a new technology compares to existing alternatives in terms of costs and benefits. Cost-benefit analysis is based on quantitative measurements, such as the cost in dollars per life-year gained. Work is also being done on ratios that reflect quality of life factors. The techniques of economic evaluation will continue to become more refined and helpful to decision-makers. There is still a great distance to be travelled to make this analysis of practical value in day-to-day decisions.

A recent article in the *New England Journal of Medicine*[10] compared hospital expenditures in Canada and the United States. After adjusting for case mix and other variables, the authors estimated that resources used for inpatient care per admission were 24% higher in the U.S. than in Canada. One of the main reasons appeared to be greater centralization of specialized equipment and personnel in Canada, leading to higher efficiency.

MRI — Magnetic Resonance Imaging — the most effective replacement to old X-Ray technology, is an example. In the U.S. there are about 3,000 MRI machines, whereas in Canada there are twenty-eight, eleven units per million population in the U.S. and one per million in this country. In Ontario, there are ten MRI units operating and one more approved, all in health science centres. We must proceed with caution in relaxing our controls on the proliferation of technology. Nevertheless, ministries of health in every Canadian jurisdiction are under some pressure to revise policies regarding MRI, and a range of other technologies.

The stakes are high. If we misallocate financial and human

---

10 Redelmeier, Donald and Victor Fuchs, ''Hospital Expenditures in the United States and Canada,'' *New England Journal of Medicine*, March 18, 1993, p. 772-778.

resources to an inappropriate technology, we are diverting resources from cost-effective technologies. And that means patients who would have benefited will not. On the other hand, if we invest wisely in technology, population health will improve.

We can also take cost-benefit analysis the next logical step and compare new medical technologies, not with other medical technologies, but with alternative investments in the broader determinants of health. Perhaps instead of buying the latest medical equipment we should insist on better driver training, add fibre to foods or invest more in job training. These questions on the determinants of health are ultimately political ones for government to decide on behalf of and in consultation with the public.

The key to getting the maximum value from technology — to meeting patient needs within affordable budgets — is co-operation among hospitals and physicians. We are beginning to see a determined effort at various levels in health care to assess technology more rigorously and distribute it more rationally. Assessments are occurring within the larger context of the managed re-engineering of the health care delivery system to bring costs under control and emphasize the larger determinants of health. Through partnership we can succeed in creating a sustainable and affordable health care system in which continuous quality improvement is a reasonable expectation.

Chapter 1
Hospital Services

Boards should meddle. To begin with, there is no way to stop
them, and if you can't lick them, you had better join them! Board
members of a non-profit organization should be committed to
the cause. They should be deeply interested and involved in it,
they should know the programmes and the people who work on
them, and they should *care*. But also, non-profit boards are
usually organized in such a way that 'meddling' is part of their
job.[1]

Managing For The Future
Peter F. Drucker

In attempting to arrive at the truth I have applied everywhere
for information, but in scarcely an instance have I been able to
obtain hospital records fit for any purposes of comparison. If
they could be obtained they would enable us to decide many
other questions besides the one alluded to. They would show
subscribers how their money was being spent, what amount of
good was really being done with it, or whether the money was
not doing mischief rather than good.[2]

Florence Nightingale, 1863

The re-engineering of health services delivery in Canada is changing

---

1 Peter Drucker, *Managing For the Future* (Butterworth and Heinemann: London,
   U.K. 1993), p. 176-177.
2 Florence Nightingale, as quoted by Mr. Frank Maynard, Deputy Minister of Health
   for Manitoba in presentation to meeting of Deputy Ministers of Health, Fall 1993,
   Hull, Quebec.

the nature of our nine hundred hospitals in many ways. Fifty-two small hospitals in rural Saskatchewan are being closed or converted to community health services. Large hospitals across Canada are closing, in total, thousands of beds. In many mid-sized Canadian cities, the existing four or five hospitals will be reorganized in the next few years into one or two facilities. In a number of two-hospital towns or small cities one hospital is to remain for acute care while the other becomes a long-term care facility. Why is this happening? Is this re-engineering or simply shutdown?

The forces driving hospital change are powerful and continuing. The changes which we are witnessing need to be accelerated, not slowed down, if our hospitals are to keep pace with the combined forces of technology and changing medical practice, and cope with reduced funding from governments. Historically, our hospitals were like hotels, where doctors and nurses provided care to patients. Hospitals were measured by how many beds they had and the task of the hospital administrator was very focussed on managing the 'inn'. Our vocabulary has lagged behind the dramatic change in the role and management of the hospital. Ask the president of a hospital to describe his or her facility and, in most cases, you will still get the bed count early in the reply. But beds are no longer the right measure. Hospitals have become a key delivery point for a vast array of services, which have been unbundled from the bed or hospital stay. Rapid movement of many services from inpatient to outpatient, the explosion in growth of day surgery and impressive technological advances to much less intrusive ways of treating patients, have altered hospitals. The new role of a hospital is as physical structure where a range of treatment services is managed, some of which may involve a hospital stay, but many of which do not.

For health services which still require a hospital stay, the length of that stay is being dramatically shortened and the quality in the outcome improved. Techniques for better management of bed utilisation have gained importance. Many hospitals are working out the consequences of these changes and finding ways of reshaping their operations. The smart ones are asking their workers for ideas. The Woodstock General Hospital in Ontario is one of the smart ones. Some comments on the Woodstock re-generation:

> We decided to reduce our days, cycle days from a fourteen-day menu cycle to an eight-day cycle menu. That depresses our food

inventories in the department. So that helps our cost and we don't have food just sitting in inventories waiting to be used.

Kris Lavoie,
food services manager

For years, the menus changed every two weeks. Then, one of the kitchen workers pointed out that patients don't stay in hospital for two weeks anymore, so they changed the cycle and that saves money. They changed the way they scheduled Operating Rooms and that saves $100,000 a year. They consolidated two critical care units and saved $300,000.

Bob Johnston,
CBC News

Just a few years ago, we used to bring them in for a couple of days to do tests on them. Before we made this change, you'd have two more days; now, we do all that testing on an out-patient basis. Just bring you in, in many cases, on the day of your surgery. And with the changes in techniques, more and more folks are going home that same day.[3]

William Pobe,
hospital administrator

The Woodstock General Hospital changed its employee suggestion programme two years ago. The new rule was that employees would be told where their idea had gone and why. The number of suggestions increased from twelve the year before the new rule, to 366 the following year.

When St. Boniface Hospital in Manitoba undertook a major restructuring project[4] in 1993, it gathered ideas from all staff at all levels. Of the 2,300 ideas submitted, a steering committee, with representation from all levels including the bargaining agent, approved 129 recommendations to proceed to implementation. These ideas will save the hospital $13.5 million over three years or nearly 10% of the hospital's budget.

These examples suggest a dangerously radical three-step plan for

---

3 C.B.C. Radio News Broadcast, Toronto 7:30 a.m. EDT, October 18, 1993.
4 Presentation by Mr. Jack Litvack, CEO, St. Boniface General Hospital, to the Canadian Institute Conference, Re-engineering Hospitals, Toronto, April 11-12, 1994.

achieving efficiencies through changing the way activities are carried out in hospitals:

Step 1. Ask the people who work there, all of them.

Step 2. Take the ideas seriously — implement the good ones.

Step 3. Have enough respect to tell them what happened to their ideas, both the good and the not-so-good ones.

The Japanese quality revolution in the automobile industry was accomplished by re-engineering the car and how it was made. Employee suggestions played a key role in Japan's automotive success, as did continuous quality improvement processes. Eventually, as their market share eroded, North American car makers had to follow suit.

Consider the dramatic changes in the automobile over thirty years. Consider also that you would have been regarded as a dangerous radical to predict in 1963 that today's cars would be lighter, more fuel efficient, safer and less polluting. In developments which have saved hundreds of thousands of lives, the automobile has advanced dramatically. The one thousand dollar plus per car of safety equipment includes seat belts, side impact bracing in doors, airbags, anti-lock brakes, and crash crumple zones, front and back. All this and cars are still about one thousand pounds lighter due to advanced materials. On the pollution side the progress is even more dramatic. The 1963 model emitted 96% more hydrocarbons, 96% more carbon monoxide, and 76% more nitrous oxide.[5] Lead fumes have been totally eliminated by taking lead out of the fuel. Can we re-engineer the hospital in as total a fashion as the automobile? Are hospitals so different from our automakers? The scale of hospital enterprise dwarfs the automobile industry. The nine hundred hospitals in Canada employ three hundred and fifty-thousand workers, the auto industry barely one hundred thousand.

Canada's nine hundred hospitals are overseen by volunteer boards of trustees. This aspect of health care governance is a significant strength, if the trustees take their governance responsibilities

5   Al Haas, "Today's cars are leaps ahead of yesterday's guzzlers," *Toronto Star*, March 28, 1992, p. K23.

seriously and if they have the tools to do their job. High quality information is the most important of these tools, without it, effective governance is thwarted and the board of trustees can be quietly reduced to fundraisers and boosters for the hospital's cause. These are both legitimate and necessary roles, but fall short of full, responsible governance. Trustees must demand sufficient information to do their jobs, and hold hospital management accountable for achieving the goals and mission of the hospital.

Advocating that hospital boards fulfil their entire role is not an argument for their intrusion into the role of hospital management. A proper balance of roles clearly separates the task of *governing* — setting direction, priorities, establishing policy, approving a strategic plan and approving the budget — from the task of *managing* — hiring and managing staff, monitoring progress towards goals, implementing policy and administering the spending of the approved budget.

What follows are my best twenty ideas for saving money and improving quality in the hospital system, gleaned from three decades of visiting hospitals, consulting in hospitals and serving in government. Where possible, I have given examples, named names and told stories. I apologize to my colleagues and many friends in the health consulting business for giving away trade secrets at a low price. However, my apology is limited by the limited time we have to keep Medicare accessible and affordable. There is also no shortage of work for health care consultants. Every single idea on the list has already been successfully implemented somewhere in Canada. By sharing, we can all climb the necessary learning curve at a faster pace.

If you are a health care manager you have a ready source of hundreds of additional ideas available from your employees, and from the physicians and other professionals, who are part of your institution. If you are willing to listen and to let them know which ideas worked and which did not, this is a well that will not run dry. If you are a trustee or board member, here are a few meddlesome questions to ask yourself, your fellow trustees and your management team. I don't completely subscribe to management guru Peter Drucker's meddlesome views of boards noted earlier. A gently managed conspiracy between the board chair and the chief executive officer should focus the meddling board on a constructive set of tasks.

Here is the hospital-money-saving-quality-improving question and idea list. A word of warning: while some of these questions should only be attempted by trained professionals, most are just organized common sense!

Informed and Dangerous
— A Few Questions Trustees
To Ask Themselves and Hospital Management

Big Questions About Hospitals

1 **Does your hospital really need to exist at all?**
We might as well deal with the toughest question first. Is there another nearly identical hospital across the street or down the road? Are you both needed or would one hospital be enough? Could the elimination of all the non-patient care costs in one hospital provide both savings and more dollars for patient care in your community? Who are the major beneficiaries of the continued existence of the hospital? Providers? Consumers? The community? Is the benefit primarily a health benefit or an economic benefit? This is one for the chair of the board to consider with a handful of key and trusted board members.

A gut-wrenching, but good litmus test for chairs of small hospitals is whether they would themselves use the services of the hospital in an urgent care situation. If the answer is no, that may be the beginning of the answer to the basic question.

In many communities, consumers are voting with their feet by seeking care in the nearest regional centre. In communities such as Sault Ste. Marie, Ontario, two hospitals across the street from each other have merged into one hospital. The bottom line needs to be resources for health care not preservation of bricks and mortar.

2 **Could your hospital dramatically alter its role with a benefit to the overall system?**
The future of Doctor's Hospital in Toronto has brought down health ministers and sparked enormous political controversies over the past fifteen years. Yet, recently the board of the hospital, the Ontario Government and the Metro Toronto District Health Council unanimously agreed to rebuild the aging facility as an innovative ambulatory care centre. Downtown Toronto is knee-deep in closed, never to be re-opened hospital beds. The Doctor's Hospital decision is to

transform into a sensible accommodation with a new and important role, which builds on the strengths of the organization without adding to a growing problem of excess hospital bed capacity.

Does it still need to be an acute care hospital? Across Saskatchewan a number of small, under utilized community hospitals are being converted to better serve chronic care needs or to become community health centres.

3 Should your hospital's role be a smaller subset of its current activities? Should you specialize or become a long-term care facility? Do more of what you're really good at and less or none of the rest?

In Guelph, Ontario, twenty-five years of discussion and a report by a Committee chaired by Bill Blundell culminated in the decision by the Sisters of St. Joseph where their hospital would become a long-term care facility and the Guelph General Hospital would focus on acute care.

When the Toronto Hospital, Canada's largest hospital, declared two years ago that it would no longer be all things to all patients, the world moved in Canadian hospital thinking. If even the biggest cannot do everything well, should other hospitals consider a narrower, more collaborative role? In June, 1994, the Toronto Hospital and the Princess Margaret Hospital have formed a Joint Venture Council to lead comprehensive cancer care services.

4 How are you restructuring services and roles with other hospitals and health service providers?

Planning for restructuring of hospital services has become a central activity in Windsor, Ontario,[6] in Victoria, B.C. and in dozens of other cities and regions across Canada. Has your hospital joined as an active participant in planning for future services or are you waiting for someone else to take the lead?

As governments continue to pressure for a broader continuum of care extending from home to community to hospital and back, your linkages with community services will become extremely important. How strong are those linkages? Do patients remain longer in hospital because relationships with home care are not well developed? Does your emergency ward fill with social admissions who might be better

6 *An Evolving Plan For Total Health System Reconfiguration* — The Essex County Win-Win Model — The Final Report of the Steering Committee on Reconfiguration, Essex County, District Health Council, Windsor, February, 1994.

served by a community shelter or drop-in centre? Have you considered an advisory board or board committee link to other service providers in the community? Have you ever considered using your hospital's ability to raise capital dollars as an asset in a partnership with community agencies who may need new facilities?

In Edmonton, a report by Dr. John Atkinson recommends extensive consolidation of hospital services.[7] In Calgary, Mr. Lou Hyndman has chaired a similar review.[8] In Winnipeg, the Bell-Wade Report[9] recommends a reordering of teaching hospital programme responsibilities. Will your hospital undertake a constructive, leadership role in the realignment heading your way? Are you preparing your board, management team and staff for change?

Some Questions on Patient Care Servies

What patient care services does your hospital provide? Where and how? Before we get to all the standard and important questions of effectiveness and efficiency, we need to consider what services are delivered and in what setting. The unbundling of services from the bed extends the full spectrum.

5 Inpatient, Outpatient or Somewhere Else?

Changing the setting for delivering health care services has been the major shift in the hospital sector over the past five years. In 1989, Ontario's hospitals had 48,989 beds. By 1994, we had reduced the number of beds by 7,889. How? Did people in Ontario become miraculously healthier in this period? No. The answer lies in a real shift in hospital activity from inpatient to outpatient and day surgery. Services increased during this period. With nearly 8,000 fewer beds, Ontario hospitals increased acute cases by 1.3 million or 8.8% (1989-90 to 1993-94) and outpatient services by 10.4%. Overall productivity increased by 18.5% due to a 20% decline in length of stay from 8.2. days to 6.5. days.[10]

7 Dr. John Atkinson, Tannis Chefurka, ''Principles and Programs for Edmonton Regional Health,'' a.k.a. the *PAPER* Report, for the Edmonton Region Health Faculties Planning Council, Edmonton, March 1994.

8 *Report of the Calgary Facilitation Group on Health Services in Calgary, Alberta,* Chair Mr. Lou Hyndman, Members, Dr. C. Wright, Mr. Ken Fyke, April 11, 1994 Report to the Calgary Regional Acute Care Planning Group.

9 Dr. John Wade, Mr. Bob Bell, *Bell-Wade Report,* Government of Manitoba, 1993.

10 ''Managing Health Care Resources 1994-95 Meeting Priorities,'' Ministry of Health Ontario, Queen's Printer, 1994, p. 5.

The Alberta Government has established targets for bed use in that province. From 1,083 patient days per 1,000 population and 4.3 hospital beds per 1,000 population in 1991/92, Alberta intends to reduce to 745 patient days per 1000 and only 2.4 acute care beds per 1,000 by 1996/97.[11] Data from elsewhere in Canada reveals the same trends.

The Saskatchewan Health Services Utilization and Research Commission (HSURC) published a study in August of 1993[12] showing that hospitals in that province could save $16 million per year by increasing day surgeries and reducing pre-surgical admissions. Dr. Stewart McMillan, who heads HSURC, noted these changes could cut costs and improve quality of care to patients. There have been dramatic increases in the use of day surgery in Canada in the past five years but we still lag well behind the American hospital system in this area. There are many free-standing ambulatory care centres in the U.S. which do nothing but day surgery and outpatient work. In Canada, day surgery is undertaken largely in converted operating rooms within hospitals. There is considerable merit in facilities which are purpose built and managed for day surgery. Staffing patterns and other major cost factors in a twenty-four hour a day hospital setting can be dramatically reduced in a centre that operates from seven a.m. to six p.m.

Reviewing the facilities and location in which day surgery is carried out, coupled with a review of inpatient stays for procedures which need not require inpatient stay, are both worthwhile efforts. Lists of procedures approved for day surgery are available from U.S. health authorities and might form the basis for a review by your hospital's medical and management staff.

Good integration and communication with home care services are required to ensure follow-up care for day surgery patients. These linkages have been discussed in general above and will require attention as you expand day surgery to more complex procedures. As well, patient education and education of patient's families will be necessary to provide an understanding and peace of mind to post-surgery patients recuperating at home.

The Mulcahy Outpatient Centre at Loyola University Medical Centre in Chicago is an excellent example of a free-standing outpa-

11 "Healthy Albertans Living In A Healthy Alberta; A Three Year Business Plan," *Alberta Health*, February, 1994.
12 Deana Driver, "Hospital days acutely overused in Sask," Deana Driver, *The Medical Post*, Vol. 29, No. 24, June 15, 1993, p. 2.

tient centre with a significant volume of day surgery. An extensive library of videos for viewing by patients in advance of their day surgery is a valuable tool in Mulcahy's patient education approach, as is the use of nursing visits for patient education purposes.

6 How are you managing utilization? How *well* are you managing service utilization?

Utilization, that is, what services and how many are used by patients is extremely important to improved management. Most Canadian hospitals have some form of utilization management review in place but there has been little formal evaluation of the effectiveness of these efforts. In the U.S., where market forces and government incentives have forced more intensive efforts, the trend is towards explicit criteria for review of bed utilisation. In a June, 1993 review of the recent Canadian experience, an Institute for Clinical Evaluative Sciences — ICES — study team found a number of techniques that demonstrated effectiveness in improving management. These included:

- screening emergency departments and using quick response teams to prevent unwarranted admissions
- pre-admission testing to reduce cancellations of surgery
- guidelines are useful in reducing lengths of stay but their development process impacts significantly on their success
- short stay units
- a range of other techniques including co-operative care and self-care units, expected date of discharge programmes

Decisions about approach to utilization of beds are best taken in a collaborative fashion by hospital management, physicians and nurses. Formal bed utilization review tools such as SWITCH, ISD-A, MCAP establish criteria for admission and days of stay. These tools are in use in Canada: SWITCH at several Ontario hospitals, ISD-A in Victoria, B.C. and Saskatchewan and MCAP at the Hospital for Sick Children in Toronto. The ICES evaluation concluded that MCAP and ISD-A were the highest scoring against the criteria used.[13]

---

13 Paula Blackstein-Hirsh et. al., ''Management of Hospital Bed Utilization in Canada,'' Institute for Clinical Evaluative Sciences, Working Paper #10, Toronto, June 1993. A6 SWITCH, ISD-A, MCAP are all acronyms for computerized tools to assess hospital performance. ISD-A — Intensity of service, severity of illness and discharge screens. MCAP — Managed Care Appropriateness Protocol. AEP — appropriateness evaluation protocol. SMI — standardized Medereview Instrument.

We are at a very early stage in applying the rigour necessary to develop a fully effective set of tools and properly evaluate their impacts in random trials. Nevertheless, the direction is clear. Much more management of admissions, discharges and lengths of stay, based on explicit criteria, are the new tool kit.

A good example of learning across Canada is the quick response team idea made prominent by the Victoria Health project in B.C. and later adopted by the Greater Niagara and Windsor Hotel Dieu in Ontario. The simple idea of screening patients prior to admission and determining whether the patient could be safely returned home without a hospital admission is a powerful and successful approach. Getting beyond "bed" management to services management is essential.

7   Benchmarking and Performance Measurement

Benchmarking is a powerful technique for comparing your performance to the performance of other similar peer organizations in comparable circumstances. In other instances, you may wish to benchmark your hospital with perceived leaders in the field. How do you compare with the best? Common measures are length of stay for patients of a particular type, percentage of surgery undertaken on a day basis, bed use and resource use, for various conditions or procedures.

For Ontario Hospitals the recently published ICES — Practice Atlas is a superb source of comparative data for benchmarking purposes.[14]

In 1992, Arthur Anderson & Co., a leading consulting firm, published a study based on a review of best practices in 120 ambulatory surgery facilities in the United States.[15] Their results showed an average time from arrival to surgery of forty minutes for the best performer, fifty-six minutes for the top twenty group of performers and ninety-eight minutes for all other facilities surveyed. The leader was saving nearly one hour per case! The study identified forty-three best practices or benchmarks in eleven areas such as patient registration, recovery, physician relations and diagnostic testing.

A leading American in the benchmarking field, James Heidbreder of the James Group Ltd., identifies four key qualities of true process benchmarking. These are:

14 *ICES Practice Atlas*, Institute for Clinical Evaluative Sciences, Toronto, 1994.
15 Arthur Andersen, "Ambulatory Surgery Best Practices," Dallas, Texas, 1992.

1. "It deals with the "how's" as well as the "what's.""[16] Benchmarking is not simply about performance measurement but it is also about how superior performance is achieved.
2. "It stimulates breakthrough thinking that results in quantum improvements."[17] Not incremental improvements but real breakthroughs with process improvement of 20% or more.
3. "It is grounded in a customer orientation."[18] What should be benchmarked should be determined by the customer. This quality is a shared foundation with Total Quality Management which is discussed below.
4. "It is a carefully structured analytical process."[19] This is a back of the envelope approach. Organized data, analysis and an intelligent plan, executed in a systematic fashion is necessary for success.

Mr. Heidbreder concludes on the following note:

As health care organizations come to test — and then to institutionalize — benchmarking, we will learn from the best and adapt that learning to our critical processes. The result will be the ability to do more with less and do it faster. We will be working smarter. And, above all, we will have a predictable ability to bring substantial improvement to our critical processes that produce both patient customer delight and superior financial performance.[20]

The Ontario Ministry of Health began sharing benchmarking software and peer hospital comparative data with Ontario hospitals in 1993. Data is available for Canadian hospitals from — MIS — or Hospital Management Records Institute — HMRI — which are merging to form the National Health Information Institute in 1994. The *ICES Practice Atlas* provides some useful advice on how to make this data of relevance to clinical practice and hospital management.

---

16 James E. Heidbreder, "Looking for the Light — Not the Heat," *Healthcare Forum Journal*, January-February 1993, p. 26.
17 Ibid., p. 26.
18 Ibid., p. 27.
19 Ibid., p. 27.
20 Ibid., p. 29.

8 Hospital Pharmacy: Managing Your Drug Costs

One of the fastest rising cost aspects of the hospital system is the drug bill. As new drugs have been developed, often with important advantages over the ones they replace, drug pricing has resulted in significant cost increase.

A lesson from down under: at an international meeting in Adelaide, Australia I had an opportunity to meet the talented CEO of the Royal Adelaide Hospital, a one thousand bed adult general teaching hospital in that city. He shared an interesting approach to drug decisions and allocation of scarce resources.

The Royal Adelaide on Drugs!

... The Hospital Drug Committee remained concerned at the continuing pressure on the drug budget and the growing request to use new drugs in the Hospital. By mid 1992, nineteen new drugs that had been assessed as clinically effective were waiting to be released for use within the Hospital. The Drug Committee devised the following methodology to address this problem.

With the increasing number of applications for drugs falling into the category of being approved on clinical/scientific grounds but unable to be available because of financial restrictions, the Drug Committee decided to develop a priority list for outstanding drug requests.

In developing a method for prioritisation, it was important that the method be:

a. simple to use (i.e., use data that are readily available through the published literature)
b. objective where possible
c. reproducible and reliable
d. discriminative

After many meetings, considerable discussion and several draft models, the RAH Drug Committee developed the following model. The principles used were:

1. Specific guidelines for each drug are developed by the relevant experts to establish the protocol for drug use at the RAH.
2. Only those requests which have received approval from the Drug Committee on clinical/scientific grounds are considered for priority ranking.
3. A ranking system based on supply and cost is utilised to minimise subjectivity and enhance consistency in the decision making process.

The goal was to provide a ranking of drug requests on the basis of obtaining the greatest benefit for the most patients for each dollar spent. For each drug request, scores are allocated for each of the subsections under —

1. Quality score
2. Cost score

Scores are obtained from the information provided with the submission. The guidelines established by the relevant experts and a further review of the scientific literature is necessary. A final ratio of total quality score over total cost score is used to rank requests (i.e., the higher the ratio the greater the priority).

1. QUALITY SCORE

    1.1 Outcome

a.	Individual patient benefit		
	cure/prevention	(30)	
	prolongation of life	(15)	
	palliation/symptom control	(7)	
	placebo	(0)	
b.	Mortality/Morbidity of Disease		
	mortality:	- high risk	(9)
		- moderate risk	(6)
		- low risk	(3)
	morbidity :	- severe	(5)
		- moderate	(3)
		- mild	(1)
c.	Response		
	expected response fraction		
	(e.g. 80% of patients respond = 0.8 response fraction)		

Outcome = (a + b) x c

    1.2 Therapy Type (Based on Literature Support)

a.	established indication/effectiveness	(5)
b.	new therapy	(3)
c.	trial/investigational studies	(1)

    1.3 Clinical Comparison with Available Alternative Therapy
(considering efficacy, side effects, administration, etc.)

a.	no alternative	(15)
b.	new treatment better than existing	(10)
c.	new treatment equals existing	(5)
d.	existing treatment better than new	(0)

2. COST SCORE

   2.1 Cost Comparison with Alternative Therapy

a.	new treatment less expensive than existing	(0)
b.	no alternative	(2)
c.	new treatment equals existing	(5)
d.	new treatment more expensive	(10)

   2.2 Total Cost per Year

a.	less than $7,500	(1)
b.	$7,500 — $15,000	(2)
c.	$15,000 — $22,000	(3)
d.	$22,000 — $30,000	(4)
e.	$30,000 — $37,500	(5)
f.	$37,500 — $45,000	(6)
g.	greater than $45,000	(7)

   2.3 Cost per Patient

a.	less than $750	(1)
b.	$750 — $1,500	(2)
c.	$1,500 — $2,250	(3)
d.	$2,250 — $3,000	(4)
e.	$3,000 — $3,750	(5)
f.	$3,750 — $4,500	(6)
g.	greater than $4,500	(7)

Final Cost Score =
Cost Comparison   + Total Cost per Year   + Cost Per Patient
   (2.1)   +   (2.2)   +   (2.3)

By using this method, the Drug Committee was able to deal with fourteen new drug requests for nineteen indications during the 1991/92 financial year. If all of these drugs were approved for use then the total cost would be $750,000 per annum and the drug budget for this year was not able to accommodate it. The chart indicating the summary data for each of the newly marketed drugs and the final rankings is attached.

The Hospital decided that it only had $300,000 to apply to new drug use in this period. As a result of the nineteen drugs forwarded for funding, the first eleven only were released for use in patient care. This process was described in full not only at the Drug Committee but at several clinical staff meetings and gained acceptance by those staff as a fair and appropriate method to rank drugs in priority for use of patient care.[21]

21 Dr. Brendan Kearney, "The RHA Drug Priority Scheme," *Physician's Executive*, Vol. 19, No. 5, p. 63

The Ottawa General Hospital achieved a $500,000 saving on their drug budget in a twelve month period through collaboration of doctors, pharmacists and administrators. The Ottawa General Hospital leaders believe 5 – 10 % reduction in hospital drug budgets are possible, without compromising the quality of patient care.[22]

9 Hospital Laboratories

Do you know how much each test costs in your hospital lab? Have you invested in lab systems and telecommunications systems to reduce costs and improve quality? What tests do you send elsewhere that you could do? Should your lab testing be a shared service with some other facility?

Dr. John Atkinson has recommended in his recent report[23] that Edmonton hospitals integrate their labs. Among the specific recommendations are a single lab manager for Edmonton, one integrated computer system and a lead site. Overall, an integrated single service, rather than each hospital's lab as an independent entity. Savings from the Edmonton Caritas Group, which has already integrated three hospital sites, are estimated to be in the millions. Atkinson suggests further savings may be possible in the $8 million range on a total budget of $42 million.[24] An ambitious target. Has your hospital considered lab integration?

10 Emergency Services

Does your hospital have an Emergency Department? How long are waiting times? How many of the people visiting your Emergency Department really need to be there? Is there another Emergency Department across the street or down the block?

In most Canadian communities fundamental questions about emergency services have not been asked. Some alternatives to visiting emergency departments such as urgent care clinics exist across Canada but there coverage is uneven at best. Only Quebec, through

22 "One Hospital's Success with Medication Budget Control," *Leadership in Health Services*, March/April, 1994. Published by the Canadian Hospital Association, p. 16.

23 Dr. John Atkinson, and Tannis Chefurka, "Principles and Programs for Edmonton Regional Health," a.k.a. the *PAPER* Report, for the Edmonton Region Health Faculties Planning Council, Edmonton, March 1994.

24 Ibid., p. 21.

its CLSC's,[26] offers a widely available clinic alternative. Quebec has been struggling to convince its citizens to use CLSC care clinics rather than hospitals. A telephone help number, as an alternative to a visit, is not commonly available in Canada although the Hospital for Sick Children in Toronto has a service and Nova Scotia has promised one.

Our American cousins have a good idea in this regard.

Ask-A-Nurse

Access Health's signature product, Ask-A-Nurse, is the country's leading telephone-based health care information and referral service. It responded to more than 5.5 million calls in 1992.

Created in 1986, Ask-A-Nurse offers health care consumers 24-hour access to specially trained registered nurse counsellors. Based on the caller's symptoms or concerns, the counsellors offer personalized, confidential information. This enables callers to make an informed decision about when, how, or whether to seek medical care, and assists them in selecting appropriate sources of care.

Sponsored by hospitals and other providers within their service areas, Ask-A-Nurse helps hospitals to increase their market share by assisting consumers with their health care needs. When appropriate, Ask-A-Nurse also helps them locate care from the hospital's network of services and affiliated physicians.

Ask-A-Nurse is currently used by 195 hospitals throughout the U.S., and has become the nation's most widely recognized health care information and referral service. Hospitals sponsoring Ask-A-Nurse offer it as a free service to their local communities to build goodwill and assist individuals in finding appropriate health care services within the hospital's network.[27]

The company that developed Ask-A-Nurse has gone on to develop a newer product — Personal Health Advisor — which combines access to an audio-library on health topics with a nursing information service. In recent trials with Blue Cross of Oregon and

---

26 C.L.S.C. (Centre locale de services communautataires) Quebec has a full network of integrated health and social service centres unlike any other province. These centres include physician, nursing and social services.

27 Access Health Marketing Inc., Annual Reports 1992, 1993 and supplementary material available from Access Health: Access Health 11020 White Rock Road, Rancho Cordova, CA, 95670.

California, Personal Health Advisor has dramatically reduced inappropriate emergency room visits and increased consumer satisfaction.[27]

Dr. Ron Stewart, an expert in emergency medicine and the Minister of Health for Nova Scotia, has recently announced that his department will reform emergency health services. One of the improvements will be the addition of health information by telephone. Why not uncouple the information from the visit?

Your Hospital As A "Factory"

Devote significant attention to the sizeable slice of your hospital budget that goes to heat, light, food, supplies and all of the other non-direct health care activities. Certainly fewer beds and shorter stays will mean fewer, sicker guests at the inn, but no matter how numerous or how acute those guests, you still have lots of room to improve purchasing and non-patient care.

11 Linking to Other Management Resources

There are many lessons to be learned about re-engineering from outside the hospital sector. Is there someone on your board who manages a manufacturing operation? An information technology-driven services company? A bank?

Perhaps the senior management team of the hospital could visit the relevant manufacturing plant or bank and meet their counterparts. Is there learning that could be shared? Are there experts who could be "borrowed" to help with a problem or issue?

This will work best as a partnership or two-way street. What expertise does the hospital have that could be of value to firms? Is a partnership with mutual learning possible? In Ontario, the Ontario Hospital Association has become active in promoting the export of hospital expertise to other countries.

The strength of this type of collaboration is that it can draw managers out of their conventional wisdom ruts causing new questions to be asked and answered.

---

27 Evaluation material on Oregon and California Blue Cross studies, unpublished material, 1993-1994.

12   Management and Purchasing

Materials management! I hear you sigh. How dull! How boring!

A recent Ontario study[28] estimated that Ontario hospitals could save $250 million per year through improvements to materials management including purchase, distribution and storage of products. Not sexy, but you sure could use the money saved to improve your performance and be a hero or heroine to your hard-pressed finance committee and board of directors. Beginning to sound less dull?

There are two joint buying groups among the Ontario hospitals, Carecor and the Ontario Hospital Association. With personnel and support from the Ministry of Health, the buying groups formed a Health Care Materials Management Task Force. What did the Task Force and its expert consultants discover? First, that Ontario hospitals lagged behind other Canadian and worldwide industry leaders in this field. Second, and more important, they identified five activities which will lead to significant cost reductions:

- more extensive use of information technology
- improvements in, and greater use of, hospital buying groups
- buying from fewer vendors
- use of just-in-time delivery (stockless supply systems)
- use of shared off-site warehousing

The Ontario situation in materials management may be a little better or a little worse than that in other parts of Canada. There is significant savings potential in every hospital in Canada in the better management of materials. Has your hospital Board ever heard a presentation from the management team on materials management? A full consideration of the potential for shared services among hospitals and others is highly recommended. What are the potential savings of shared services and a systems approach? In 1992, I met Scott Parker, the calm, thoughtful Chief Executive Officer of Inter-Mountain Health Care (IHC). This charitable, non-profit health care system serves communities in the states of Utah, Idaho and Wyoming. Scott Parker had commissioned Ernst & Young Management Consultants to examine IHC. In particular, they studied nine services

---

28   Report of the Ontario Healthcare Materials Management Taskforce, by Carecor Health Services Inc., Ontario Ministry of Health, Ontario Hospital Association, October 1993.

provided by the corporate office to IHC hospitals.[29] The savings attributable to the system were $36.7 million for the year 1990, allocated as follows:

Purchasing	**$9.3 m**
General liability, Malpractice and WCB	**7.7 m**
Data processing	**6.2 m**
Financing	**5.2 m**
Cash management	**1.1 m**
Collection agency	**3.5 m**
Clinical engineering	**2.8 m**
Equipment rental	**.8 m**
Central laundry	**.1 m**
	$ 36.7 m[30]

Although each and every hospital cost is not comparable between the U.S. and Canada, enough similarities exist to make Scott Parker's IHC a system worth investigating. Canadian hospitals are less likely to need a collection agency but just as likely to benefit from rethinking purchasing decisions.

13 Food Services

We have already considered the menu cycle cost-saving idea from our leaders in Woodstock. What about the bigger question? Catering management firms have streamlined food service production across the country. Does a hospital in the 1990's need to prepare all its own meals from scratch? Airlines don't. In many cases hotels don't. Even many restaurants don't! Has your hospital considered buying meals, prepared foods, becoming part of a commissary group? The Ottawa hospitals own the Ottawa Commissariat and are saving significant costs through shared food services. The Commissariat serves hospitals and other institutional customers, such as the homes for the aged. The result is smaller kitchens, less expense and more attention to patient care.

Seven Oaks Hospital in Winnipeg is in the process of working out a new menu option approach jointly with Nestle Canada which could lead to a total re-engineering of food services in that hospital. The Toronto Hospital and Bitove are teaming up on a venture which

---

29   "Ernst & Young Report Savings from Corporate Office Activities to Intermountain Health Care," Salt Lake City, 1991. Further material can be found in the Intermountain Health Annual Report, 1992.
30   Ibid., p. 4.

could signal the beginning of mini-commissariats serving several hospitals.

Are you in the health care business or the food services business?

14 Energy Management

Energy conservation sounds almost passé but what about co-generation? Have you devoted a senior management meeting or a finance committee meeting to hearing from experts in the energy conservation and energy management fields?

Energy Costs

- How much energy does your hospital use each year?
- Have energy conservation actions been undertaken?
- Has your management team explored energy co-generation options?
- Is a regular energy audit part of your management plan?

15 Management of Labour Relations Matters

Hospitals are people-intensive organizations, 75% + of the budget is the payroll, with potential for very difficult labour relations if serious effort is not devoted to managing this area. Early warning signals are the numbers and types of grievances being filed. An abundance of grievances may reflect a lack of skills on the part of front-line managers, or it may reflect an insufficient delegation of authority by senior management to settle grievances at early stages. Front-line supervisors need to be able to problem-solve with the bargaining agent. If the bargaining agent is willing, joint training of union and management staff, in dispute resolution, can lead to dramatic improvement. Left to fester, bad labour relations only get worse with expensive and disruptive results. With proper attention, good labour relations can save dollars, aggravation and contribute sound ideas to the savings process.

16 Employee Benefits, Workers Compensation, Workplace Health and Safety: Hospital Heal Thy Self

In recent years hospitals have eclipsed the construction industry as a growing site of workplace injuries. As older, heavier patients are cared for by older, more easily injured workers, the result unsurprisingly, has been a steady growth of at-work injuries.

To heal themselves, hospitals are going to need a greater focus on workplace health and safety. This is cost-avoiding. Today's injury is a workers compensation claim for tomorrow and tomorrow and tomorrow. Hospitals can also play a key role in early rehabilitation services which prevent a short-term injury from becoming a chronic condition. Needless to say, this is part of being a decent employer and human being, not just a cost-saving measure.

The results can be startling. In Whitby Psychiatric Hospital in Ontario total Workers Compensation Board costs were reduced by 20% in a three-month intensive effort with full labour-management cooperation.[31]

What about employee benefit plans? Have you moved your drug benefit plan to a mail-order pharmacy with much lower dispensing fees? Have you insisted on less expensive but equally effective generic drugs in your employee benefit plan?

17 Insurance and Financial Management

When I met with the London Teaching Hospital Council and the Thames Valley District Health Council in 1992 they told me about the substantial savings the London, Ontario hospitals had achieved by purchasing their insurance as a group. Does your provincial hospital association offer a plan? Would you benefit from joining it?

Do you have an ATM (automated teller machine) in your hospital? Is your bank paying for the privilege of using your facility to shelter their machine? How about cash management? Have you undertaken a thorough review of factors that could improve your financial efficiency and lower costs?

A few constructive thoughts would include better terms from major suppliers and direct deposit of payroll cheques for employees. Have you examined the merits of a payroll service? How much does it cost you to issue a single paycheque?

18 Selecting and Managing Consultants and Other Advisors

If they are well-selected and well-managed, external advisors can provide a worthwhile addition to a hospital. The external "team" is

---

31 Whitby Psychiatric Hospital, Ministry of Health-OPSEU project team, 1993.

typically composed of the accounting firm represented by a partner, the legal firm represented by a partner, and one or many consulting firms advising on strategy and managing projects. Under-managed or completely unmanaged external advisors can be a very expensive and redundant proposition. Getting the most out of your external team is important. Often the experience of the external advisors is vast, and they can help identify major versus minor problems or issues to be tackled.

A good first rule is not to ask external advisors to do work which properly belongs to the management team. If your vice president of finance is not up to the challenge, then you should recruit a new vice president of finance, not expect your external audit partner to cover inadequacies. If your strategic planning is a once-in-four-year affair, then a consultant is probably a good person to lead the way. If you are a large hospital and the change effort is permanent perhaps you need a fully dedicated member of the management team for planning.

If you require the expertise of an external team of consultants, insist on a partnership. Insist that the consultants train staff at the hospital and that data used for the restructuring remain connected to your decision-making process. Consultants earn their fees if you have both an immediate result and a value-added process left after their departure.

Recruit a high quality team and use their talents well.

Total Quality Management (TQM)

19 **How to Benefit From TQM**

What is TQM or Total Quality Management? It is an approach to customer-centred quality management focused on doing the task right the first time. A Total Quality Management approach can yield important benefits, but requires leadership from a very committed CEO and management team. A purely externally-led TQM effort will fail due to lack of understanding within the decision-making structure of your hospital.

To encourage the application of Total Quality Management approaches to health care, in 1992 the Conference of Deputy Ministers of Health hired Ernst & Young Management Consultants to undertake a study. They reviewed seven case studies of excellence in quality management in Canada with companies as diverse as Inco and Bombardier. The consultants identified the major thrusts and captured their implications for health care in Canada. The following chart indicates their findings.[33]

Quality Champions

ORGANIZATION (sector)	RESULTS OF TQM APPROACH
Whistler Mountain Ski Corporation (Tourism)	- premier customer services - development of measurement systems to evaluate impacts of customer service initiative
Nodak Associates Inc. processes (Information Technology Consulting)	- quality embedded in management - has not lost a customer in 7 years of operation
Inco Ltd. Manitoba Division (Mining)	- involvement of union from the start - redefinition of customers to include both internal and external
Bombardier Inc. (Manufacturing)	- value system linked to teamwork - shared vision of customers and shareholders as important
Maritime Telegraph and Telephone (Utility telecommunications)	- measuring results on a continuous basis (customer satisfaction surveys, etc.) - quality as integral to jobs, not an add-on
Standard Aero (Aircraft engine servicing)	- targets to be 50% better than the world's best in every business activity - focus on value-added activities with others dropped
MDS Laboratories	- cost reduction and improved (Medical labs) service levels - MDS transformed from a collection of labs into specimen-collection centres - consolidation of information - consolidation of existing 150 indicators of performance into Quality Improvement Binder

ASK STAFF HOW do you know do you do well you

33 Adapted from Ernst & Young Report to Deputy Ministers of Health, Steering Committee on Quality and Effectiveness, *Quality Champions: Case Studies and Implications for Health Care in Canada*, June, 1993, p. 5-42.

Outcomes and Resource Allocation

20 Applied Clinical Epidemiology: Tapping the Best and Brightest

Applied clinical epidemiology — gasp! But it's not as obscurely technical as it sounds. Epidemiology looks at patterns of disease and their occurrence in the population. Clinical epidemiology looks at patterns of outcome from various medical interventions. "Applied" is my own addition to underscore the practical bent of it.

Across Canada there has been a wave of "best and brightest" approaches to increasing the effectiveness of the health care system. These are new ways to make public policy choices. In each the focus is outcomes. This shift from examining inputs — how much we spend — to examining outcomes — what works and how well it works — is a major shift.

In Manitoba, Dr. Nora Lou Roos heads the Centre for Health Policy; in Saskatchewan, Dr. Stewart McMillan is Chair of the Saskatchewan Health Services Utilization and Research Commission (HSURC), and in Ontario, Dr. David Naylor heads The Institute for Clinical Evaluative Sciences (ICES). Whatever the name on the door, these institutes are research tanks filled with very bright researchers focused on how to judge outcome: what works and how well it works. Their goals are not simply to do good research driven by intellectual curiosity and publish the results in technical journals. Governments have funded these initiatives to focus on improving both quality and affordability through *applying* knowledge and intelligence to the measurement of outcomes. Governments also believe that practitioners are more likely to accept the results and findings of independent think tanks. The results are available in user friendly formats.

Let us examine a few examples of a non-technical sort. ICES published a study in October of 1993 which calculated that if all vasectomies were done in doctor's offices, rather than in hospitals, the saving would be about $4.26 million per year in Ontario alone.[33] The cost for a vasectomy in an outpatient department of a hospital was found to be $324 versus a fee paid in a doctor's office of $10.30. How many vasectomies per year does your hospital perform? How

---

33 Wendy Young and Vivek Goel, *The Impact of Relocating Vasectomies from Hospital Outpatient Departments to Non-Hospital Sites*, Institute for Clinical Evaluative Sciences, Working and Research Paper Series #19, October 1993.

many other procedures are better performed in other settings? How could you create incentives to shift work to the most appropriate setting?

The bottom line for hospital managers is clear. Each study released by ICES, or the Manitoba Centre or the Saskatchewan Commission is a source of good, well-researched ideas. Why not ask your vice president medical and the president of your medical staff to co-chair a group to review these ideas and findings as they apply to YOUR hospital. Successfully managing change in health care is probably 80% implementation and 20% bright ideas. The work of the health service researchers needs to affect behaviour changes in hospitals and in the delivery of health care. It must be a key driver of intelligent change. The tough, essential job is to build bridges between what we *know* and what we *do* in health care.

Managing Non-Government Revenues

21 Meals, Parking and All of That (extra-bonus special idea No.21!)

In difficult economic times it is easy and tempting to devote too much effort to schemes to attract additional revenues. This can have a negative effect on organizational performance, if it diverts management and board attention away from pressing challenges in the expenditure management side. Here are a few initiatives worth taking. Be careful — do not divert your attention from the real management challenge of doing more with less. The revenue side can be seductive and treacherous.

The sad story of the financial crisis[34] which engulfed St. Michael's Hospital in Toronto flowed from a wholesale shift of management effort to a revenue project, contributing to both large losses and a rapid growth in deficit and debt in the late 1980's and early 1990's. The current hospital president described the situation at St. Michael's Hospital during their troubled period as follows:

Management team — out of control

Board — asleep at the switch

---

34 Lone et al. *Report of the Investigation of St. Michael's Hospital*, August 30, 1991, Details the difficulties of St. Michael's presented by Jeff Lozon, Canadian Hospital Association Conference, Halifax, June 7, 1994.

Medical Staff appetite for new technology — insatiable
Owners — trusted the wrong people[35]

The happy news is that the dynamic team of Sister Mary Beth Montcalm, Board Chair Patrick Keenan and President Jeff Lozon, who replaced the previous revenue-fixated folk, achieved a remarkable turnaround by putting their focus back on the expenditure side of the ledger. They have reduced St. Michael's Hospital spending by 15% without damaging care services. This was accomplished with a 25% reduction in overall management, a 55% reduction in senior management and the closure of 126 beds. Total staff reductions were 500 positions with 300 actual layoffs.

There is reason to ask your financial team to review all revenue possibilities, including options such as the sale of surplus land assets. Revenues from parking and other non-health care services should be at market rates and effectively managed. "Are we in the health business or the parking lot management business?" and other such questions are worth asking. What hidden subsidies do you have in place for direct employees or doctors? Are these still justified, if they ever were? But, don't let the great revenue search become a dangerous diversion from managing.

Advocating Change Is Easy, Doing It Is Hard

These ideas focus much more on re-engineering hospital activities than on the human consequences for the hospital workforce. This is not a pointless or thoughtless omission. The people aspects are dealt with in Part 2. Hospital boards, managers and other key players have the challenging task of pursuing change rapidly enough to get the necessary job done but taking sufficient time to bring along their health care people. Without their support little lasting and constructive change can be accomplished. With their active support and participation, this process can be interesting and very productive.

Our wins in health care in the next while will require a daily "grinding it out on the ground" in re-engineering care delivery. We need a lot of help from trustees. It is worthwhile to note that the British are scrambling to create what they call trust hospitals, i.e. hospitals with boards from the community. We have that. It is a tremendous asset. If the trustees can be persuaded to ask the difficult

---

35 Presentation by Jeffrey Lozon, Canadian Hospital Association Conference, Halifax, Nova Scotia, June 7, 1994.

questions, we can see a rationalization of the system that will maintain affordability and quality.

Look West — Look Way West

Canadian hospital trustees and managers looking for inspiration should look to the Greater Victoria Hospital Society (GVHS) and to Ken Fyke, its remarkable CEO. In the past decade, since the three hospitals on four sites in Victoria have been brought under one governance and management, a virtual transformation has occurred. All of the progress has been achieved despite the high portion of Victoria's population over the age of sixty-five. Fully 20% have reached this age in Canada's retirement capital. Far from overwhelming the hospital system, as some have predicted, the GVHS is using fewer hospital beds than nearly anywhere else in Canada.

With a reduction from 25% to 2.3% in the number of beds utilized by people best served elsewhere, and with an emphasis on home nursing care, including pain control and palliation, the GVHS has returned dying to the home. The benefits include both the creation of a more compassionate end-of-life setting and the availability of resources for other needs. Significant progress has also been made in the quest to improve community care. Through patient education, the number of nursing home visits associated with cataract surgery had been reduced from twelve to one per patient.

So, learn about Ken Fyke and the Greater Victoria Hospital Society — they are 80% of the way to the future of hospital services.

Good Stuff To Read

Re-engineering the Corporation by Michael Hammer and James Champy. Published by Harper, New York, 1993. This is a powerful book of insight and advocacy for starting from scratch in the redesign of how we do business. The authors argue persuasively for an abandonment of orthodoxy and a thoughtful, participatory reworking of the processes and organization of the enterprise. Their case studies have application to customer service in the health care sector.

Rx for Hospitals New Hope for Medicare in the Nineties by Philip Hassen. Published by Stoddart, Toronto 1993. Phil Hassen is the president of St. Joseph's Health Centre in London, Ontario. He is also a leading Canadian advocate and practitioner of Total Quality

Management (TQM). A first rate book which brings together the practical and the theoretical, it is a must-read for hospital board members, hospital managers, hospital based nurses, physicians and those who sit on various health planning bodies. It offers sound practical ideas on how to make continuous improvement through TQM in a hospital setting.

The Challenge of Organization Change or *When Giants Learn to Dance*, London, Simon & Schuster, 1989 or *The Change Masters, Corporate Entrepreneurs at Work*, London, Unwin, 1985 both by Rosabeth Kantor. Any of these books by this Harvard professor are a wonderful read with strong ideas on how organizations can manage change.

Quality Champions: Case Studies and Implications for Health Care in Canada. "A Profile of Findings" for the Conference of Deputy Ministers of Health, Ernst & Young, September, 1993. An excellent review of the experience of seven major Canadian corporations. Implications for health care management are clearly outlined.

Report of the Investigation of St. Michael's Hospital by Edward Lane, Ralph Coombs, Donald Holmes, August 30, 1991. Available from St. Michael's Hospital. A guidebook on how not to manage the affairs of a hospital. A gripping read.

Get on the Mailing List

Institute for Clinical Evaluative Sciences
G-2, 2075 Bayview Avenue
North York, Ontario
M4N 3M5
The ICES Working Paper series is an excellent source of ideas. A variety of key topics from surgical rates to drug utilization to surveys of key medical literature are included in the series. The ICES monograph, *Patterns of Health Care in Ontario — ICES Practice Atlas, First Edition*, 1994 published by the Canadian Medical Association is available from the CMA at 1867 Alta Vista Drive, Ottawa, Ontario K1G 3Y6. It is an insightful and data rich source for all concerned with health policy and managing the delivery of health services. Issues covered include patterns of drug use, variations in surgical procedures by region, variations in lengths of stay and day

surgery use. This is the most thorough work in Canada on these issues. It is a must read for health policy makers and health care managers. It is also a powerful tool for consumers and consumer groups.

Saskatchewan Health Services Utilization Commission
Box 46
GMO 41
Saskatoon, Saskatchewan
S7N 8W8
(306) 966-1500

The Manitoba Centre for Health Policy and Evaluation
St. Boniface Hospital Research Centre
409 Tache Avenue, Room 2008
St. Boniface, Manitoba
R2H 2A6
(204) 233-8563

Council for the Evaluation of Health Care Technology
522 Pine Avenue West
Montreal, Quebec
H2W 1S6

Hospital Annual Reports — Another excellent source of ideas and advice is to obtain annual reports from individual hospitals which are leaders and learn from their experiences. My own list of hospital annual reports always includes Foothills Hospital in Calgary, University of Alberta Hospital in Edmonton, St. Boniface Hospital in St.Boniface, Manitoba and a range of Ontario hospitals including The Hospital for Sick Children, Mt. Sinai, Wellesley, Sunnybrook, Toronto, Kingston General, St. Joseph's in London, Chedoke — McMaster in Hamilton and CHEO (Children's Hospital of Eastern Ontario).

International Benchmarking Clearinghouse — Part of the American Productivity & Quality Centre, the Clearinghouse is an excellent source of books and other publications on benchmarking and can be reached at 1-800-366-9606.

Chapter 2
Long Term Care Services

The elderly benefit as much as other age groups from good nutrition, regular exercise and other health promoting activities.[1]

Long-term care is likely to be the 'sleeper' health issue in Canada. As a baby-boomer, I realize that re-engineering for the aging of my generation will create major change, as it did in the school system, universities and labour markets. Soon, in planning terms, the long-term care system will feel aging boomers' demands. Countries with older populations, such as Germany and the United Kingdom, are already experiencing these enormous pressures. Occasionally, in stories about the inability of current levels of contribution to sustain the Canada Pension Plan, we get a glimpse of a much tougher future ahead. The good news is that we are living longer in good health. The bad news is that a small percentage of a larger group of us needing long-term care can devastate current funding arrangements. Our need to better balance health care approaches to mental illness between institutions and communities is directly linked to the long-term care issue.

Mental and physical health are both part of long-term care. As we live longer and become more frail a variety of health issues arise. Many of these correspond to issues addressed later in the book having to do with advance directives for our care. Much of the dilemma of treating the elderly in need of care, stems from disorders

---

1   June Engel, ed., "Keep up the quality of life with advancing years," Chapter 15, *The Complete Canadian Health Guide* (Toronto: Key Porter, 1993), p. 392.

such as Alzheimer's disease, which rob people of their ability to decide for themselves about care. A vast majority of seniors experience greater needs for company, companionship and a social context than for intensive medical care.

In the long-term care sector we are seeing the same shift to community and broadening of continuum of services as in the acute care sector. The unlinking of services from institutions, and the desire of most elderly persons to remain in their own homes and live independently, is providing opportunities for rapid growth in non-institutionally-based services. For example, in the United States, there are estimated to be three thousand day care centres for the elderly, a growth rate of 50% in the last three years and forecast to soon reach ten thousand centres. The benefits of these centres and other efforts of a non-institutional nature are supported by a range of studies. One such study conducted by California's Department of Aging in the early 1980s concluded that between 87% and 96% of people who attended senior citizens' day centres either improved or maintained their functional abilities in such daily activities as bathing, dressing, problem solving, and so on. There is both a humanity and a cost-effectiveness embodied in this approach. In some cases these types of services will delay institutionalization by a period of months or years; in other cases they will prevent its necessity all together.

Of the myriad issues in the long term care field this chapter focuses on three key challenges:

- the need to integrate health and social services in a comprehensive and manageable fashion
- the need to examine the financial issues sooner rather than later at a national level
- the role technologies can play in long term care services.

Integrating Services

Across Canada changes are going on in how long-term care services are organized. In Ontario, after two successive governments engaged in lengthy policy analysis and extensive consultation, a movement toward a reformed system is underway. The key elements of the Ontario reform can be summarized as a more needs-based funding approach on the institutional care side and significant new investment to build a high quality, comprehensive, set of services in the home and community setting. One of the most interesting aspects of the Ontario long-term care policy process was the surprisingly strong impact of advocacy organizations for seniors in the policy process.

Consultation changed the government's programme design in a fairly dramatic way. The government's original intention had been to establish placement coordination agencies to perform the gatekeeper function, replacing individual physicians and institutions. Advocacy by seniors' organizations pushed the government a step further, into the more radical reorganization of the system just beginning. At its core is the principle of one-stop shopping. Seniors, as consumers, indicated their very strong preference for a more accessible and centralized service provision network. At present, thousands of small agencies deliver services ranging from meals on wheels to home care to visiting nursing services. The clear message from seniors was to pull these together and put the access to them under one roof. The policy response, called multi-service agencies, offers the prospect of both administrative efficiency in a system which suffers from fragmentation, as well as the much sought after one-stop shopping. The process of moving the thousands of small agencies into perhaps one hundred to two hundred larger multi-services agencies will be an enormous political and managerial struggle.

Evelyn Shapiro, the founder of Manitoba's innovative home care programme and a sound thinker on health policy and delivery captured the need to integrate in a very practical fashion:

> ...the problem is that most provinces have not included representation from their community care program in their overall planning for health care. In some provinces, this occurs because community care reports to the Minister of Community Services or to the Ministry of Social Services, whereas other health care sectors report to the Ministry of Health. In provinces that do not have this division of responsibility, community care, probably because it is not a major spender, is regarded as nice and maybe even necessary, but peripheral. Each province, in my view, should have some conjoint vehicle for:
>
> 1) reviewing what changes in treatment modalities require changes in the kind or amount of home care services delivered,
> 2) anticipating what effect changes in one sector will have on another

3) deciding whether a new type of service should be delivered, and

4) ensuring that serving a new sub-population does not jeopardize serving vulnerable elders.[2]

Financing For Future Needs

Other nations are also examining their long-term care system. One of the most intriguing policy processes is underway in Germany. The European countries, including Germany, have much older populations than Canada. They provide a window on the future which Canadians would be well advised to look through. With a larger proportion of the population in the seventy plus and particularly in the eight-five plus age group, the German system is experiencing rapidly increasing costs for long-term care. The conclusion the Germans are reaching is that they need a separate form of insurance for long-term care. They delineated insurances for health services, for unemployment, for injury, in short, for the major risks in life. The purpose of an organized national societal approach is to share these risks on a broader basis rather than having them fall on individuals. The options are to create a marketplace in which individuals can insure themselves privately against such future risks, or take the risks on as a collective responsibility as a society. In Canada we have taken health insurance as a societal risk. Through Unemployment Insurance we have shared the burden of insuring the risk of unemployment among employees, employers and governments.

With regard to long-term care, Canada has not set an overall approach in a comprehensive way. We do not have a long-term care system yet. At present, there are a range of approaches in the different provinces. In general, individuals are expected to contribute some or all of their room and board charge while governments pay the health care component. In the home or community setting, there is a mix, with governments paying for a number of services, and individuals being charged cost-sharing in the form of co-payments for some other services. As well, there is an enormous voluntary sector active in the care of the elderly and the provision of services to the elderly. In some ways, the long-term care system shows the mix of funding sources and approaches evident in health care,

---

2   Evelyn Shapiro in Deber and Thompson, *Restructuring Canada's Health Services System* (Toronto: University of Toronto Press, 1992), p. 103.

generally prior to the introduction of Medicare. Some aspects of long-term care are, of course, covered under the Canada Health Act and the health insurance acts of the provinces. Medical care and hospital services are insured, drug costs are insured in institutional settings. There is an array of different approaches to drug coverage among the provinces in the home and community sector.

The institutional side of the long-term care system supports a range of institutions including guest homes with minimal care; nursing homes with a moderate amount of care; homes for the aged, both municipal and charitable; and, at the more intensive end of the spectrum, chronic care hospitals. These different institutions have evolved historically on a very fragmented basis. They have become part of the system largely through the development of government funding and therefore standards. Until recently, when several provinces moved toward needs-based or levels of care funding, there was no particular connection between the needs of any individual and the funding received by the institution. The general tendency to have dollars follow patient needs in the system is a good one. If sufficiently sound methodologies can continue to evolve, it will provide a way of increasing both the fairness and the effectiveness of care services within the institutional system.

We have also come to realize that not institutionalizing elderly people who aren't in need of institutionalization, and who could cope in their home on an independent basis with a range of support services, is a far better option. The growth of home care in various provinces is illustrated by a dramatic increase in spending through the past two decades. This mirrors the acceptance by government of care in the home as an alternative to institutionalization in acute care hospitals or long-term care facilities.

We need to have a hard national look at the trends and the numbers. Do we need an additional insurance approach for long term care? Should it be modeled on Germany or the Canada Pension Plan or the Registered Retirement Savings Plan approach? There is a lot to be gained by answering the design questions early.

The Chip Meets Seniors - Welcome to The Caring Network

For a fascinating example of a product which utilizes modern information and telecommunications technology to improve both quality and affordability, a visit with a British company, Tunstall PLC, is worthwhile. Tunstall started out in the alarm business and thirty years later has evolved into a high-technology manufacturer. One of their leading-edge products is called The Caring Network. In their own description:

> A British technology company - Tunstall PLC - has developed a very interesting product by combining software, hardware and a lot of common sense. The Caring Network is a clever use of telecommunications technology and people to provide the elderly with security in their homes while assisting the management of in-home services.[3]

The elements of the system are straightforward: a special, modified telephone for your home, a control switchboard staffed by trained personnel and a computer capable of tracking and storing an accessible record of all care provided.

The Caring Network system allows elderly persons to remain in their home with the security of immediate access to care and a friendly, familiar voice by telephone. By including the record keeping function for all home visits the system begins to reduce dramatically the paperwork burden on providers. Paperwork is not just a hospital phenomena!

Good Stuff to Read

The Eldercare Sourcebook, by Ann Rhodes, Key Porter, Toronto, 1993 ($18.95). Until one-stop shopping is achieved this is a good guidebook of services for seniors. Very readable and current. There is an intention to update annually which will keep it current.

Anything written by Evelyn Shapiro on home care and long term care is highly recommended.

When Older is Wiser: A guide to health care decisions for older adults and their families, by Patricia Parsons and Arthur Parsons, Doubleday Canada, Toronto 1994. A very user friendly guide to rights issues and to various seniors organizations. Accessible and practical in its tone.

---

3   "The Caring Network," Tunstall PLC Corporate brochure, 1993.

Chapter 3
Drugs and Pharmacy Services

Statistics Canada estimates that in 1989, four thousand Canadian seniors died as a result of inappropriate medication use.

- Up to 20 % of seniors entering hospitals are there because of a "drug problem" — too many drugs, the wrong dosage, drug interactions, or the failure to take drugs properly.
- Inappropriate medication use is "one of the five most important quality of care problems among the elderly in terms of morbidity."[1]
- Seniors are being "drugged silly," given medications they don't need or given new expensive drugs that don't work any better than the older, cheaper ones.

Doctors need drugs, but do drugs need doctors? Could the pharmacological revolution ultimately cast aside the physicians? Many patients regulate their own medicines rather skilfully after an initial diagnosis and medical advice. Many simple remedies are available over the counter in pharmacies and their numbers will grow as patents expire on relatively safe medicines like ibuprofen. Large research-intensive pharmaceutical houses are buying up generic manufacturers and suppliers of inexpensive drugs directly to patients.

The challenge is for physicians to develop greater skill and understanding in the use of therapeutic drugs. If they do not,

---

1 *Consumer Response*: Prepared by the Senior Citizens Consumer Alliance for Long-Term Care Reform, Ontario, 1993.

their role in the treatment of many common conditions may become marginal.[2]

Drugs and their use is an area of miraculous breakthroughs, rapid cost growth and horrendous misuse. We have been able to eliminate whole classes of disease and the pain and suffering they cause through drug therapies. But our ability to manage drug therapies has not kept pace with advances in the products or with the market power of the pharmaceutical industry. Technological change is rapidly overtaking our traditional drug distribution systems and replacing them with new, information-rich approaches. Pharmaceutical companies quest for an extended monopoly on new products is giving way to purchase of generic companies and a drive for greater, non-prescription, over-the-counter-sales.

Four ideas are presented which will greatly improve the Canadian situation in the drug policy area. They go to the heart of the needed re-engineering in how we evaluate drugs, how we distribute them and pay for them. By adopting a cost-effectiveness approach to assessing new drugs, re-engineering the drug distribution system and re-skilling the pharmacist, we can create significant efficiencies. By adopting a new national approach, Canada can improve the fairness of the access to necessary drugs.

Drug Use and Abuse

All recent studies of the problems of drug misuse reach two key conclusions. The first is adverse drug reactions are common due to mis-prescribing, inappropriate consumption and lack of conformity to the optimum use of drugs. The second conclusion is that adverse reactions are a high cost to the total health care system, measured in unnecessary human suffering and in millions, perhaps billions, of dollars. Available studies reach roughly the same conclusions on the need for better management of drugs and greater efficiency in the distribution system. As Dr. Barry Sherman, president of generic drug manufacturer, Apotex Inc., argues: "Drugs cost Canada $6 billion to $7 billion per year. With rational prescribing and competition that could come down to $2 billion."[3]

A somewhat remarkable statement for someone in the drug

2   Sir Colin Dollery, "The Harveian Oration," Royal College of Physicians, London, U.K. October 19, 1993.
3   "Profile of Dr. Berry Sherman," *Profit Magazine*, Sept., 1992, p. 37.

manufacturing business! It underscores the huge potential for improvement in the drug use field.

A Changing Marketplace

The day Merck decided to pay $6 billion for Medco Cost Containment the pharmaceutical industry was forever transformed. Merck paid sixty times the earnings for a company that, far from manufacturing drugs, makes its living by managing the cost and distribution of drugs. Medco has its original roots in finding a better way to deliver drug benefits to organizations like the International Ladies Garment Workers Union. Through rapid growth, it has expanded to cover nearly one in every eight Americans for drug benefits. Merck is the largest global pharmaceutical manufacturing firm with sales greater than the GNP of many small nations.

A new drug costs some $300 million to bring to market. Merck have decided that Medco is a better investment than 20 new drugs — a remarkable shift.

WalMart is coming to Canada. The giant U.S. retailer has purchased the Woolco stores and is preparing their conversion to Wal-Marts. Among the areas in which WalMart is known as aggressive price competitors is pharmacy. Large advertisements in the national *Globe and Mail* are recruiting pharmacists to staff these new Wal-Mart pharmacy operations.

What will a changing marketplace mean for Canadians? Certainly more price competition and a wider array of ways of obtaining drugs. But, also, the fundamental reordering of the pharmaceutical and pharmacy industries.

The Chip Meets Norman Paul — Result: Meditrust

Norman Paul is a pharmacist. When he was in his twenties he was part of the Shopper's Drug Mart revolution in Canada. In this first wave, a large chain of pharmacies was assembled by Murray Koffler and significant results achieved. Many more products were added and Shoppers became the drug supermarket. The corner drugstore gave way to the mall superstore as the franchise overwhelmed small businesses owned by the pharmacist. Shopper's Drug Mart used the leverage of a customer flow to sell all sorts of other merchandise. The pharmacy is always at the back of the store and few of us can resist the other products enroute to our prescription. Now, thirty years later, Norman Paul is leading the second revolution in pharmacy distribution in Canada. His company, Meditrust, is often labelled as Canada's first mail order pharmacy, an inadequate description. A better way of looking at Meditrust is as a fundamental re-engineering of the pharmacy business. From the computerized data base record on each client, to the arrival of prescriptions by fax, to the automated assembly line for filling orders and courier delivery, the entire operation is the application of information technology to re-engineering. Without the information and telecommunications technology made possible by the silicon chip, this revolution would not be possible.

Norman Paul is also providing a higher quality service for his customers. Into each dispensed prescription, an information sheet on the drug is included. The patient receives much more than the traditional tiny label with "take before each meal." As well, patient profiles maintained by Meditrust allow them to identify and prevent potential, harmful drug interactions before dispensing. In New Brunswick, Meditrust is piloting interactive telephone booths connected to its national operation along a state of the art information highway.

Meditrust will face competition and resistance in this revolution. Already traditional pharmacies in Ontario have resisted. The largest U.S. mail order pharmacy, Medco Cost Containment, with thirty-three million Americans enrolled, will look to Canada for new markets. Aggressive expansion in Canada by Medco is likely. As well, the advent of WalMart competition in the pharmacy market will bring extremely low prices. WalMart assisted by its massive purchasing clout will push other pharmacies out of business. If this competition follows the course of reducing prices charged to both patients and insurers, including governments, as well as increasing information to patients, then it will assist our Medicare challenge. This second pharmacy revolution has significant potential to simultaneously improve affordability and quality.

A Good Idea: Re-skilling the Pharmacist

Another piece of the pharmacy reform puzzle are pharmacists, their training and their model of practice. Dean Perrier of the University of Toronto, Faculty of Pharmacy, sees a major shift in the role of pharmacists. In a February, 1993, paper he noted that historically, pharmacists were very product-focused but, by the middle of this century this role had been largely taken over by pharmaceutical companies. This narrowed the pharmacist's role to drug distribution. Gradually, many of these tasks passed to the pharmacy technician or dispensing assistant.

Are pharmacists to become more and more, de-skilled assistants to the pharmaceutical industry? Dean Perrier sees a new and evolving role, which is patient-focused rather than product-focused. He calls this expanded role the "pharmaceutical care" model. Perrier describes it as "the responsible provision of drug therapy for the purpose of achieving definite outcomes which improve a patient's quality of life."[4]

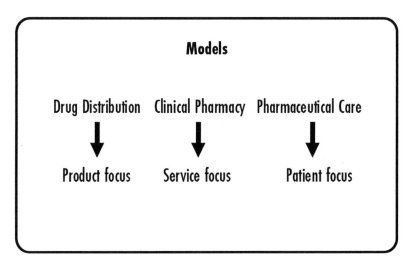

4   Dean Perrier, "The Pharmaceutical Care Model," (Toronto: University of Toronto, 1992).

Pharmaceutical Care Model

In the following pharmaceutical care model three distinct functions can be detailed for the pharmacist. These are:
- Identifying a patient's actual or potential drug related problem (DRP)
- Resolving a patient's actual DRP
- Preventing a patient's potential DRP

Eight categories of problems pharmacists can solve:
1. The patient is taking/receiving a drug for no medically valid indication
2. The patient is requiring drug therapy (a drug indication) but not receiving/taking a drug for that indication
3. The patient is being treated with the wrong drug or drug product
4. The patient is being treated with too little of the correct drug (subtherapeutic dose)
5. The patient is being treated with too much of the correct drug (toxicity)
6. The patient is not receiving/taking the prescribed drug appropriately
7. The patient is experiencing an adverse drug reaction (any undesirable effect from the drug which is not dose related)
8. The patient is experiencing a drug-drug, drug-disease, drug-food, drug-laboratory interaction

There are several prerequisites for a pharmacist to successfully undertake Dean Perrier's vision of an expanded and very desirable role. The first is a diversification in pharmacy training programmes to properly prepare pharmacists. This is underway.

The second necessary reform is the application of information technology to pharmaceutical care activity. Only with full patient information at the point of service can the pharmacist successfully treat the range of problems identified above. Computerized information systems which provide point of service information have been created in Saskatchewan, and started in several other provinces, including Ontario. These information networks will allow a pharmacist to know all the drugs a patient is already taking and how those drugs might interact with the prescription to be filled.

The third necessity is for a fundamental shift in the method of payment for pharmacists. As long as the only two sources of income for community pharmacy are prescription dispensing fees and product mark-ups, it will be difficult to move from a transaction or product-focus to a patient-focus.

With these three improvements, two of which are substantially underway, pharmacists can perform an expanded and needed role in tackling our very serious over-medication and inappropriate medication problems.

Good Ideas: A National Drug Benefit Plan for Canada

As more and more health care services are delivered in a home or community setting, one of the weaknesses of the Canada Health Act has become evident. Because drugs administered in the community setting are not insured medical services under the Canada Health Act, each province has devised its own drug plan, without the benefit of a national standard or framework. The consequences are unfair and expensive. This state of affairs is the major unfinished piece of phase one — the removal of the financial barrier between the individual and appropriate care — of Medicare.

The drug cost issue is very real for Canadians. Their access to appropriate medication is determined by their province of residence. Access to medical and hospital services are reasonably comparable across the country. Variations in access exist, but they are minor and predictable, for example, bigger cities have more sophisticated hospitals than smaller centres. There are, however, major and as yet unexplained variations in use of services. This is not true of how drug costs and benefits are organized. Here access and financial barriers vary dramatically, depending on which province you reside. In Ontario, those over sixty-five years of age or on welfare do not pay for their drugs. If you are working at a low wage you are likely to receive no help from government with your drug bills. Your employer may or may not cover you. Next door in Manitoba, everyone has some coverage under the government Pharmacare plan. A senior citizen would pay the first $117.25 per year of their drug costs and 30% of the balance. Others would pay the first $206.90

per annum and then 30%. In Alberta, seniors pay 20% per prescription but no deductible. Others, under sixty-five pay $50 annually plus 20%. In P.E.I. only seniors and social assistance recipients are covered. Seniors pay $7.85 for the dispensing fee and $4 towards the drug cost. In Ontario, if you are over 65 and wealthy you can send your chauffeur to the pharmacy and the taxpayer will pay the whole cost for your drugs. But if you are without coverage and trying to pay your own drug costs while working, you get no help.

This patchwork of provincial programmes illustrates the problem of unfair coverage across the country. The inequity of this situation is getting worse as the smaller, poorer provinces have been forced to raise deductibles and co-payments. And the very real issue of misuse of drugs through inappropriate prescribing and dispensing require national efforts to tackle. This work need not be undertaken by the federal government, although federal leadership has historically been key to achieving interprovincial cooperation in the health field.

A national plan with provincial discretion over both the scale of their formulary (what drugs are covered) and the level of premiums collected, would better serve our country than the current inequitable and inefficient hodgepodge of programmes. There are two major advantages of a national drug plan approach. The first is that it would allow far better management of drug use. Canada has a limited number of experts in the drug evaluation field (also known as pharmacological epidemiology). By having the relative merit and cost-effectiveness of each existing and new drug assessed once and the results shared among the provinces, better decisions could be made. The second major benefit is increased bargaining power to obtain lower prices.

A national plan would also benefit Canada's drug manufacturers. Many complaints have been voiced by manufacturers about the fragmented nature of Canada's drug market. Because each province operates a separate plan with different rules for listing products and paying for them, the companies incur considerable additional costs conforming to variant prices and policies in the different provinces. A national plan could reduce company costs in this regard. A good case could be made that some of these savings should flow through to taxpayers and consumers in the form of lower prices. Recently the industry, through the Pharmaceutical Manufacturers Association of Canada, has undertaken to promote better use of drugs. As noted earlier, this area requires significant attention in Canada.

The Australians have a national approach to drugs. The Pharmaceutical Benefits Scheme PBS is a monopoly purchaser of drugs in Australia, accounting for approximately 80% of the market and directly influencing the prices of drugs in the hospital market (12%). Expenditure in 1989/90 was approximately $1 billion, accounting for 8% of Australian Federal Government health expenditure.

The PBS has a long history. It was originally developed in 1950 to pay for 'lifesaving and disease preventing drugs' to the community at no cost. The list was originally quite small but has grown to about 1300 items, including different strengths and dosage forms.

Co-payment, that is payments by patients, for general users was introduced in 1960, and is now $15 per script. Co-payments for pensions were introduced for the first time in 1991 and are set at $2.50 per script (prescription), the same as for other subsidized users, with a safety net.

The Australian PBS

The goals of the PBS balance health care, economic development and fiscal objectives of the government. They are designed to:

- provide access to safe, efficacious and high quality pharmaceuticals to the Australian population, irrespective of income
- limit the budgetary cost to Government
- encourage the development of an Australian pharmaceutical industry

The PBS prices are determined taking into account eight pricing factors:

i the prices of alternative brands of the same drug
ii comparative prices of the drugs in the same therapeutic group
iii cost information supplied by the manufacturer
iv prescription volumes, economies of scale and other factors such as expiry date, storage requirements, product stability and special manufacturing requirements
v prices of the drug in reasonably comparable overseas countries

vi the level of activity being undertaken by the company in Australia including new investment, production and research development

vii other relevant factors which the applicant company wishes the Authority to consider

viii other directions as advised by the Minister

Drug companies can launch a drug onto the market after it receives general marketing approval from the Australian Drug Evaluation Committee. In reality true market access is only provided through a drug attaining PBS listing. Companies lodge applications for listing on the PBS to the Pharmaceutical Benefits Advisory Committee (PBAC) after marketing approval is received. PBAC considers applications and advises the Pharmaceutical Benefits Pricing Authority (PBPA) of its recommendation for listing. PBPA is then responsible for negotiating the price with the company. The PBPA determines prices taking into account factors such as the advice of PBAC on the therapeutic benefits of the drugs in comparison with other drugs and the cost of manufacture, or import, plus an amount meant to cover indirect costs such as research and development, administration and profit. A gross margin of 30% over direct costs is used as a guide although this varies with the level of usage of the product and other factors.

More recently a number of companies have indicated an increased willingness to de-list products, or not to seek listing not being prepared to accept the price determined by the PBPA. The private prescription market may eventually provide a greater share of the total market, but under existing arrangements it will probably always be small.

In addition, an increasing number of drugs listed on the PBS have restrictions on use. This is done by an authority system where drugs are rationed by making it difficult for patients to fill prescriptions and by building in delays between scripts. Restricted listings include products for which prescribing is permitted only after the doctor attests that all cheaper alternatives have been tried. These include cancer drugs and human growth hormone.

> The list of restricted access drugs is likely to grow because of the increasing numbers of effective but very expensive drugs.[5]

How Would We Pay For This Programme?

The major obstacle to a national drug plan — the perilous state of public finance in our nation — will be readily and rapidly identified. This dictates a careful approach, without new public dollars, but it is not an excuse for inaction. The savings inherent in a national approach, plus a revenue stream from fair, monthly premiums, plus existing provincial spending would be a good start. The necessary federal investment may well be political will, leadership and a small amount of funds. The gains to a strengthened Canadian Medicare and a true adherence to the principles of comprehension and portability in the Canada Health Act are well worth the effort.

Major savings would be realized from improved utilization and tougher price bargaining. The cost of the plan could be born by the Government of Canada through price rebates negotiated nationally, the governments of the provinces, and individual Canadians through payment of modest monthly premiums. This would spread the burden more fairly. It would also put drug costs on the same footing as medical or hospital costs, rather than continuing a patchwork quilt coverage that resembles the current, and discredited, approach of Americans to health care in general. Where employers are now paying for drug coverage they would continue by paying premiums for their employees.

It would be a fitting twenty-fifth anniversary of Medicare to replace the inequity inherent in our fragmented approach to drugs by a fair national plan, administered by each province.

Good Stuff to Read

Reflections on a Month in the Life of the Ontario Drug Plan, by Warren McIsaac. C. David Naylor, Geoffrey M. Anderson, Bernie J. O'Brien, published a ICES Paper #004, April, 1993.

The Real Pushers — A Critical Analysis of the Canadian Drug

---

5   Adapted from Brendan Kearney paper. Presented to the King's Fund International Seminar, October, 1992, Adelaide, Australia.

Industry, by Joel Lexchin, New Star Books, 1984. Although nearly a decade old, Joel Lexchin's book asks all the tough and necessary questions in a critical and readable fashion. Dr. Lexchin's criticism caused more questioning of the industry's role by policy makers in Canada and lead to some improvements.

Controlling Drug Expenditure in Canada, the Ontario Experience, by Paul Gorecki, 1992, published by the Economic Council of Canada. A data-rich analysis of the Ontario Drug Benefit Program.

Part 2

The 3 R's of Human Resource Management: Restructuring Re-skilling Redeployment

Health care services are a labour-intensive, person to person endeavour. Of the over $64 billion expended on the health care delivery system in Canada in 1994, about 80% will be taken home as a paycheque by a nurse, doctor or other health care worker. Health care creates jobs for nearly 750,000 Canadians.

Within Canadian health care the trend has been toward increasing expenditures on the wage component. In 1961, 68.6% of total hospital spending was wage costs. By 1988, wage costs had climbed to 76.3%. Managing change in how we deliver services is about managing the human issues, about managing transformation in careers and lives. The human side of the equation must be central to achieve success, as work is restructured to coincide with a re-engineered health care delivery system. Restructuring will require us to shape our training and our retraining systems on the assumption that once-in-a-lifetime training is not the route to success in a world with significant technology advances.

There are 3R's on the human side of the re-engineering challenge in our health care delivery system:

- restructuring of work;
- re-skilling of workers;
- redeployment of workers.

With serious attention to these 3R's and a new infrastructure for the people side, a humane transition from our current health care system is possible. How do we manage our most important health care resource — our health care providers/workers — through this re-engineering period? First, we must recognize the need to alter the work itself. Second, we must recognize the need for all health workers, whether physicians or orderlies, cooks or nurses, to gain the new skills to undertake restructured work. And, thirdly, we must implement redeployment mechanisms. Redeployment is a fancy term for moving health workers to the new work from the old. Redeployment mechanisms will allow continuity and permit workers to follow health care work as it moves from inpatient to outpatient, from the hospital to the community and the home. Where an overall reduction in the workforce of a hospital or other health sector employer is required, effort must be made to maximize voluntary exits through measures such as enhanced early retirements or leaves of absence. Involuntary exits, i.e. layoffs should be a last, not a first, resort.

We have badly undermanaged human resources in Canadian health care. Unfortunately this situation is not unique to the health care sector of our economy. Generally, we focus on training young people, rather than retraining our existing workforce. Health care has been no better or worse than the steel industry or retail trade. We are now turning the demographic corner into a country of middle-aged workers. The only rationale response is to shift from a pure focus on initial training to ongoing workforce training for new skills.

The second major force driving change in human resources is technology. As it alters how and where we work, our skills are being surpassed. It goes without saying, revolutions in information and telecommunication technologies have created powerful new tools which we must learn to use effectively. We need skills to manage these new tools and to adapt to restructured work. These skills will not appear by magic. Training is essential.

Human resource management, training and redeployment apply to *all* health care workers, physicians, orderlies, nurses and managers. The Canadian policy effort to tackle the physician resource issue provides important lessons.

Job security for individual health workers will not come from opposing all change. The necessity of change is too great, the timing too urgent. Instead, we require careful attention to minimize the adverse consequences for individuals. Continuity of employment will depend upon ability to cope with modifications and evolution.

Bargaining agents in the health care sector are gradually acknowledging these realities, without much enthusiasm. They seek mechanisms to protect their members by equipping them for change in the work environment. We need new infrastructure to ensure re-skilling opportunities and redeployment. Successful creation of new structures and opportunities for workers depends on increased labour-management cooperation, often difficult to achieve in an atmosphere of reduced financial resources and layoffs.

It is essential nevertheless that management fulfil their entire obligation to their employees by finding ways of cooperating. It is also essential that unions participate fully in joint activities with the potential to create new opportunities for members to gain skills and access to new jobs. For this process to succeed, management must be open and direct about change; hiding consequences will not work.

It will only erode trust. Bargaining agents and individual workers need to accept the inevitability of evolution and work to adapt.

Re-engineering health care services turns on the acceptability of reform. In turn, the acceptability depends upon each individual's perception of their own risk. This risk is accessed personally. Will I lose *my* job? Will *my* income be reduced? Successful management of reform requires good answers to these questions. Answers which must be found as a result of communication and sharing between management, employees and where applicable, bargaining agents.

These are troubled, tough, times for those leading change in health services delivery. Just surviving is difficult in an environment of turbulence and uncertainty. As a people–intensive business, health services are shaped, to a considerable degree, by perceptions of the individual health workers, as well as the realities of the situation. These are essential steps for those leading change:

- Clear vision and objectives
- Have a *plan* developed with lots of workforce participation and based on objective data that people can understand
- Take care of people in the process of change: address their loss and their needs for support in a period of adjustment
- Commit resources to training, education and communication
- Be consistent and visible in the implementation of change with a transparent timetable
- Meet at frequent intervals with the representatives of the bargaining agents or other worker representatives; a direct and informed discussion in advance of announcements will assist management of the change process; do not allow surprises
- Be honest and open about mistakes — they are inevitable — keep listening and learning

Leadership of people in health organizations must take into account several complexities. Health organizations assemble an array of professionals with varying degrees of professional autonomy. This complexity is deepened by a major professional group who derive most of their income from sources other than the organization's budget. Fee-for-service physicians participate in the financial and organizational structure of health care services on a different basis than most other health workers. This in turn, generates further layering in the management of change.

Our health institutions must become learning organizations if they are to survive and manage transition among their people in more effective ways during rapid transitions. Some of our hospitals predate the creation of Canada (and have life spans far longer than that of many corporations). They have already demonstrated one characteristic of a learning organization — an instinct for survival.

What is a learning organization?

Consultant and M.I.T. Professor Peter Senge sees five disciplines converging to innovate learning organizations. He views them as "component technologies" of the learning organization. They are:
- systems thinking
- personal mastery
- mental models
- building shared vision
- team learning

Of these disciplines, systems thinking acts as the fifth discipline, because it brings the others together.[1]

There is also a qualitative and power dimension to the human issues. Most vividly captured in recent actions to reduce sexual abuse of patients by health providers, the above mentioned cluster of issues is really about authority and responsibility.

Remember, There Is No New Money For Health Care

The best assumption for health care managers to make is that they must provide with existent dollars in the health care system. While reallocation of funds from low-priority to high-priority areas is inevitable, the overall picture in the resources available to health care will either shrink or maintain very slow growth. That makes all of our jobs tougher. The most reasonable national prognosis for the next three to five years is no real growth in health care spending and up to 3% per year real reduction. The form may vary greatly from province to province. Alberta is proceeding with real funding cuts of about 15%. Other provinces will freeze funding and let slow inflation grind away at the existing purchasing power already of the health care system. Whether radical surgery or a diet is the treatment, financial resources will diminsh or stay the same.

---

1   Peter Senge, *The Fifth Discipline — The Art & Practice of the Learning Organization* (New York: Doubleday, 1990), p.5-11. Peter Senge does a very fine job of explaining the learning organization. Read this book!

Pace of Change

Change is stressful. Pace of change is a real issue. A lot of health care leaders and providers are wearied by the pace of change and wish everything could just decelerate. Circumstances won't allow it. People are going to have to continue a juggling act of doing a superb job of managing their existing programmes while being involved in innovative redirection of programmes. That is stressful.

This overwhelming feeling is felt all the way up and down the line. We will need to be skilful in managing the 750,000 of us who work in the delivery of care and in the promotion of health in Canada, to arrive at a new and better place. We will need to support each other. This is a real opportunity to make change in a constructive way, while being aware of the mounting pressure to move rapidly. We are in the early stages of a major transformation of health work. Our working lives in health will be irreversibly altered and, if we are able to balance efficiency with compassion, improved.

Chapter 4

Restructuring Health Work

In his presentation to the 1993 *Financial Post* Conference on Restructuring Health Care in Canada, Mr. Peter Ellis, CEO of Sunnybrook Hospital, vividly underscored the need to restructure health
work. Utilizing the following table from a Booz Allen Hamilton Inc.
U.S. study,[1] he noted that as little as 16% of hospital staff time is on
actual patient care, less than one out of every six hours!

Traditional U.S. Hospital's Typical Allocation of Hospital Staff Time

Nearly twice as much time — 30% — is spent on documentation or

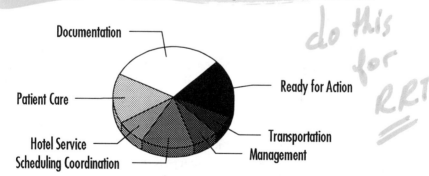

1   Booz Allen Hamilton study of American Hospitals from a presentation by Mr.
    Peter Ellis to the *Financial Post* Conference, 1993. Similar data is contained in
    other studies of time allocation in the hospital sector such as the work of Philip
    Lathrop, "Where Your Wage Dollar Goes," *Healthcare Forum Journal*,
    July/August, 1991, p.18. Philip Lathrop calculated that 24% of hospital employee
    time was direct patient care versus 29% on institutional and medical
    documentation.

paperwork. "Ready for Action," a positive way of indicating waiting, consumed 19% of total time. Peter Ellis reached the obvious conclusion: there is significant room for improvement.

In the context of restructuring health work, these are very powerful numbers. They provide a possible answer to the often-asked question "From where will the resources come to meet new health care needs?" Patient care time can be increased by finding more efficient means of handling documentation through new information technology. When nearly twice as many hours are spent on documentation as on patient care, there is an opportunity as well as a problem.

The objective of restructuring health work is two-fold: maximize the portion of health work allotted to providing patient care, and minimize all other work by health workers. This is a basis on which to re-engineer health work. It is important to start from a patient or consumer-centred view with a thorough process of examining how work is carried out.

New information and telecommunication technologies will be key enablers of the restructuring and re-engineering of health work. Because of our computer capacity to store and instantly retrieve information we have enormous potential to reduce the amount of time spent on documentation of patient records. Converting rooms full of files and paper records to data storage on computers can free up a significant portion of health care worker's time. This applies particularly to nurses, for whom paper-dominated record keeping has been a major misuse of their skills and time. As hand-held data entry computers replace the patient chart, nurses will have more time to nurse. Automation of records, and the ability to access them over telephone lines, will also allow physicians to utilize their time more effectively.

One of the activities undertaken by the Ontario Health Ministry in 1993 was movement to physician billings in a machine-readable form. By convincing Ontario physicians to submit their billings in this form, the Health Ministry redeployed nearly two hundred staff to other duties. There was also dramatic improvement in the percentage of claims free of processing errors.

The Ontario Health Ministry has conducted a pilot study with "smart cards," health cards with an embedded silicon chip containing full personal health records. While there were benefits to the use of the so-called smart card, the technology still proved too expensive for universal use. Automation, in addition to saving time and improving accuracy, also reduces inappropriate care and outright fraud within the health care system.

Any heath care organization should fully investigate the potential of information and telecommunication technology to assist them in re-engineering the processes of providing quality care. It is time to get going or risk being left behind. Many corporations have created the position of Chief Information Officer to underscore the importance of this expertise and to lead their investments in technology.

Multi-Skilling of Health Workers

Sunnybrook CEO Peter Ellis also noted that among the 1200 non-union staff at his hospital there had been 263 different job classifications. Compartmentalization is seen as a barrier to both care and performance in the hospital setting. Peter Ellis's remedy includes a matrix organization, multi-skilling of employees, a patient-centred care approach and larger service units.

Multi-skilling of health workers is a must as we move more services to the community and home. While many separate health providers visiting a patient's hospital bedside is inefficient, the inefficiencies grow dramatically when the many providers must travel to a patient's home. Without multi-skilling the move to greater in-home care will not achieve its full potential.

Teams and Super Teams

Self-managed teams is one useful approach to restructuring work and work organizations. Cross-functionality, an awkward word, is about connecting people in different jobs and functions, allowing them to problem-solve quickly and effectively. This contrasts sharply to a hierarchical organization, where decisions are delegated upward and instructions move downward. In a team-organized workplace, responsibility, accountability and decision-making rest with self-managed action teams.

Experience in the industrial sector shows the benefits of self-management. Over the last decade so-called super teams, between three and thirty workers who take responsibility for cross-functions and high performance, have been organized in about 7% of the U.S. workforce, according to a study of five hundred large American companies by the American Productivity and Quality Centre in

Houston.[2] Super teams make sense if a job entails a high level of dependency among three or more people. The more complex the job, the more it is suited to teams and super teams. The complexity and interdependence of health care work is indisputable. Teams and super teams could be the way forward in health care.

In companies that have introduced teamwork a dramatic improvement in quality and efficiency, an acceleration of decision-making and implementation have resulted. General Mills, a major food manufacturing company with all of its factories organized in super teams, reports productivity 40% higher than in traditional factories.

Plants with self-managed teams need fewer middle managers. De-layering is a part of the restructuring of work, but it needs to be accompanied by organizing, resourcing and empowering teams. Simply removing middle management layers will not realize the potential gains offered by a more comprehensive approach. In hospital settings or in community health care, significant movement towards interdisciplinary teams is afoot. Much more energy in that direction is needed if self-managed teams are to succeed. The relationships among different providers — physicians, nurses, physiotherapists, orderlies, in fact all those who have a role to play vis-à-vis service to the patient — will need to be carefully considered.

Allowing teams themselves to decide how to tackle the organization of work and other workforce challenges is essential. You cannot impose decisions from above and expect teams to own and be accountable for the results. Areas in which responsibility has been given to teams include work schedules, goal-setting and development of appropriate benchmarks to measure progress towards goals. Communication, flexibility and ownership of decisions made and their consequences, are key factors that make this approach more productive.

Among those involved in studying and implementing team concepts, there is a lively debate as to whether it is vital to tie compensation to the new team organization. Everyone agrees there must be recognition for teams and team members that do an excellent job. Whether the reward system must extend to compensation is unclear; there are strong views on both sides. Certainly, there ought to be motivation for the teams. Most involved in teamwork report enjoying

2   "Who Needs a Boss," *Fortune Magazine*, May 7, 1990, p.5.

it more than working in a hierarchy. One consequence of removing middle management is that there are fewer opportunities for advancement. This seems however, to be more than offset by career ladder shortening and opportunities for rewarding work.

Re-organizing from a hierarchical structure to a team approach is neither a panacea nor a short-term quick fix. It will require changes in everything from information available to employees, to the physical structure of the offices, including the furniture and how it creates relationships. And take a significant amount of time. In recognition of this innovative move in the work place, one large American furniture manufacturer now produces a line of "team" furniture which creates "neighbourhoods" or small areas for work teams, and a central work area with a meeting table, while desks nearby provide privacy.

These are some of the shapes of future work. Many of them are already evident in hospitals as leaders such as Peter Ellis at Sunnybrook Hospital and Jack Litvack at St. Boniface Hospital move their organizations towards a service unit approach.

Technology and Restructuring

Technology is restructuring work in the health sector by altering work activities. As in the industrial setting, the work of actually doing a task has been replaced by tending the machine that does it. In factories this evolution moved people from the shop floor into control booths. In the health care setting it has moved doctors from wielding the scalpel to overseeing machines.

An excellent example is the emergence of lithotripsy technology. A lithotripsy machine smashes kidney stones without surgical intervention. The patient sits in a bath of water. Sound waves bombard the kidney stones, breaking them into pieces small enough to be passed through the body. In the past, urologists would have performed surgery to remove stones to eliminate obstruction and the excruciating pain that would result. Now, some of these same surgeons spend part of their time watching the lithotripsy machine at work. Their role is machine-tending rather than active medical treatment. From performing to watching.

Generally, when machines take over functions there is a tendency to have the skilled worker of the past watch the working machine. Is this really necessary? Would a technician be just as competent? Naturally, in medicine, as in other fields, technology will de-skill particular tasks. This need not be negative, instead, coping with new technology will require retraining and a refocussing of effort.

Labour Relations

One problem in restructuring health work is a relatively dysfunctional labour relations system. There have been major upheavals in labour relations in the Canadian private sector, but the public sector need serious improvement. Historically, the roles of management and labour were clear, separate and apart. Labour relations was about dividing the "pie" between the two parties — labour and management. The labour relations system viewed its role only as distributing wealth, not creating it.

In the private sector, the Steelworkers Union — the United Steelworkers of America — has played a major leadership role in restructuring the American steel industry. They understand the trade-off between wages and jobs and the survival of the enterprise. They also comprehend the vital need to reskill their members. This is evident in Canadian Steel Trade Employment Congress (CSTEC), an innovative training initiative in which the United Steelworkers Union is an equal partner with the steel companies.

Job loss and rigidities in how work is organized are real consequences. Compartmentalization and fragmentation is not beneficial for workers or the health care system. To the extent that labour relations are unable to solve problems, they become part of the problem.

How do we change dysfunctional labour relations? Because the system is built around distributing wealth rather than creating it, bargaining agents must take some responsibility for the process that creates wealth. Management must be accountable for ensuring access to training and greater security for workers, as alternatives arise. Training security is essential to the survival of the enterprise and its success. This has happened well in some places and not so well in others. For example, when Canadair, the Montreal-based aircraft manufacturer, was purchased by Bombardier and they launched a new product, the president of the union at Canadair went to the Paris air show with the management team to help sell the plane. At Algoma Steel, the employees became owners to save the enterprise. The United Steelworkers Union played the decisive role in salvaging the company from bankruptcy. Historically, this has not been the role played by labour leaders. The old "no truck or trade with the bosses" approach to the world of labour relations is giving way to the new realities of technology, knowledge-based work and relentless financial pressure. There is enlightened leadership, in pockets, on both sides of the labour-management divide but also strong clinging at times to old confrontational approaches.

In labour relations, an adversarial system built around staying up all night, pounding tables, yelling and eventually, when everyone is sleep-deprived, coming to some sort of agreement is not constructive. Neither is an approach which looks to the past. Too often, bargaining starts with both parties soliciting criticisms with the existing agreement. This insures backward-looking. To begin with the premise that you want to deal with legacies from the last round rather than questioning where the enterprise must go is unhealthy.

Health care management needs to improve its attitudes towards unions and collective bargaining. Bargaining agents need to overhaul theirs toward the process and management as well.

New Roles For Managers

What about a new framework for the work of managers? This is absolutely essential to the overall healing of our system where the traditional barriers between workers and managers dissolve. As James Champy, co-author of *Re-Engineering The Corporation* observes in a recent article: "The role of managers becomes one of empowerment — providing workers with the information, training, authority and accountability to excel in a re-engineered business process."[3]

Champy cautions against three dangers for managers in this process.

1) Retain supervisory accountability:

Work may be self-managed but it is not unmanaged. Instead, managers periodically must inspect the work, measure the performance of the process and its contributors, and coach the workers to even better performance.[4]

2) Leadership and vision:

...Managers must take on more leadership tasks — holding a vision for the business, articulating it to workers and customers, and creating an environment that truly empowers workers.[5]

---

3   James Champy, "Time to Re-Engineer the Manager," *Financial Times*, London, January 14, 1994, p. 16.
4   Ibid., p. 16.

3) New style:

    ...Shedding the traditional 'command and control' model for one of 'lead and enable' is proving a difficult transition for most managers.[6]

This is a transition of management style that not all managers can successfully achieve. Some individual managers, with self-awareness, will take themselves out of the line of fire. In other cases, board's will need to assess whether an executive or executive director is able to lead the change. Without vision and leadership, the restructuring of work in the health sector will be needlessly confrontational and painful.

Managers in health care have additional complexity in their working lives in that they deal with independently regulated professionals. Physicians are primarily not employees. Empowerment of workers must be balanced with physician accountability; a challenging task for managers.

Restructuring Health Work in Canada – Some Initial Progress

Formal Canadian experience with work restructuring in the health sector has been confined to a few hospitals. Many are in the early stages of planning. Much of the effort undertaken as quality improvement — either Continuous Quality Improvement(CQI), Total Quality Management(TQM), or as organizational redevelopment — has involved significant elements of work redesign. Often severe financial pressure has driven change. Frequently, incremental change has bogged down due to resistance.

In a recent presentation, Tom Closson, the Chief Operating Officer of Sunnybrook Health Sciences Centre, reached four conclusions on re-engineering hospitals.

Focus On The Customer
Think Big Changes
Use Data
Make Big Changes [7]

---

5   Ibid., p. 16.
6   Ibid., p. 16.
7   Tom Closson, ''Gold Star Options: Lessons From Sunnybrook Health Science Centre,'' The Canadian Institute Conference, Re-engineering for Hospitals, Toronto, Ontario, April 11-12, 1994.

The sentiment expressed here of thinking big and making it big is reinforced by many in the work restructuring field. These are profound alterations to organizational culture and process. To avoid "vicious circles," where the organization cycles back to its previous inefficient or dysfunctional state, it is essential to make the shift permanent. Managing in a humane fashion will avoid unnecessary stress.

The best advice on work restructuring is to go and see for yourself. Visit the leaders in Canada: Sunnybrook in Toronto, St. Joseph's in London, St. Boniface and Health Sciences Centre in Winnipeg, University of Alberta Hospital in Edmonton, Foothills in Calgary. Talk to Jack Litvack, Don Schurman, Phil Hassen and others. Learn from their experiences. Work restructuring is going to be with us as a central challenge for the rest of the 1990s. It will carry different names, but it is a major trend. Learn the available approaches and select the right one for your organization. Better still, have your organization, itself, choose where it is going.

Good Stuff to Read

In Search of Excellence, Lessons from America's Best-Run Companies, by Thomas J. Peters and Robert H. Waterman Jr., Harper & Row, New York, 1982. The key book which began the new age of management change in the corporate sector. Because the health sector in Canada is about a decade behind the manufacturing industry in transforming itself, this is a very relevant book.

Meeting Materials, prepared by the Task Force on the Organization of Work, Ontario Premier's Council on Economic Renewal, May 21, 1993. Excellent background material from a joint labour-management perspective on the restructuring of work and workplace issues in their entirety. This material and further work on these themes may be obtained from the Premier's Council, 1 Dundas Street West, 25th Floor, Toronto, Ontario M7A 1Y7.

Chapter 5
Re-skilling Health Workers

It had struck us as peculiar that, on the one hand, everyone seems to agree that the pace of medical knowledge and medical technology is indeed pretty remarkable. Yet on the other hand, everyone seems relatively complacent about the fact that we train physicians over periods of five to ten years, then we set them loose on patients for up to forty years and sometimes longer without even requiring that they demonstrate that they are keeping on top of this constantly changing knowledge and skill-base. [1]

Morris Barer, 1993

Our basic challenge in skilling and re-skilling health workers is to ensure that all training is relevant to our population's current and emerging health needs and is consistent with technological progress. Re-skilling is fundamental to success. Once is not enough in health training. Evolution is far too rapid and profound to allow any health worker — nurse, technician or physician — to perform effectively for very long without acquiring significant new skills and knowledge. As health work is rearranged by efforts to enhance quality and reduce cost, new skills will be demanded.

What has been undertaken in Canada? Are we investing in new skills for health workers? Are they relevant skills health workers can adapt to new work in new settings? Let's consider a few examples of initiatives taken in Canada.

1 Morris Barer, National Media Briefing on Physician Resource Policies, February 18, 1993. Dr. Barer is director of the Centre for Health Services and Policy Research, University of British Columbia.

Physician Resource Policies — Barer-Stoddart and National Policy

The actors in the drama which created a new national physician resource included all thirteen of the ministers of health in Canada, their deputy ministers, two talented academic researchers, Greg Stoddart, Morris Barer and an assembled chorus of the provincial medical associations. The Royal Commission on Health Care headed by Justice Emmett Hall and the Banff Communiqué from January 1992 were two crucial papers in the overall discussion. The Barer-Stoddart Report and the articulate and forceful voice of health reform advocate Jane Fulton, were the other equally important components to the National Health policy devised. The central public question was "Does Canada have too many doctors?"

Barer-Stoddart Report

Two thoughtful and diligent academics, Morris L. Barer of the University of British Columbia Centre for Health Services and Policy Research and Professor Greg Stoddart of the Centre for Health Economics and Policy Analysis at McMaster University in Hamilton, were charged with completing an in-depth examination of physician resource policy. In their report, entitled, the Barer-Stoddart Report they devised a set of policy recommendations which caught the interest and commitment of Canada's previously mentioned assembled health elite. A number of factors led to it being openly embraced with the rapid implementation of its recommendations into policy.

The commissioning of the Barer-Stoddart report was rooted in a problem and a story. The first part of the problem is physicians are Canada's most expensive health workers. This is true not just in their remuneration for the practice of medicine, but also and more so for the cost of their training. As a nation, we invest very heavy subsidies to physician education. About 80% of the cost of educating a Canadian doctor — over $500,000 — is borne by the taxpayer. We fund physician practice through our single payer, taxpayer supported health insurance system. Unless on salary at a hospital or university, Canadian physicians are paid fee-for-service for their work, guaranteed by the government.

The second part of the problem was from the 1970s until very recently Canada was experiencing much more rapid growth in physician payments than in either population, even adjusted for aging, or in government ability to pay. A number of studies corroborated findings that when the number of physicians increased so, too, did the total billings to the government insurance system by those physicians. Contrary to the market logic of increased supply meeting or even saturating fixed demand, the addition of more physicians to any particular geographical area of Canada produced more supply and more demand. This phenomenon is not unknown in other areas of public policy. Building a new highway, for example, often generates more traffic rather than simply providing a means for existing traffic to move more swiftly. Say's law of economics, that supply creates its own demand, has particular application to physicians in an open-ended, fee-for-service environment. Governments in Canada, in particular deputy ministers of health, came to the view that managing the supply side of the system and its capacity would achieve more manageable costs. In commissioning Barer and Stoddart, they sought a comprehensive set of policies to implement supply-side management of physician resources.

The story which galvanized people to action, the over supply of physicians, was illuminated by Jane Fulton, a dynamic and controversial figure in Canadian health care policy. Jane Fulton is a public advocate for health care reform, an author and an extremely entertaining speaker. As Barer and Stoddart were preparing their report, Fulton brought to light that the original work of the Hall Commission had projected wrongly on Canada's population growth. Whereas the Hall Commission expected that by the early 1990s Canada's population would be 31.5 million people, it was only twenty-seven million. Physician requirements were calculated to supply services to 5.5 million extra Canadians, or a population 25% larger than it is. Fulton provided a solid explanation as to how the health care system's flawed planning created a situation of physician over-supply.

"... this issue of physician personnel is not something that arose simply during the 1980s. The issue really does go back thirty years. It goes back to the early 1960s and over that whole thirty year period there has been a steady increase in the number of physicians in Canada faster than the population and that is how we have come over that period to double physician supply in relative terms. Or put another way, there are only about 450 people per active civilian physician today compared with about 860 in the early 1960s. So we have gone through a long and extended period of massive increase in supply.

The second point is that this increase was an accident. It was not unplanned in one sense because the Hall Commission [the Royal Commission headed by Justice Emmett Hall which created the foundations for Canadian Medicare as a national programme] did present a plan. The Hall Commission put forward recommendations for a dramatic increase in the supply of medical school places and the remarkable thing is that twenty-five years later the number of places, first-year places, in Canada was still very close to what the Hall Commission recommended in the early 1960s. The problem was that the population was not. The Hall Commission reported just before the massive collapse in the birthrate in the mid-60s. So their 1991 estimate of Canadian population is 37 million and the actual is 27 million — 10 million did not show up. They also overestimated the amount of outflow, out-migration of physicians and underestimated the inflow and that is how we get the problem that the number of places they recommended as sufficiency to maintain the physician population ratio, in fact, led to a doubling of it."[2]

2 Professor Robert Evans, National Link of Experts in Several Canadian Cities, coordinated from Toronto, Media Briefing on Physician Resource Policies, University of British Columbia, February 18, 1993. He is director of Programmes for the Canadian Institute for Advanced Research and Professor at the University of B.C.

In their report, Barer and Stoddart avoided the obvious trap of developing a blueprint. Instead, they offered a set of linked policy proposals. Their preface states that: "Physician resource policy in Canada is plagued by historical and political inertia, professional and geographic territoriality, incomplete and inconsistent information, frustration and a great deal of nervous apprehension." It suggests, "we need to get over our collective Canadian-style fear of changing directions even when such redirection in clearly called for."[3] Barer and Stoddart identified priority areas in needed directions. They provided a clear and readable executive summary which, including fifty-three recommendations, totalled only twenty-nine pages. For busy ministers and deputy ministers, it was a welcome relief as documents go.

As a result of Barer-Stoddart being endorsed by deputy ministers of health, the provincial and territorial conference of ministers of health announced national strategic directions for Canadian physician resource management in a document entitled the "Banff Communiqué" of January 1992. Ministers accepted the fundamental findings of Barer and Stoddart that we should cease searching for the exact optimum number of physicians. Instead, we should recognize that annual increases in the numbers of physicians are in excess of population growth. The notion of matching needs and resources was fundamental to Barer-Stoddart and all of its recommendations. While disarmingly simple, this flies in the face of nearly two decades of governmental indecision on this aspect of health policy.

3   M. Barer, G. Stoddart, *Towards Integrated Medical Resource Policies for Canada*, Report prepared for the Federal/Provincial/Territorial Conference of Deputy Ministers of Health, 1991, preface p.v.

Excerpts from the Banff Communiqué:

NATIONAL PHYSICIAN'S
STRATEGY ANNOUNCED

BANFF, Alberta — January 28, 1992

To strengthen the Canadian health care system and preserve the principles of the Canada Health Act, the Provincial/Territorial Conference of Ministers of Health today adopted a series of strategic directions for physician resource management.... The Ministers were in Banff to discuss the training, supply, distribution and payment of doctors within Canada's health care system. Across the country, governments are faced with spiralling health care costs and issues such as shortages of physicians in some areas and surpluses in others.... Physicians are one of the key players in Canada's health care system. Decisions they make have enormous impact on access to care and costs to the taxpayer. The Ministers recognize that working with the medical profession is essential and their plans include ongoing consultation between government, the health care professions and other partners.... Recognizing variations in health care priorities, each province and territory will develop its own plan in the context of this national agreement.

The Provincial/Territorial Conference of Ministers agreed:

National Policy Directions
1. To reduce by the fall of 1993 Canadian medical school entry class size by 10%. Future adjustments will reflect progress on other physician resource initiatives. The Ministers will ask the Canadian Council of Ministers of Education for endorsement.
2. To reduce national postgraduate medical training positions by 10%.

3. To reduce the recruitment of visa trainee graduates of foreign medical schools into Canada for postgraduate medical training.
4. To support the development and implementation of national clinical guidelines with an emphasis on health outcome research, that can serve as a basis for the funding and provision of both ambulatory and institutional medical services.

Coordinated Provincial/Territorial Policy Directions

1. To establish predictable medical care expenditures through a combination of regional and individual practitioner budgets.
2. To replace fee-for-service wherever that method of payment aligns poorly with the nature or objective of the services being provided.
3. To increase utilization of alternative service delivery models.
4. To restructure and rationalize the funding of academic medical centres to align with educational objectives based on identified community health status needs.
5. To introduce a series of initiatives to improve access to clinical services in rural communities.
6. To establish initiatives and processes to ensure the continuing competency of physicians.
7. To eliminate exclusive fields of practice and replace these by a more circumscribed set of exclusive acts and reserved titles through legislation.
8. To enhance the information base and share information for improved physician resource management, clinical practice and consumer education.[4]

---

4   Communiqué from the Provincial/Territorial Conference for Ministers of Health, Banff, Alberta, January 28, 1992.

The "Banff Communiqué" is a significant achievement of consensus among health ministers. Even more significant were the action's of provincial governments. Medical school enrolments have been reduced, in accordance with strategic directions. Consistent with Canadian Medicare, each province has taken a slightly different course. Provinces have worked together and two government officials, Dr. Stephen Gray from British Columbia and Bonnie Hoyt-Hallett from New Brunswick, have demonstrated incredible leadership in the transformation process. At various times, some of the provinces have backed off because of pressures in their own jurisdictions, however, the overall directives are being implemented and progress is happening.

In February 1993, a national media teleconference was organized where a number of deputy ministers of health as well as other health experts participated in a briefing. Throughout this process, one of the confidence builders for ministers was the sense that not only were they on the right track but there was enough detailed work being done involving all of the stakeholders, that progress could be achieved. One of the early steps endorsed by the ministers was the national conference on physician resources where all key health care partners were invited. Although there was some grumbling, particularly from provincial medical associations, there has been no fundamental challenge to the basic assertion of Barer and Stoddart. The Ministers accepted that we could do a much better job of getting the right number of physicians in the right place at the right time.

What will be the eventual result of this process approach? First, it's likely that a better overall match will be achieved between physician supply and physician requirements in Canada. Second, there will likely be better geographical and specialty matching. Third and most importantly, all of the crucial players — the teachers, the academic health sciences centres, governments and regulatory bodies — are working together with the expectation that sensible recommendations which emerge will be implemented.

An interesting dilemma was illustrated by Barer-Stoddart with the recommendation of 10% reduction in undergraduate medical enrolment in Ontario. Ontario has five medical schools. When Barer-Stoddart was released, the annual, first year enrolment for the five medical schools totalled 617; the target was to reduce it to 540. This could have been achieved in two ways. Either by closing one of the four smaller schools, McMaster, Ottawa, Queen's or Western, or the largest medical school, the University of Toronto, with an entering class of 250, could have been reduced in size. An across-the-board cut would have diminished the smaller medical schools to below the minimum feasible level. Arguments in favour of closing one of the smaller ones ran up against the unique qualities of each. Ottawa is the only place in Ontario for training French-speaking physicians to provide service to Franco-Ontarians. McMaster has a international reputation in population health and a significant portion of its graduates tend to enter teaching, research and public health careers. Similarly Queen's, in its rural and northern focus, and Western, in its service to southwestern Ontario, had appropriate claims to uniqueness. The policy dilemma became how to reduce the medical entering class at the University of Toronto by seventy-five students. A compromise was reached by University President Rob Prichard and Bernard Shapiro, then Deputy Minister of Colleges and Universities for Ontario, later principal of McGill University. It was decided that for a period of years, the government would protect the funding base of the University of Toronto Medical School. The University would reduce its Medical School enrolment, bringing Ontario in line with overall national goals and funds freed up from the teaching budget would be reallocated to a research fund. I am a strong advocate for increased investment in research. As we find ways of making the health care delivery system more efficient, and of growing healthier, lessening demands on physician services, the sensible redirection of funds is towards research. In downsizing the University of Toronto Medical School, reallocation of dollars to research proved an elegant means of meeting all objectives. Cost savings for the government, from the reduction in the number of physicians entering practice in Ontario, may total as much as $40 million a year. The funding transferred from physician education to research will average about $4 million per year.

Other provinces have shown likewise flexibility and creativity in policy implementation. The reshaping of the most entrenched and feudal of our educational institutions — the medical school — has begun. Surely we can add skills to other workers delivering health care.

Physician Supply, Priorities and Pogo

... What the data says is if you keep turning out physicians, each of them will remain, on average, at about the same level of employment and they will cost you proportionately more money. So you have in a sense mortgaged your budget to decisions that were made on mistakes 20 years old.

Now taking off from there you say, alright, if we don't know that the new supply is going to have a major impact on our health, we do know that it is having, has had, substantial budgetary impacts, so what follows from that? Well, one of the things that follows from it is that it distorts any efforts or prevents any efforts that you might be trying to make to reallocate resources within your existing health care budget. Every commission that has looked at the Canadian health care scene has said the priorities have changed. One of the reasons they have said that is because that is what people have told them loud and clear, that an aging population has different priorities for care than does the population of 30 years ago but you cannot re-deploy resources from one sector to another if you have already committed a continuous expansion of resources to the new physicians who are coming into the field. And yet, on the other hand, if you continue to increase the supply of physicians but then re-deploy the resources away from them the mathematics, the arithmetic of that very simply is that you are talking about trying to push physician income steadily down and that is going to be pretty contentious stuff too. So the political conflicts that you see arising now between physicians and provincial governments are a natural consequence of the inconsistencies of a policy of trying to re-deploy our resources from one sector of health care to another, combined with the continuing expansion of the numbers of people in that sector.

So that kind of growth distortion shows up in the great difficulty in trying to develop new kinds of personnel. Nursing associations all over the country have told us, and they are right, that there are many opportunities to use nurse practitioners, for example, to substitute for physicians. But if you are continuing to increase the supply of physicians then any nurse practitioner growth would be on top of that and, in fact, the nurse practitioner movement was killed off 20 years ago when we found that we were into a dramatic increase in the supply of physicians. If you look back, there were very strong pressures to introduce nurse practitioners at that time and they all died because of the physician growth.

And, finally, the bottom line distortion you get is that in a time of general economic contraction, very slow growth, if any, what we have found is that our health budgets continue to increase as a share of our national income, not because anybody has based a priority on them to this effect but because the overall economic base is not growing nearly as fast as it did prior to the eighties.

So, we are really now having to face up to questions that everybody knew were serious questions for the past 20 years, that the economic climate has become sufficiently severe that we are finally starting to think about what we should have been thinking a long time ago. And I think the relevant line may be from the Pogo cartoon strip which is that "man never reads the writing on the wall until his back's against it."[5]

Re-skilling Nurses for a Changing Environment

An important think tank on nursing and nursing research in the economic context was held in April 1992.[6] The organizers drew upon experts in the health economics and nursing economics field.

There has been a significant increase in the number of nurses in Canada. The ratio of nurses to population increased from one nurse for every 256 people in 1966 to about one nurse for every 120 people in 1989. Most nurses were still employed in hospitals, about 70%, but there has been a steady, accelerating shift toward greater nurse

5   Professor Robert Evans, national media briefing on Physician Resource Policies, Coordinated from Toronto, February 18, 1993.
6   Jan Dick, *Canadian Journal of Nursing Administration*, May/June, 1992, p. 7.

employment in community health and nursing homes. It is likely that, with reforms and restructuring, this trend will increase. As with other health professionals, nurses will need to acquire skills compatible with the new roles in the community and accommodate to greater community reliance on multi-disciplinary teams.

One issue is enormously important. Because nurses are largely employed by hospitals or other agencies funded by government on a transfer payment basis, their concerns occupy far less of the policy decision making time of ministers of health and their officials than those of physicians. This is a structural problem. Because ministries of health pay physicians directly, they spend a great deal more time battling with the physicians over the annual increase or decrease in fee schedules. Nurses are one step removed from the health ministry and receive correspondingly less policy attention. There are negotiations with the nurses' union, but these are typically centralized with the hospital association, at arm's length from the government. Nursing is central to quality care. Ministers and ministries of health need to incorporate nursing issues more centrally into the reform agenda. Nursing organizations are going to have to be aggressive, not simply about opposing change which they view as detrimental to their members, but in recommending constructive alternatives.

In this regard, the Canadian Nursing Association has been the leader for twenty years in advocating policies which look to a broader vision of health. We have much to learn by listening carefully to nurses when they give advice. We should take as much time or perhaps more to hear the economic issues raised by doctors as to the care issues raised by nurses.

An opinion poll done by Environics Research[7] occasionally tracks numbers as to the credibility of different professions. Nurses were at the top of the list with over 70% of the population surveyed saying they believe a nurse on an issue of public policy; some 55% had a similar view of physicians. Not surprisingly, given the times, political leaders ranked somewhere farther down the list somewhere near the single digits. The rest of us should listen more attentively to nurses. Nurses need to speak more forcefully than they have in the past.

Nursing leaders need to focus on the changes which health reform is bringing about and the fundamental economic reasons. The

---

7   Focus Ontario, Environics Research, Quarterly Report, 4th Quarter, 1992.

April 1992 conference previously mentioned, identified ten key areas of nursing economics.

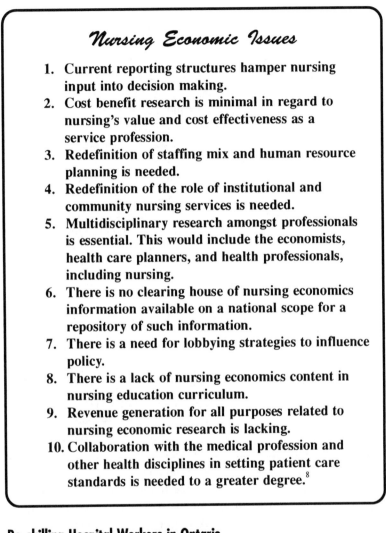

Nursing Economic Issues

1. Current reporting structures hamper nursing input into decision making.
2. Cost benefit research is minimal in regard to nursing's value and cost effectiveness as a service profession.
3. Redefinition of staffing mix and human resource planning is needed.
4. Redefinition of the role of institutional and community nursing services is needed.
5. Multidisciplinary research amongst professionals is essential. This would include the economists, health care planners, and health professionals, including nursing.
6. There is no clearing house of nursing economics information available on a national scope for a repository of such information.
7. There is a need for lobbying strategies to influence policy.
8. There is a lack of nursing economics content in nursing education curriculum.
9. Revenue generation for all purposes related to nursing economic research is lacking.
10. Collaboration with the medical profession and other health disciplines in setting patient care standards is needed to a greater degree.[8]

Re-skilling Hospital Workers in Ontario

Like many innovations in health care management, The Ontario Hospital Training and Adjustment Panel (HTAP), was born of urgent necessity and politics, rather than scientific study and research. In

8   From editorial by Jan Dick, *Canadian Journal of Nursing Administration*, May/June, 1992, p. 7.

the fall of 1991, the fiscal situation of the Ontario Government led the Cabinet to determine a much lower rate of increase in transfer payments to the hospital sector for the fiscal year starting April 1, 1992, than in any previous time. After a decade of double digit annual funding growth — averaging above 10% per annum — hospital transfers would increase by only 2%.

Reactions were swift. In a flurry of emotional statements, reported as banner headlines in the daily newspapers, the Ontario Hospital Association forecast that this inadequate funding increase could cause 12,000 layoffs across the 223 hospitals in Ontario — almost 10% of the total workforce of 140,000. The Canadian Union of Public Employees (CUPE) forecast was slightly higher at 13,000. The Ministry of Health estimated job loss at a maximum of 2,500 or less than 2%. However, in a sector which had enjoyed two decades of nearly uninterrupted growth, this was uncharted territory. Whatever the actual number was, one reality was clear: there were no provisions for hospital worker retraining or redeployment and no infrastructure or mechanisms devoted to these. Some collective agreements contained extended notice periods, but collective bargaining in good times had focussed on dollars rather than on re-skilling or redeployment provisions.

In this atmosphere of concern and, at times, forceful disagreement, the Hospital Training and Adjustment Panel was created. Because there were no real models for a re-skilling and redeployment initiative in the Ontario public sector, HTAP was modelled on the successful joint labour-management initiative in the steel industry, the Canadian Steel Trade and Employment Congress (CSTEC). Then Health Minister Frances Lankin took three decisive steps to launch HTAP. First, Lankin approved $30 million to be transferred from unspent hospital funds in the Ministry of Health to HTAP as a three-year fund. Second, Lankin appointed Dr. Peter Warrian, the Executive Director of CSTEC, as the founding HTAP Board Chair to lead the start-up. Finally, Lankin invited the Ontario Hospital Association and the hospital workers unions (CUPE, OPSEU, SEIU, Allied Health)[9] to name representatives to the Panel. This was an offer they could not refuse. Anger at the government's funding decision did not preclude availing themselves of the opportunity to assist their member hospitals and hospital workers. HTAP was born.

---

9   CUPE-Canadian Union of Public Employees, OPSEU-Ontario Public Service
    Employees Union, Allied Health, SEIU-Service Employees International Union.

HTAP developed its policies and programmes at arm's-length from the Ministry of Health and with the active participation of these labour and management partners. Two years later, HTAP has created the following:

- joint management-employee committees in 210 of the 223 hospitals in Ontario
- over 650 displaced hospital workers in-training programmes
- a forum for labour-management discussion
- accurate information on layoffs in the system
- an agreement to expand the approach to the entire health sector.

HTAP Activity Summary as of December, 1993[10]

HTAP joint committees	210
Hospitals with reported layoffs	160
Committees accessing HTAP funding	142
Layoff notices* issues since October 1, 1991	3800
Workers accessing HTAP programme	2100
Approved training requests	600
Hirings through HTAP registry	19

* includes those whose hours were reduced by 75% or more[11]

One of the earliest and most important achievements of HTAP was actually a byproduct of its creation. HTAP's information system allowed a more accurate assessment of the hospital labour market. Instead of 12,000 or 13,000 or even 2,500 layoffs there were only a few hundred in the first year. Why? A number of reasons. Hospitals managed to make cuts that did not cause layoffs. Early retirements and normal retirements diminished the size of the labour force in a less painful fashion than layoffs. Significant reductions were made in hours of work for part-time hospital positions. The forecasted job loss "carnage" was replaced by a managed transition with support for re-skilling. A new mechanism, and a real commitment from government, management and labour found a better way.

10 HTAP unpublished material.
11 Ibid.

HTAP Works with You

The Ontario Hospital Training Adjustment Panel helps all public hospital employees, permanently laid off after October 1, 1991, to find employment. The panel oversees a programme, funded by the Ministry of Health, that fosters cooperation between unions and management through joint committees at individual hospitals.

The focus of the programme is local people working together. HTAP provides funds to hospitals through the joint committees, which are made up of equal numbers of management and employee/union representatives.

You Are Not Alone

HTAP has made a commitment to help you through your hospital's joint committee. The committee's first step is to develop a list of laid-off employees. To help you find other employment, HTAP provides assistance with:

- counselling
- determining your needs
- job placement assistance
- re-training and education
- family support
- retirement planning

HTAP's employment databank provides a valuable opportunity to access and share information. And, we're working with prospective employers in the public and private sector who are interested in hiring — and re-training — laid off hospital employees.

Funding Is Available

HTAP field staff will work with joint committees to develop a plan and budget for assisting laid off employees. Budgets are based on a formula of up to $500 per employee for first level assistance and up to $5,000 for training and relocation.

The funds are not paid directly to individuals. Once the plans are approved by the panel, joint committees will be granted lump sums. This funding structure is flexible — hospital joint committees may want to pool funds to maximize community resources.

Get Involved

To find out if there is a joint committee where you work, contact your hospital's administration office or your local union representative.

If you are a prospective employer call either HTAP or your local committee.[12]

Fortunately HTAP is not the only effort underway in Canada to re-skill and redeploy health workers. Many provincial jurisdictions have initiated activity in this field. The following chart provides an overview of these efforts

The Deborah Feltham Story

When Deborah Feltham received a letter last July telling her she was going to be laid off, she burst into tears. Her worst fear had come true.

"I'm a single mother with $1,000 to pay in rent each month," she said. "I was devastated. I felt betrayed and very alone."

Feltham worked full-time as an RN in gynaecology at Scarborough General Hospital. She spent years training to be a nurse and put in a lot of time. Two years later it was all over, and the prospects looked pretty grim.

Today, just seven months later, Feltham says being laid off is the best thing that could have happened to her. She is back at Scarborough General working part-time in critical care and taking home almost as much money as she made before.

12 HTAP brochure, published by HTAP in 1993.

"Thanks to HTAP, I was able to take a training course that changed the course of my career," she says. "A friend told me about HTAP during my last week of work. On my last day of work I went through the hospital's in service workshop for laid-off employees where I learned about what HTAP had to offer."

Two weeks later, an HTAP peer supporter contacted Feltham and discussed the programme with her. Within days she was enroled in the six-week, full-time East Metro Critical Care Education programme at Centennial College. Funding for tuition and books came through Scarborough General's HTAP joint committee.

"The peer supporter programme is wonderful," she says. "Before I spoke with the supporters, I felt if I was the only person in the world this had ever happened to. They gave me so much emotional support and good advice — it was just the boost I needed. I told a friend to go and she had the same experience."

While taking the course, Feltham managed to pick up a few shifts in emergency where she heard about a position available in coronary care. The day she graduated, she got the job. She started the following Monday.

Feltham says she wouldn't have gotten the job if she hadn't taken the course. And she never would have taken the course had she not fast-tracked through the HTAP programme and made use of the services available to laid-off employees.

"I never would have made the move to go back to school and improve my skills," she says. "Now, I'm planning to continue taking courses. I feel more positive about my future now than I did before."[13]

---

13 "*On the fast track to a bright future,*" *Communiqué*, Volume 1, Number 2, February/March, 1993.

Healing Medicare cannot be achieved by inflicting excessive hardship on a small minority of health workers. We need to continue to create schemes for re-skilling and redeployment. The HTAP story illustrates the need for problem definition and ownership of the problem by people with an ability to solve it. The Minister of Health could not successfully define the scale of the crisis and address it; she could only engage in a futile shouting match with the stakeholders. By creating HTAP, the key stakeholders were given both the structure to define what was happening and the tools to address it. There was also the capacity to achieve a win-win outcome for both labour and management. The Ontario Hospital Association and the hospital workers' bargaining agents delivered something positive to their respective members.

In its first two years, HTAP has achieved progress measured against its objectives. There has been significant, constructive investment of time and energy in problem-solving by the HTAP members, on behalf of their respective organizations. HTAP has broadened its mandate and focus from hospitals to the entire health sector in Ontario. As a result of the Ontario Social Contract Health Sector Agreement, the Panel, now known as HSTAP (Health Sector Training and Adjustment Panel), will also take on responsibility for the 140,000 or so health workers who do not work in hospitals. This includes workers in long-term care institutions such as nursing homes and homes for the aged.

Re-skilling and Redeploying Health Workers — Some Canadian Initiatives[14]

Program Name	British Columbia Healthcare Labour Adjustment Agency	Manitoba Provincial Health Labour Adjustment Committee	Quebec Health and Social Services Placement Service	Saskatchewan Health Reform Transition Program
Mandate	- placement of displaced employees - facilitation of employment security in hospitals	- address the needs of employees affected by health care reform (hospitals only, voluntary basis) - maximize redeployment, empower affected employees, provide information and guidance to employees and managers	- provide employment security to employees laid-off following bumping or closing of health care services - redeployment of laid-off workers - management of movement of employees, not restructuring of system	- provide funding for Career Assistance, Career Adjustment, and Severance Enhancement programs for employees laid off as a result of health care restructuring (ie setting up of 30 District Health Boards province wide as employers)

14 Adapted from HTAP Evaluation Report, 1994.

	British Columbia Healthcare Labour Adjustment Agency	Manitoba Provincial Health Labour Adjustment Committee	Quebec Health and Social Services Placement Service	Saskatchewan Health Reform Transition Program
Structure	- under Framework Agreement - Board of Directors — 6 organizational reps (3 union/3 employer), Chair by consent - Labour Adjustment Committee at facility level - Labour Adjustment Officers facilitate LACs, advise employees (each covers 2 regions and 40 hospitals) - HLAA is final arbiter of whether labour adjustment purpose is being served	- Letter of Understanding signed by participants - PHCLAC has 10 union reps, 10 employer reps, 2 co-chairs - government-appointed Chair - PHCLAC oversees program - facility Employment Adjustment Committees are being set up	- under S.C.F.P.— C.H.P. collective agreement - SPSSS administered by 1 MSSS person and 1 person designated by each association - general manager executes all decisions by SPSSS - Committee on Retraining has 4 employer reps and 4 FTQ reps - Parity Committee (SPSSS and 7 union reps) settle disputes under redeployment program	- Provincial Joint Committee — 11 members union/management, 1 gov. rep; 1/mo mtg.; sets policy guidelines - Sask. Assoc. of Health Organization (SAHO): administration of applications based on guidelines set by Prov. Cttee. Any non-standard applications go to Prov. Cttee for approval (in future District Health Boards — the new employers — may administer program, but so far handling everything centrally is proving most expedient and manageable)
List of Services	- Priority placement - secondments - early retirement program - lay-off option - job sharing - voluntary transfer, relocation - funding of some retraining related to placement	- redeployment program/job line registry - employee/employer handbooks - supportive counselling, referrals	- placement service - lay-off indemnity (indefinite period) - continuity of benefits - retraining programs - moving expenses, relocation compensation	- Career Adjustment Program — funding for: training/retraining career counselling/job placement services relocation assistance alternate employment assistance - Enhanced Severance

Learning New Tricks

All the machinery for re-skilling and redeployment will not alter one reality. We're all going to need to cope personally with change. Whether we are writing health policy on a new and unfamiliar computer or learning a new surgical technique, it's made easier by a willingness to learn. Without it, change will be abrupt, jarring and damaging to health! With this willingness *and* the right machinery to connect people and opportunities, change may be bearable.

The U.S. Dept. of Labour, Bureau of Labour Statistics had estimated in 1975 that the average person would change careers once or twice in a lifetime, and jobs between four to five times. By 2010, the Bureau estimates that the average person will change careers four to five times and jobs ten times. To survive we must all learn a number of new tricks.

Whether we are professionals such as doctors, nurses and pharmacists, or the more numerous hospital orderlies and community health workers, two points are clear. Everyone is affected by the re-engineering of the Canadian heath care delivery system. *All* need new skills to cope successfully.

Employers, managers and funders of our health care system must ensure that investment in training and re-skilling are enhanced in this period of transition, not diminished.

The three key needs that prompted HTAP were the absence of accurate information on job impacts, the absence of a re-skilling "safety net" for hospital workers and the need for a new partnership, in which the government had a visible role. These concerns, and the development of new infrastructure to address them, have application to other groups of health workers.

There is no magic to training or re-skilling. It may take the form of a one-hour talk over lunch in your workplace, or a learning system embedded in the software on your computer work station, or a several year stint back in the classroom. The only universal truth is we need retraining to face the transformation we are undergoing.

Redeployment and Change

Significant redeployment measures are a necessary component of managing change. From HTAP to Sunnybrook Hospital to Vancouver, people in Canadian health care are leading and managing transitions for our most important resource — the people who work in health care. By building the new infrastructure of redeployment: committees, registries, linkages to re-skilling and accessible information on opportunities, we can achieve the needed affordability without sacrificing the humanity, morale and commitment of the health sector workplace.

Good Stuff to Read

The Fifth Discipline, The Art & Practice of the Learning Organization, by Peter Senge, Doubleday, New York, 1990. A brilliant book which has strong ideas on the management of organizational change. Senge is particularly good at explaining why change works in some organizations and not in others. A "must read" for those involved in managing change in health care.

Toward Integrated Medical Resource Policies for Canada, better known as the Barer-Stoddart Report in recognition of its co-authors Morris Barer and Greg Stoddart. This report was commissioned by the Federal/Provincial/Territorial Conference of Deputy Ministers of Health in 1990 and reported in June 1991. The Report is an excellent and comprehensive analysis of physician issues in Canadian Medicare. It is also one of the most significant health policy success stories in recent times. This report actually got implemented! Unlike a mountain of Royal Commissions, Task Forces etc., Ministers took the advice they sought. Available from Health Canada, Ottawa.

Unions and Economic Competitiveness, edited by Lawrence Mishel and Paula B. Voss, M.E. Sharpe Inc., New York, 1992. The section on Work Organization, Unions and Economic Performance by Ray Marshall is powerful and insightful in advocating a higher quality and productivity approach to the workplace. The message is one of a strong role for unions in competitiveness and productivity issues. The authors advocate greater union involvement in productivity improvement with a fair sharing of gains between workers and the employer.

Chapter 6
Redeployment of Health Workers

Redeployment of health workers captures the increasing shift of health work from institutions to community, and the profound demand of rural and northern citizens for health services closer to their home. The enabling aspects of telecommunications technology have a role to play, but redeployment is based on the principle of workers following work. This voyage may be from institution to community or it may be a journey from a large city with doctor surplus to a rural or northern community without local physicians. The concept of redeployment also includes movement of health workers to non-health sectors where their skills are in demand. For example, the transfer of a displaced cook from a provincial psychiatric hospital to a vacant cook job in the provincial jail across the street.

The core belief embedded in redeployment is that workers are our most valuable resource not an expendable, throwaway commodity. Even in a period of rapid transition, people who have devoted their training and working lives to caring for others deserve more than a pink slip. People deserve, within the limits of reason, the opportunity to follow work as it is restructured by the financial, technological and public pressures. There is an obligation to uphold this opportunity principle. Everyone will need to be flexible and willing to learn new ways of working and proficiency in new areas. Job security will be a direct result of new work created from arrangements which support re-skilling and redeployment.

Sometimes, there are simple solutions to redeployment issues. At the Queen Street Mental Health Centre in Toronto, 25% of the psychiatric hospital workers have followed patient needs into the community. Over time, with the movement of programmes to an outpatient and community base, functions previously performed on the campus of hospital have relocated into the community. Workers have moved with the programmes and retain their benefits. Unfortunately, this model is not appropriate in every location.

Redeployment Possibilities

```
┌──────────────────┐
│ New job in same  │
│ organization     │
└──────────────────┘
         ▲
┌──────────────────┐
│ Re-skilling and/or│
│ redeployment     │
└──────────────────┘
         ▲
┌──────────────┐     ┌──────────────┐     ┌──────────────┐
│ Displaced    │ ──▶ │ Re-skilling  │ ──▶ │ New job in   │
│ Health       │     │ Redeployment │     │ new health   │
│ Worker       │     │              │     │ organization │
└──────────────┘     └──────────────┘     └──────────────┘
         │
         ▼
┌──────────────────┐
│ Re-skilling and/or│
│ Redeployment     │
└──────────────────┘
         │
         ▼
┌──────────────┐
│ New job in   │
│ non-health   │
│ organization │
└──────────────┘
```

Getting Doctors in the Right Places

One preoccupation of national health policy has been to improve the distribution of doctors throughout the country. Historically and at present, Canada has a doctor surplus in the major cities such as Toronto and Vancouver, and shortages in the north and in southern rural communities. This is not unique to Canada. It's a situation which has consumed a great deal of time and energy on the part of policy makers and it has been a concern to the public, particularly to residents in southern rural and northern areas. Their assessment of the adequacy of the Medicare system is viewed largely through their experience of whether and what doctors are available. Doctors and hospital beds define health care services. It's not surprising that the inability of a community to secure a doctor or a sufficient number of doctors to meet a real or perceived need leads it to conclude that there is a fundamental problem with Medicare.

In all professions, whether law, accounting or medicine, professionals gravitate to larger centres. The fee-for-service system has produced the same situation for doctors. Often rural, northern or remote areas, because of relative scarcity of doctors, have larger numbers of patients, and therefore larger incomes than their colleagues. This is most true of general practice, and yet this has not been sufficient to assure a smooth geographical distribution of physicians. It's worth noting here that one would not want an absolute equal distribution of all physicians. There are specialty areas where the most appropriate situation is to have a few experts in the major centre and transport patients to them. This suggests that there should always be a greater endowment, particularly of specialists involved in tertiary care, in the major urban centres. On the other hand, specialization could be undertaken in regional centres were the medical and other personnel available to carry them out. For example, the Ontario Cancer and Treatment and Research Foundation (OCTRF) runs eight regional centres that deliver a high quality of care across Ontario in smaller cities such as Thunder Bay, Sudbury, as well as in Ottawa and Toronto. OCTRF operates on a different basis than the more open market, fee-for-service system.

Over the years a variety of methods have been attempted to secure physicians for less-serviced areas. In Manitoba, student loans to physicians have been forgiven at an accelerated rate if they move to an underserviced area. And the Manitoba fee schedule slightly favours service in more remote areas. That is, a doctor in rural

Manitoba would be paid a bit more for the same procedure than a Winnipeg colleague. Some other provinces such as Ontario have been unwilling to differentiate the fee schedule regionally. Quebec has undertaken the most prolonged and elaborate series of measures to bribe, cajole and force physicians to locate in underserviced areas. They include: limited access to facilities, fee differentials and compulsory service of various sorts. Ontario has stuck significantly to financial incentives rather than disincentives and has veered away from differentiating the fee schedule. In the most recent agreement between the medical profession and the provincial government, however, grants are provided for contract positions for physicians willing to locate in so-called under serviced communities.

As a result of the Barer-Stoddart Report on physician resources, described earlier, there have been a number of efforts made across the country to better match supply to needs. The following outlines Ontario's initial directions in this regard:

- better aligning the educational supply of physicians to the health care needs of the province
- modifying the medical education experience to better prepare physicians for the settings in which they will eventually practice
- exploring ways to better distribute physician human resources geographically and by health care setting
- creating a system of linked regional, multi-disciplinary referral networks to effect a mix and distribution of physicians that provides a more rational means of accessing health care providers[1]

Almost all measures have succeeded to some extent, although nothing has solved the problem. Our significant physician surplus has meant significant additional costs, with dubious additional medical value in larger centres, and continuing chronic problems in some of our smaller centres. Some rural, northern and isolated regions of the country have relied heavily on immigration of foreign-trained physicians to fill gaps. In light of the Banff agreement to manage physician resources, including restricting entry of foreign-trained doctors, this source will be curtailed somewhat.

Redeploying physicians depends significantly on changing the context in which they practice. In those parts of the country where

1 *Managing Health Care Resources*, Supplementary Paper, Ontario Budget, May 1992, p.20-21.

solo practice, particularly for a family practitioner, is the norm, the most frequent complaints from doctors working in underserviced areas are about compensation. There is a lack of backup support to take calls and a limited access to continuing medical education and other amenities. To solve the problems of under service, Canadian provincial health ministries will need new organizational structures, including more inclusive partnerships with physicians. Solo medical practice does not provide opportunities for work-sharing, nor does it provide for sufficient technological support. It is likely that physicians, like other groups, will need to form partnerships, even where individual practitioners are not in the same geographical location. Linking physicians together with information telecommunication technologies of various sorts will be a step in the right direction. So, too, will changing compensation arrangements so that physicians will be hired to work in the areas in which they are needed. They don't necessarily have to be employed by provincial governments, instead hospitals, community clinics or other health management organizations that emerge might take them on. The test of our ability to redeploy health workers must include a redeployment of the physician population to more appropriately meet the needs of all Canadians.

There are some encouraging signs. Recent graduates of faculties of medicine show very different attitudes from their predecessors. They are not assuming they will practice fee-for-service medicine as some divine right of physicians; rather, it is seen as an option to possibly pursue. Many others would prefer various compensation arrangements, particularly if they allowed the doctors more flexible hours. Real progress has been made in increasing the number of women in the medical profession. Women now constitute about 50% of graduates. Recognition of their approach to practice patterns can possibly lead to alterations in the overall approach of the profession to compensation issues. Younger physicians are generally more open to different models than just fee-for-service.

Another emerging direction in Canadian health care is a new look at academic health science centres. Previously, academic health science centres were seen significantly as locations for teaching and research. They were linked to teaching hospitals which were an integral part of the academic health science centre. Two interesting notions have recently emerged regarding academic health science centres. The first is that they could take on broader responsibilities for population health by harnessing broad expertise, including disciplines other than nursing, medicine or health (such as those in sociology, economics). The second notion is that academic science centres might take greater responsibility in the management of physicians in practice. There are already some isolated and successful examples of this. For a number of years the University of Manitoba Faculty of Medicine has operated a northern medical unit that educates young physicians and provides needed medical service to the north. In Ontario, a similar situation exists between the Mushkegot Tribal Council and Queen's University. The concept of academic health science centres taking greater responsibility for the delivery of care in under-serviced areas needs to be more fully explored. All partners, including physicians and future physicians, need to be involved in these discussions, if there is to be success.

Redeployment of Nurses

Canadian nurses have faced a rapid and uncomfortable shift from a nursing shortage to a surplus in a few short years. This happened so quickly that the Ontario government was still providing special bursaries to encourage nursing entrants when a moratorium on the programme was declared. In its second year, nurses graduating from the programme could not find placements. Four forces have simultaneously impacted on nurses: more appropriate payment for nursing services, the restructuring of everyone's work to free-up nurses to do only nursing work (this will be explored further in the next chapter), the shift from inpatient to outpatient services at the hospital level, and the shortened length of stay for inpatient services. The consequence of these forces is the reduction of nursing hours required in hospitals.

For nurses, redeployment will require creativity. There are opportunities for nurses in the community and home sector. There should also be openings in independent practice. Nursing clinics will require careful management, to ensure they are not a pure cost add-on to the system. The experience in the U.S. and elsewhere is that nurses can provide very good quality care in independent practice. Naturally, protocols for referral from nurses to other providers, such as physiotherapists or physicians, would be necessary. The second major opportunity for nurses may be in providing advice and helping to manage care over the telephone.

The Hospital for Sick Children in Toronto has operated two phone lines staffed by nurses since 1977. Their Poison Centre line handled 95,000 calls in 1993. The Medical Information line had 65,000 calls in 1993. It is estimated that these calls cost an average of $7.00 as compared to an average of $100 for an emergency room visit, though not every call substitutes for a hospital visit. Surveys have indicated that 75% of patients would have gone to the emergency room in the absence of the telephone line.[2] The benefits are not purely financial. Individuals worried about their health or the health of their children are greatly reassured by picking up a telephone and talking to a knowledgeable nurse. The benefits to the overall health system are significant in terms of improved patient confidence, improved quality of care and, particularly, more appropriate access to services.

Nurses will need to be organized and aggressive to seize the new opportunities and to ensure that as their work is restructured they can follow it through redeployment.

Good Stuff to Read

What Colour is Your Parachute, by Richard Bolles, Ten Speed Press, Berkeley, California, U.S.A. With over five million copies in print since its 1970 debut, and now in its 1994 edition, *What Colour is Your Parachute* is an excellent survival guide for the changing working world in which we live. It contains very useful tools to assess your real skills and interests. Investing in this book could help you on the road to a discovery of skills and interests hidden by the job or occupational label we all tend to stick on ourselves.

Updated annually, this is worthwhile companion for the voyage through a restructuring world of work.

---

2   *Journal of Nursing Administration*, March, 1993.

Chapter 7

Health Providers and Outcomes

Autonomy is not a right of professionals, nor a prerequisite to being a professional. It is a social reward, exchanged in recognition of the professionals' pursuit of knowledge for the purpose of better service to others. Professional autonomy is granted when society can trust practitioners to pursue goals which are consistent with the greater good of society.[1]

Ken Fyke, 1993

One of the consequences of Canadian Medicare's original great deal with physicians was the continuation of a provider-dominated health care delivery system. The political compromise necessary to bring in Medicare committed the government to act as insurer/payer and offer little "interference" with professional health providers. Consumers, no longer paying directly for their health care, became unaware of its actual cost. Government was only to pay the bills, not to manage the system. Taken together, these two conditions reinforced provider domination of delivery. The focus of health care debate for twenty-five years has been inputs: how many dollars are we spending on health care? How many hospitals can we build or rebuild? How many new health initiatives and programmes can governments launch? Evaluation of outcomes did not occur. The judgment of health care activities, on the basis of whether and how

1   Ken Fyke, "The Autonomy of the Medical Profession Must Be Earned," *Beyond Provider Dominance*, King's Fund, London, U.K. 1993, p. 48.

well they worked was always deferred because of the dominance of measuring inputs.

Physicians, although having had to endure some government restrictions in terms of practice in a hospital and incomes in the offices, have been in general, well protected from the effects of the recession. Compared to many other professionals such as lawyers, accountants, engineers, we have been able to maintain relatively stable income over the last four or five years. Many of us have friends, children and relatives who have suffered tremendously with the recession from job loss and reduction in pay to difficulty in obtaining meaningful work.

It is a difficult time for physicians but let's look around and we will see that it is a stressful time for a large number of Canadians. It is time for us to work together, to regroup, to replan and above all, to carry on our practice of medicine with great compassion and pursuit of scientific treatment. Difficult times bring forth the true art of medicine.

Profound changes will occur in the Canadian society and, in particular, in the delivery of health care in this country. We should be talking to each other, we should be adapting to these new situations and we should be, above all, keeping our cool in the face of adverse conditions of practice. Although it may appear that the grass is greener south of the border, I do not believe that Canadians need to embark on such a drastic course. Our country has a lot to offer, it has many challenges ahead and needs the participation of every man and woman to make it even greater. In terms of medicine, the trends will be to a diversified practice of medicine. We must be prepared to work with colleagues from other professions. We must discuss and plan new types of practice for the years to come. In general, governments agree that global budgets are the cornerstone of their financing for the next few years. With this in mind, we should be looking at new delivery methods of health care to our population. Group practice will become more and more important and through this, obstetricians and gynaecologists may be able to plan a better family life for themselves and better lifestyles in general.[2]

2   Andre Lalonde, "From Time of Reflection," *SOGC News*, March, 1994, p 1.

Beyond Provider Dominance: Easy Theory, Hard Practice

There are Canadian examples of the tensions involved in the struggle to rebalance health care with a stronger consumer and citizen/payer role.

Lesson #1 — Witness — Quebec

In December, 1990, Quebec's then Health Minister Marc-Yvon Côté, launched provincial health and social services reform, focused on the consumer/citizen. These reforms identified the citizen as the focus, with three roles and nine 'orientations' with those roles:

For the citizen as consumer:
1. Citizens whose rights are recognized and respected;
2. Citizens who benefit from services adapted to their needs;
3. Citizens who receive services as close as possible to where they live;
4. Citizens who are welcomed, assisted and treated by staff dedicated to their task.

For the citizen as decision-maker:
5. Decision-making as close as possible to the action;
6. Citizens at the centre of the decision-making process;
7. Citizens accountable for their decisions.

For the citizen as payer:
8. Citizens who get their money's worth;
9. Citizens who must assume the cost of the services.[3]

By seeking to shift the authority within the system from providers — particularly physicians — to consumers, Minister Côté found himself in a noisy, difficult battle with physicians. Physicians advanced their critique of the reforms by portraying government as anti-health care quality, and themselves as in favour of it. The reforms were slowed down and amended because of the ability of

---

3   *A Reform Centred on the Citizen*, Report by Ministère de la Santé et des Services Sociaux, Gouvernement du Québec, December, 1990.

physicians to rally public support, or at least the appearance of public support, to their cause. This scenario has been all too common whenever health care reform, effecting physicians, is introduced.

As in all long campaigns, it's not the battles that are decisive but the general direction. Quebec is still leading a debate that will eventually be resolved in favour of greater citizen involvement.

Lesson #2 - Legislating a Tougher Regime for Patient Sexual Abuse — Ontario Bill 100

In 1991, the College of Physicians and Surgeons of Ontario (CPSO) became concerned about sexual abuse of patients by physicians. A task force, headed by a tough-minded Toronto lawyer, Marilou McPhedran, was appointed.

Based on survey work conducted by the Canada Health Monitor and Price Waterhouse Management Consultants, the McPhedran report estimated that 8% of Ontario women reported sexual harassment or abuse by doctors.[4] The Ontario task force advocated a philosophy of zero tolerance.

> We do not tolerate sexual abuse by physicians. We do not tolerate the ways sexual abuse by physicians is implicitly supported. We work towards the development of sufficient support for victims if they can come forward and they can heal. We work diligently towards educating doctors and the public about appropriate behaviour and attitudes so abuse cannot occur out of ignorance on the part of either doctor or patient. We continue to support touch as a crucial healing part of the practice of medicine when that touch is caring, nurturing and not sexually exploitive.[5]

Issues which go to the heart of power relationships in our society and to challenging past, implicit acceptance of abuse of power will always be controversial. A great deal of our energy as a society will involve assisting those damaged by the abuse of power by healers. Much of the healing is through various self-help networks and support groups, rather than the formal medical system. As Marilou McPhedran notes in the preface to the report:

4   *The Final Report*, Task Force on Sexual Abuse of Patients, Commissioned by the College of Physicians and Surgeons of Ontario, November 25, 1991, p. 4.
5   Ibid., p. 15.

Readers stay with us through the journey of this report, be open to the voices in it who speak urgently to us about doctors, lawyers, teachers, clergy, nurses, social workers, hospital administrators and others who have been vested with status, trust and power. If we allow ourselves to hear them, we will be able to move beyond the collective denial and resistance that have enabled abusers and allowed the suffering of patients for too long.[6]

I do not believe that the majority of professionals have abused their status, trust and power. It is clear on the evidence, however, that a minority have, and haven't been accountable for their actions. We have had a collective conspiracy of denial and silence in our society around sexual abuse. This is not, by any stretch of the imagination, exclusive to medical practitioners. Those without power, significantly women and children, have, for the most part been victimized, whether at Mount Cashel or in their family practitioner's examining room. A necessary part of both the personal healing and the social change is to bring this abuse out of secret denial. Acknowledge its existence. Our fundamental challenge is to ensure that none of it occurs in the future.

As a result of the CPSO initiatives, there is now a minimum penalty for any sexual offence by a doctor against a patient of a five-year suspension and a provision for a fine of up to $35,000. Recently, a parallel report to the McPhedran Report was done by a committee led by Dr. Anne-Maran Ponton for the Quebec Corporation of Physicians.[7] The president of that corporation, Dr. Augustin Roy, who has been criticized for both his comments and views previously, rejected the findings of the report. The Quebec proposals, which parallelled those in Ontario in measures such as penalties, more investigators and a toll-free hotline where patients can check doctors' records, were opposed and rejected.

At about the same time as the Quebec rejection a new national study found that 40% of gynaecologists and obstetricians answered "no" to the question "Do you think sexual involvement with a patient is always an abuse of power?"[8] Clearly we have a great distance yet to travel as a society to achieve understanding of this issue.

6 Ibid., p. 6.
7 André Picard, "Doctors in Quebec Reject Sterner Rules," *Globe and Mail*, January 14, 1994.
8 Ibid.

Provider dominance is a product of history and the structure of our health care system. It is not a permanent fixture. Although moving beyond provider dominance is a difficult struggle, we must. Determination and persistence will turn the tide to a healthier system.

Broadened Responsibilities — Prevention and Information

Health providers must take more responsibility for providing patients with high quality information. Providers have an important role to play in improving health status and in treating illness.

A 1993 study by the Kaiser Permanente Research Centre in Portland, Oregon developed some interesting insights on the smoking issue. Although smoking is the major preventable health danger for those who smoke, most physicians did not ask patients whether they smoked. Further, physicians did not record this vital health information on the patient's medical record. Kaiser's researchers developed an intervention where doctors asked patients whether they smoked. If the answer was yes, they asked if the person intended to quit. If the answer was yes to quitting, a date was set. Nurses followed up this very brief intervention by providing an informational video and a phone call at the planned "quit" date. This very modest and cost-effective intervention significantly increased the rate at which smokers successfully quit.

In Canada, we have been slow to provide sufficient information to patients. While patients have an obligation to take responsibility they can't do it unaided. We also have a great deal of room to expand multi-disciplinary approaches. This is not to suggest that health care providers will have the greatest role in decreasing tobacco consumption for example. Quite the contrary. Tough legislation, social marketing advertising and taxation all have an impact but health professionals can contribute both through advocacy and thoughtful interventions with patients. Even with the recent, and deplorable, reduction of tobacco taxation brought about by the Government of Canada, we have higher levels of tobacco taxation than other nations. As President Clinton increases U.S. levels of tobacco taxation to finance his health reform plan, Canada may have an opportunity to revisit its disastrous decision.

Canadian dentists have done an excellent job on patient education and prevention. The last time I took my son for his dental checkup the waiting room featured a very effective wall rack entitled, "The Dental Information System — Helpful Information for Patients." The display contained a series of excellent brochures on: *The Checkup* and *The Dental Office: Healthy and Safe*. *The Dental Information System* is provided by the Canadian Dental Association. It is a very thoughtful guide for people committed to better dental health. The physician's waiting room immediately adjacent to our dentist's had the usual collection of old magazines but no health information.

Good Stuff to Read

Beyond Provider Dominance: Managing Change and Transition by Fiona Hastings, stimulated by papers from a King's Fund International Seminar. Published by the King's Fund, London, 1993. Copies are obtainable from Bournemouth English Book Centre, P.O. Box 1496, Parkstone, Poole, Dorset, U.K., BH12 3YD. A provocative and intelligent series of papers addressing the questions of moving beyond provider dominance in the delivery of health services. The book is idea-rich and Fiona Hastings is able to wrap a thought provoking framework of Harvard guru Rosabeth Kantor's management insights (relevant books by Kantor noted in Chapter 4) around the health policy issues. It is both a good read and a road map to many of the tough questions among providers, consumers and payers. Questions that will occupy centre stage for the balance of the 1990s in all nations debating and implementing health care reforms.

The Final Report, Task Force on Sexual Abuse of Patients, an Independent Task Force commissioned by the College of Physicians and Surgeons of Ontario, November 25, 1991. Marilou McPhedran chaired this task force which brought to light the very serious extent of sexual abuse of patients by doctors. This report caused both a furore and new legislation on a very important issue which needs to be understood and resolved.

The Canadian College of Health Services Executives (CHESE) produces some excellent material for health care managers and others. Information is available to both CHESE members and non-members from CHESE, 350 Sparks Street, Suite 402, Ottawa, Ontario K1R 7S8. Material includes:
- *A Guide to Career Management for Health Services Executives*
- *Contracts and Compensation for Health Service Executives*

- *Management Control and Funding Systems* – Lawrence J. Nestman
- *Certification Preparation Materials – Self-Assessment and Certification Bibliography*
- *Ethical Dimensions of Health Administration* – Ed Chown
- *Case Studies in Health Services Management – Leadership and Caring Visions in an Environment of Constraints*
- *Seeds of Health – An Anthology on Health Promotion*

Promote Your Patient Care Focus Through Programme Management, a new video from the Canadian College of Health Services Executives with the support of Peel Memorial Hospital.

Viewing the patient as a customer has become crucial for health services since the mid 1980s when some hospitals began adopting a programme management approach. The key to ensuring efficient and effective quality services is to end the traditional hierarchical structure where departments work within their defined boundaries. We need to adopt a programme management approach where services are offered by cross-functional teams to best meet patient needs.

This video features presentations on programme management. Specific issues such as development, implementation and evaluation of programme management are addressed by a panel during a discussion sponsored by the College with the support of Peel Memorial Hospital, and held in conjunction with the Ontario Hospital Association Convention in November, 1993.

The panel included:
- Dr. Peggy Leatt, Professor and Chair, Faculty of Medicine, University of Toronto
- Marilyn J. Bruner, President, Markham Stouffville Hospital, Markham
- Bruce Harber, FCCHSE, President, Peel Memorial Hospital, Brampton
- William MacLeod, CHE, President and CEO, Women's College Hospital, Toronto
- David Martin, CHE, President and CEO, The Hospital for Sick Children, Toronto

Part 3
Taking Control of Health and Health Care

Is it beyond our ability as individuals to help save Medicare? Should it be left to the experts, the doctors, nurses, managers and health ministers? The experts need help in two very important ways:

- Stay healthy and be an informed consumer — use health services appropriately
- Be an active and informed citizen — help build a healthy community

One of the challenges in Canada is to become more involved as individuals, as consumers and as citizens, in our health and health care. When governments stepped in as the insurer for most medical and hospital services, we gained great security and benefit. The financial barrier to accessing care fell away. But Canadians, as consumers, lost a key role in the health care system. We were no longer individual purchasers. The marketplace process of consumer demand shifted responsibility to governments. Health ministers and ministries became the complaints department for the health care delivery system. Health care delivery issues became very political. Daily question period in every provincial legislature became the forum for consumer feedback.

Our reform efforts to date have concentrated on the supply side of the health care delivery system. Getting the right number of doctors, making our hospitals more efficient and shifting attention to outcomes are all essential to better care services. Healing Medicare requires us to go further and manage the demand side. Demand for health care services is not straightforward. We encounter the health care system for a variety of reasons. Sometimes we are ill. Other times we are fearful that we may be ill. Often we go seeking information. There are also times when the system provides care that we don't really need or want. To succeed in reforming Medicare we must take action to manage the citizens demands. We can accomplish this by enabling individuals to have much greater access to information about choice and control over their care.

How significant are the challenges in health terms? Consider the following data. Ontario will spend about $17 billion on health services, through the Ministry of Health in 1994. Many of these costs however, are generated by behaviour which could be changed. The

Addiction Research Foundation estimates that approximately 30% of this budget is due to excess expenses generated by legal or illegal alcohol and drug abuse.

Our health care system is situated in a social context which society shapes and affects. It can be assisted by our choices about our behaviour.

Chapter 8

Be An Informed Consumer

One of the most striking revolutions in our history as a species on this planet is the information revolution now upon us. If knowledge is power we are the most empowered group of humans in the history of our species. But do we act on the information? Do we take the time to consider how it affects our lives?

Staying Healthy

The most obvious way in which we can be informed consumers of health care is to reduce the need to use such services. By staying healthy we can defer or reduce our encounters with the care system. We can also enjoy life more.

What are the best steps you can take to stay healthy and enjoy a long life? When you scrape away the endless studies, a list of the top 10 ways to stay healthy is refreshingly straight-forward and sensible:

1. DON'T SMOKE
2. DON'T SMOKE
3. GET ENOUGH SLEEP
4. EXERCISE REGULARLY
5. EAT PROPERLY
6. LIVE SAFELY
7. PRACTICE SAFE SEX
8. DRINK MODERATELY
9. BUY A SAFE CAR AND WEAR YOUR SEAT BELT
10. DON'T SMOKE

If the list seems a little repetitive, don't worry. You only need to remember to stop smoking and seven others. Why the annoying repetition about smoking? Simply because smoking is many times more of a hazard to your life expectancy and health status than anything else within your personal control.

I am not the only list maker in the health world. The former U.S. Surgeon General is a fellow list addict.

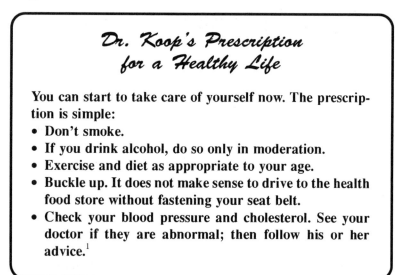

Dr. Koop's Prescription for a Healthy Life

You can start to take care of yourself now. The prescription is simple:

- **Don't smoke.**
- **If you drink alcohol, do so only in moderation.**
- **Exercise and diet as appropriate to your age.**
- **Buckle up. It does not make sense to drive to the health food store without fastening your seat belt.**
- **Check your blood pressure and cholesterol. See your doctor if they are abnormal; then follow his or her advice.**[1]

By now we are all knowledgeable about the role of tobacco in causing cancer but how many of us understand the impact of smoking on increased numbers of heart attacks and strokes? Tobacco kills more Canadians each year than traffic accidents, suicides and AIDS combined. Almost five times more, according to Dr. Richard Schabas, Chief Medical Officer of Health for Ontario.

There is a silver lining in the lethal cloud of tobacco. If you quit you regain considerable health ground, some of it rapidly. Within one year of quitting your additional risk of heart disease drops by one-half. The risk of lung cancer takes ten years to drop in half, but by the end of fifteen years, your risk of death from lung cancer drops to an almost identical level with someone who never smoked.

It's also important to note that smoking rates are declining in

1   Dr. Everett Koop, *The Memories of American's Family Doctor* (New York: Random House, 1991). I don't support Dr. Koop's focus on cholesterol level measurement. If you take the rest of the advice you will also lower your cholesterol level.

Canada. About 27% of Canadian adult men and 28% of adult women are still smoking. This is a significant drop from 50%, or one in two men twenty-five years ago but a much smaller drop from 32%, or about one in three women, over the same period of time.

In planning a take-control approach to your own health you need to assess your starting point. A few key questions need to be answered:

What are your most likely health risks?
Do you smoke?
Drink to excess?
Exercise?
Eat a balanced diet?

Once you survive being born, as 993 of 1,000 do in Canada, your main and manageable risks are dealt with by the advice above.

Taking control of your own health is linked to becoming involved in the health of your community. No matter how well you eat or how thoroughly you exercise, a drunk driver can shorten your life. So can polluted air or water. Environment *is* a health issue. Our health as individuals is shaped by environmental factors, some of which are amenable to community action.

Staying healthy is not just a good idea for us as individuals. Studies document the overall cost to the system of a lack of individual responsibility. The lifetime health care costs in the U.S. average about $225,000 per person. The lifetime costs for smokers, despite their shorter lives, are as much as a third higher than for non-smokers. Increased physical activity is associated with fewer visits to doctors. A study by J.J. Sokalov indicated in a large corporate environment that claims costs for those who had three or more of the risk factors — including smoking, obesity, diabetes and hypertension — were double those who had no risk factors. This strongly suggests that staying healthy is not only good medicine for you but a vital part of healing Medicare.

It is also worth considering the costs imposed by these behaviours.

What It Costs Ontario Each Year Because of Alcohol and Other Drug Use

BILLIONS OF DOLLARS

	Alcohol	Illicit Drugs	High Level Use of Legal Drugs	Total
Excess Health Care	2.6	1.2	1.8	5.6
Excess Law Enforcement	.5	.3	.4	1.0
Value of Reduced Labour Productivity	1.2	.5	.7	2.4
TOTAL	4.3	2.0	2.9	9.2^2

Be An Informed Consumer

Throughout the heyday of doctor-dominance in America, physicians kept a tight choke-hold on medical knowledge. Prescriptions were written in Latin, providing the profession with a semi-secret code, as it were, which kept most patients in ignorance. Medical journals and texts were restricted to professional readers. Medical conferences were closed to the laity. Doctors controlled medical school curricula and enrolments.

Contrast this with the situation today, when patients have astonishing access to medical knowledge. With a personal computer and a modem, anyone from home can access data bases like Index Medicus, and obtain scientific papers on everything from Addison's disease to zygomycosis, and, in fact, collect more information about a specific ailment or treatment than the ordinary doctor has time to read.[3]

Managing Your Own Care

Successful management of your own care is not a rejection of physicians, nurses, pharmacists or other very useful health care

2 Estimates based on research done by the Addiction Research Foundation, Toronto, 1989.

3 Alvin Toffler, *Powershift*, Knowledge, Wealth and Violence at the Edge of the 21st Century (New York: Bantam, 1990), p. 7-8.

providers. Self-management is the notion that you, the consumer, should not simply be a passive recipient of care. Multiple studies have shown savings from self-management. An article in the *New England Journal of Medicine*, in July 1993 estimated these savings from information and guidelines about self-management to be in the range of 7% to 17%.[4] This works two ways. Better information and increased confidence that much illness is self-limited. The *New England Journal* study also comments, in terms of self-management, that if confidence can be increased through education, there is a reduction in the cost of long-term health care even in people with chronic disease.[5]

Self-management is several parts Sherlock Holmes and a few parts your grandmother. Among the active steps needed are getting sound information from the beginning. Additionally, you need to build a home health kit with the following grandmother-inspired elements:

- Common cold kit
- First aid

Next, you need to understand informed patient choice as more than an idea. Finally, you need to make provision for health care in a situation where you cannot readily make decisions by writing a "living will."

If there were one right answer for each distinct health problem it would be easier to leave it to the experts. Your task would simply be to locate the best person. Unfortunately, there isn't one right answer or treatment for each condition. More often, there are a range of options with different consequences; potential risks and benefits are associated with each.

Getting Good Information

1. **Secure an information base.** This can be as simple as buying a book or visiting the library or as complex as linking to databases with your personal computer.
2. **Network of advisors.** Meet knowledgeable people you trust who can provide advice and link you to

4 Fried, Koop, Beadle et al., "Reducing Health Care Costs by Reducing the Need and Demand for Medical Services," *New England Journal of Medicine*, Vol. 329, No. 5. June 29, 1993, p. 322.
5 Ibid.

appropriate care. Often there are support networks of those who are coping with the same disease or condition. Breast cancer support groups are an excellent example — they've been there. They know.

3. **Subscribe to ongoing information sources.**
   These are the Sherlock Holmes steps.

It is probably advisable, in addition to books like *The Complete Canadian Health Guide* to subscribe to a health or wellness magazine. *The Berkeley Letter* is among the most popular, but there is a Canadian version available from the University of Toronto. A number of hospitals have health letters of various sorts as well. Their usefulness is that you are more likely to read something when it arrives than you are to browse through a health guide book. These letters are focused on new information, seasonal health tips and common issues. By devoting a small amount of your time and energy to making yourself informed, you will be able, in general, to manage your care. You will also be able to use services more appropriately when necessary, with a better understanding of what a particular health care service can provide.

In the case of treatment decisions involving significant medical surgical intervention, new information bases, supplemented by specific research on the condition or procedure, will vastly increase your confidence in asking relevant questions. Asking questions is an essential ingredient of getting more appropriate care. By asking questions you can state your preferences and also obtain more information.

Home Health Kit

Two or three components are suggested for your home health kit. One of the key ones is a simple first aid kit including bandages, gauze and ointment to prevent infections. Most homes would have a kit or a drawer with these items in it. Add to that, information on head injuries and cuts. You may wish to copy this information out of *The Complete Canadian Health Guide* or obtain it from other sources.

A second element is the very clever use of a "grandmother" approach of simplicity rather than high technology initiated by Kaiser Permanente, the largest U.S. health maintenance organization. In looking after their 6.6 million subscribers, Kaiser Permanente decided to take an active approach to enabling people to self-manage the common cold. The items in their common cold kit include:

- some chicken soup
- some generic aspirin
- a very good booklet on the common cold
- other cold treatments sold by your pharmacy over-the-counter

The point of the common cold kit, produced in both adult and children's versions, was to push back to the patient responsibility for a self-limiting illness. Colds come and go. The booklet contains the necessary precautions about going to the doctor if a fever or other symptoms persist. Generally your doctor can do little or nothing for the common cold. What she or he can do you can do just as well yourself.

Another useful ingredient for your home health kit is a diary in which to record illnesses, treatments for those illnesses and what seemed to heal you. With the proliferation of over-the-counter drugs and ointments, many common conditions can be appropriately treated by the individual. You can learn over a period of time about how your body reacts by keeping track of your minor illnesses and the successful treatments of them.

Informed Patient Choice

On several previous occasions in this book there has been discussion of informed patient choices as a means of making the health care system more effective. It's important to realize that informed patient choice is not only a good idea for the health care system, it's beneficial for you too. Take control of your own health care, understand the choices and participate in making them. We all have an understandable, human tendency, when faced with illness or a medical condition, to throw ourselves into the hands of the professional and say, "Whatever's necessary, doc, just do it." Part of our desire is denial. We don't like reminders that we are mortal. In many instances the advice offered by a health professional will be precisely the right advice, but how can you be sure?

Another major aspect to being an informed consumer is to seek within the health care system itself access to information. The Dartmouth technology of interactive video disks is one way. There are others like the CHEPA decision board. The main point here is to seek out more detail on the possible outcomes of various approaches to your conditions. In simple cases, such as a broken bone or an infection, there may be very few options. But in many other cases, the range may run from drug treatment to surgical intervention to a change in your lifestyle. The point is that you are a participant in that choice. Do you want back surgery or are you prepared to lose some weight and lead a more active life? Do you want to take drugs to lower your cholesterol level or are you willing to change your diet? Have you examined and felt fully informed about the consequences of particular interventions?

All of this is bound up in informed patient choice. The system can organize itself to better support patients but determination is needed on your part. If you are too passive you are unlikely to get access to full information.

Helping Patients Share Decisions with Their Doctors

The King's Fund Centre is piloting and evaluating an interactive video system designed to tell patients about the risks and benefits of treatment choices open to them. It makes information accessible to patients at the time they need to make decisions about treatment with their doctor. The system has two components—the hardware and the software.

The hardware consists of a personal computer (PC), a laser disk player, a video monitor, a video card for the PC and a printer. This compact collection of equipment fits on a desk in an outpatient clinic office.

The software 'asks' the patient to enter details about his/her age and symptoms. The system can then provide information about the risks and benefits associated with the treatment options available. The information is presented using a variety of formats—text, graphics, sound and full-motion video. The content of the programmes was assembled to answer specific questions about patient care raised as areas of concern by 'focus groups' of patients. Material is derived from work done by a patient outcomes research team (PORT) in the United States. This continuing initiative reviews research data from selected areas of health care to determine expected outcomes of treatments for common conditions.

The use of television and video can avoid the sense of confrontation and judgment sometimes associated with giving information through person-to-person contact. Interactive video programmes provide information which is standardised and consistent in presentation and content. An advantage of this technology over leaflets or conventional video is that patients don't need to apply their particular information to a more general population because the data is tailored to their own circumstances. This also means that the information can be personalized, using 'you' and 'your situation' instead of a general statement directed to the patient as part of a group.

The system is not applicable in all circumstances, for instance, patients in urgent need of treatment and where the choices are limited. Deciding whether a patient would benefit from the video is at the discretion of her or his doctor. Guidelines have been developed to help ensure that the information contained is relevant to the treatment choices.

The video does not make a decision about treatment for patients; it is designed to supplement the usual explanation given by the consultant or general practitioner in a way that means that the decision can be shared between doctor and patient. Programmes are available for the following conditions:

- benign prostatic hyperplasia (BPH)
- choices of surgery for early breast cancer
- chemotherapy after surgery for early breast cancer
- mild raised blood pressure
- the treatment of low back pain

The King's Fund Centre will evaluate all the programmes and assess the part this technology can play in the National Health Service. The evaluations involve studies of how patients and those involved in their care respond to this method of providing information.

Clinical trials have started on the BPH and hypertension videos in a hospital and in a general practice setting. How patients feel about the content of the video and how satisfied they are with the choices they make are of particular interest. The evaluations are being conducted in conjunction with the London School of Hygiene and

Tropical Medicine and the Health Services Research Unit at Oxford University.

The opinions of professional groups and patient organizations are being sought, as well as those of individual patients and doctors, to help decide whether the content of existing interactive videos needs adaptation before being introduced more widely into the NHS. A logical development is the production of British versions. Plans are being considered for this next stage.[6]

Managing Medications

Most of us already manage a range of medications. When we give our children an aspirin or rub ointment on a cut we are managing medication. Our role is certain to expand. Professor Michael Cooper, an insightful health thinker from New Zealand, offers his thoughts on self-medication:

Self-Medication

Virtually everyday of our lives we are subject to an array of discomforts the majority of which we either ignore or treat ourselves without attending a doctor. Surveys conducted in numerous countries suggest strongly that nine out of every ten people suffer from at least one condition of sickness during the course of any four week period. To be ill appears to be quite normal. Despite large variations in both scope and methodology a measure of consensus seems to emerge from the studies conducted to date which suggests that between 45–55% of all health conditions are largely ignored, 27–29% are self-medicated and 18–23% treated either by a doctor visit or by a prescription medicine already to hand from with the house. The percentage of conditions which prompt an immediate doctor visit, however, shows little uniformity ranging from 4% to 11% with one study suggesting that only 1 in 37 symptoms result in a doctor visit. Overall, it seems that at least 75% of all illness is

6   Adam Darkins, *KF News,* Vol. 26, No. 2, King's Fund, London, 1994.

coped with by the individual alone without recourse to a doctor....

...Self-medication is undoubtedly here to stay. It is as Rottenberg has put it, "a self-reliant attempt to solve a medical problem in the simplest, most economical way." In the UK, with medicine which is largely free at the time of consumption and low access costs to the general practitioner, market forces appear not to favour self-medication as strongly as overseas but the great majority of people are anxious to collaborate with their doctors and to use his services sparingly and to the best advantage. It is a tough job being a consumer, however, and we need assistance in determining when a consultation is appropriate, what conditions to self-treat, and how. As the Royal Commission studying medical education stated, "when adequate arrangements for health education and prophylaxis have been established, the typical patients of the future — who will be better educated and better informed about health dangers — can be expected to take more responsibility for the management of trivial and self-limiting complaints, provided that he is given the necessary encouragement and guidance by the medical profession.... The pharmacist, too, has an important role and one which must be more fully recognized. There can be no doubt that at present we fail to fully utilize his skill, knowledge and three years' training.

Much of future progress in health will come from what people are able to do for themselves in terms of collective and individual decision making about their life style and the socioeconomic environment. The rules of healthy living are fairly well known (if rather uninviting), and there is a rising tide of public opinion in support of the notion that people have become too dependent upon experts who make decisions on their behalf. Indeed, central to the future of primary care is the need for greater self-reliance and self-determination in matters relating to health. Responsible self-medication has an important role to play in this future.[7]

7   Professor Michael Cooper, "The Economics of Self-Medication," *Social Policy and Administration*, Vol., 19, No. 3, Autumn 1987, p. 238.

Make a Living Will

The fourth recommended step in utilizing care more appropriately is to provide direction about your care in case you are unable to give it directly.

Dr. Peter Singer describes a living will as:

> a written document containing your wishes about life-sustaining treatment. You make a living will when you can understand treatment choices and appreciate their consequences (i.e. when you are "capable"). A living will only takes effect when you can no longer understand and appreciate treatment choices (i.e. when you are "incapable"). There are two parts to a living will: an *instruction directive* and a *proxy directive*.
>
> An *instruction directive* specifies *what* life-sustaining treatments you would or would not want in various situations. A proxy directive specifies *who* you want to make treatment decisions on your behalf if you no longer can do so.[8]

Living wills are now legally recognized in Quebec, Nova Scotia and Manitoba. Recognition in Ontario is expected in 1994 and other provinces are likely to follow. Living wills go by a variety of names, including *health care directive* and power of attorney for *personal care*.

Dr. Singer notes that "a living will speaks for you when you are no longer able to speak for yourself."[9] An excellent description.

Why take this step? There are two types of burdens in treatment imposed by uncertainty. The first is a very human one. Your loved ones: spouse, children or others, must make decisions without knowing what you might really want. Many of us err on the side of more treatment for/to others than we might wish for ourselves. I lived through these decisions with a terminally ill father and probably insisted on too much treatment, the type that extended death rather than restored life. It's common for families to insist on heroic and often intrusive efforts because of a desire, a hope to prevent the inevitability of death.

The second burden is one of excessive costs. With 18-30% of health system costs incurred in the last year of life,[10] I would have

8   Dr. Peter Singer, *Living Will*, Centre for Bioethics University of Toronto, Toronto, 1993, p. 1.
9   Ibid., p. 2.

no desire to add to these costs by leaving choices to others. Recent studies indicate that 70% of people request no life-sustaining treatment for themselves when they are dying. 89% desire living wills, yet fewer than 10% have actually made an advance directive.[11] Clearly, the potential for vastly expanded use of these directives could allow both more appropriate care and a reduction in overly intensive terminal care.

The *instruction directive* requires you to think about possibilities and admit your own mortality. Making these decisions was not the most fun I've ever had. Nevertheless, upon serious reflection, the following are the choices I arrived at. These are not choices I want to burden my children with.

Bioethics Living Will Instruction Directive

Directions: Refer back to "Health Situations" and "Life-Sustaining Treatments" for the definitions of terms used in this directive. Write your treatment decision (YES, NO, or UNDECIDED) in the boxes below for each combination of health situation and treatment. For example, if you want tube feeding in severe dementia you would write "yes" in the bottom right hand box; if you do not want tube feeding in severe dementia, you would write "no" and if you are undecided, you would write "undecided." On the other side of this page, under "further instructions," you may express in your own words the situations in which you would or would not want various life-sustaining treatments.

10 Fuchs, V.R., "Though much is taken: reflections on aging, health and medical care," *Milbank Memorial Fund Quarterly,* Q Health Soc; 1984; 62:143-66.

11 Greco, P.J., "The Patient Self-Determination Act and the Future of Advance Directives," *Ana Intern Med* 1991;115:639-43. Emanuel LL, Barry MJ, Stoeckle JD, Ettelson LM, Emanuel EJ. "Advance directives for medical care -a case for greater use." *New England Journal Medicine* 1993; 24:889-95 Podrid PJ. "Resuscitation in the elderly: a blessing or a curse?" *Ana Intern Med* 1989;111;193-95

	CPR	Respirator	Dialysis	Life-saving Surgery	Blood Transfusion	Life-saving Antibiotics	Tube Feeding
Current Health	yes	yes	yes	yes	yes	yes	yes
Permanent Coma	no	no	no	no	no	no	no
Terminal Illness	yes	no	yes	yes	yes	yes	no
Mild Stroke	yes	yes	yes	yes	yes	yes	yes
Moderate Stroke	yes	yes	yes	yes	yes	yes	yes
Severe Stroke	yes	no	no	yes	no	no	no
Mild Dementia	yes	yes	yes	yes	yes	yes	yes
Moderate Dementia	no	no	no	no	no	no	no
Severe Dementia	no	no	no	no	no	no	no

Good Stuff to Read

The Complete Canadian Health Guide, Editor June Engel, University of Toronto & Key Porter Books, Toronto, 1993, $29.95. A marvellous new addition for your health "take control" library has just arrived. The University of Toronto Faculty, in cooperation with Key Porter Books, has just published a really, really fine guide, comprehensive in nature in a very open, readable style. Place this at the top of the highly recommended list. The Canadian content is also very helpful. The seventeen chapters cover the gamut from What Good Health Is All About? to Nutrition to Specific Diseases and Disorders.

Living Will, Centre for Bioethics, University of Toronto. Dr. Peter Singer, Associate Director of the Centre for Bioethics, has produced an actual Living Will. You complete it and it becomes a personal, legal document. The Living Will is available from the Centre for Bioethics for $5.00 per copy. It is a major step forward in allowing *you* to take control and make decisions now rather than someone else making them later. The document comes complete with directions and a form that can be completed and copied on legal-sized paper. You can get it by writing: Centre for Bioethics, University of Toronto, 88 College Street, Toronto, Ontario M5G 1L4, telephone: (416)978-2709, Fax: (416)978-1911.

Health News, University of Toronto Faculty of Medicine. Available for $18.95 per year. Six issues per year from Hilborni, The Newsletter Group, 205 – 109 Vanderhoof Ave., Toronto, Ont. M5S 1A8. A recent issue contained the following:
 * review of birthing in the '90s
 * first aid in the age of AIDS
 * dry eyes and eyecare tips

Healthy Life Guide to Self-Care — An Apple A Day Isn't Enough. American Institute for Preventive Medicine, 30445 Northwestern Hwy., Suite 350, Farmington Hills, MI, USA 48334, Fax: (313) 539-1818. This is an excellent guide to key issues of self-care health.

Deadly Choices Coping With Health Risks in Everyday Life, by Dr. Jeffrey E. Harris, Basic Books, New York, 1993. A solid review of the most recent evidence on health risks at the personal level and what you can do about them. The use of individual cases makes it more readable.

Tobacco and Your Health, Report of the Chief Medical Officer of Health, Ministry of Health, Ontario, 1991. A short, extremely readable review of the available and horrifying data on the impact of tobacco on the health of Ontarians. A good report to share with adolescent children during a necessary parental talk on the effects of tobacco on every aspect of your children's health. If you can convince your children not to start smoking it may be the single most important contribution you can make to their good health and long life. Better than all those vitamins and beets! The report can be obtained free of charge by writing to: Communications Branch Ministry of Health, 8th Floor, Hepburn Block, 80 Grosvenor Street, Queen's Park, Toronto, Ontario.

The 1992 and 1993 Reports by Ontario's Chief Medical Officer of Health can also be obtained from this address.

Mayo Clinic Family Health Book. First class medical reference available on CD-ROM from Interactive Publications.

The *Get Well Quick Kit,* by Linda Allison and Tom Fergusen M.D., Addison-Wesley. For children ages seven and up. A good health primer and modest "kit" of useful stuff.

Chapter 9

Be An Active Informed Citizen

Why is this important? Does it really matter how involved we are in health care? Why not leave it to the experts and the leaders we elect? The best answer is that both the experts and our elected leaders sincerely need your help. The changes necessary to make us live longer in good health and to re-engineer our health services cannot simply be imposed by legislation. Active involvement is essential. Without your help progress will be too slow, services will be discontinued and resources wasted on ineffective and inappropriate endeavours. From a personal standpoint, you may lose years of potential good health.

Helping Make Healthy Public Policy

To succeed in reforming Canadian Medicare we need health goals. We also need healthy public policy.

There are two key ingredients to healthy public policy:
- leadership and vision;
- new ways of making public policy.

Fortunately, both seem to be in evidence in Canada in the 1990s. Health goals however are meaningless without the means to achieve them.

There is, it is often said, only one group of taxpayers — us — and therefore the magic solution to access significantly more revenue is non-existent. Another dimension of public policy-making in health is the emergence of not one but two major advocacy coalitions. These are the Coalition to Keep Medicare Healthy, largely spearheaded by the Canadian Union of Public Employees with some

400,000 members, (100,000 of whom work in health care), and the Health Action Lobby (HEAL) coalition, with some 500,000 members (largely providers, although the Consumer Association of Canada is part of HEAL).

The Coalition to Keep Medicare Healthy has a seven-point plan. This coalition, with its roots in hospital workers' unions feels that we need to:

1. Stop the fee-for-service treadmill
2. Give non-physician staff a larger role in patient care
3. Eliminate health care for profit
4. Elect hospital boards and democratize health-care institutions
5. Reduce dependency on prescription drugs and make them more affordable
6. Guarantee that health care is of the highest quality, whether it is provided in the home, the community or an institution
7. Encourage preventive care

The HEAL group has ten principles or goals with three specific requests to health ministers. One is to ensure that consultations with consumers and providers, in developing health goals, are meaningful and occur at early opportunities; they want to be involved. The second request is to establish a stable financial planning horizon to consider transition funding and invite HEAL to participate in the forthcoming review of major federal transfers to the provinces. Thirdly, they want to establish a national task force to clarify the five Medicare criteria and develop more effective methods to ensure its attainment. HEAL and the Coalition have met with five of the provincial ministers, to agree on which of the two groups (or none or both) to hear. The federal ministers have met with HEAL, and provincial ministers have met with each of the two groups. Not everyone is quite at the same table yet, but movement is afoot. The National Health Forum proposed by the Government of Canada may improve the dialogue. Already many of the provinces have engaged their citizens, at the community level, in constructive conversation about health and health care.

There is an odd verbal puzzle to health care reform debates. First, everybody agrees that the status quo is not working, that we are in a period of change. Two, everybody puts the rhetorical umbrellas of health care reform and quality over the changes that are taking place. The crunch comes because there is fundamental disagreement inside that umbrella about what is meant by health care reform. Meanings are not necessarily diametrically opposed, but certainly the prescriptions of the Coalition to Keep Medicare Healthy and those of HEAL, diverge significantly. It is understandable that provider organizations, which are largely what the two coalitions represent, are concerned with protecting the interests of their constituent members. The national organizations have embraced change at the level of their statements, speeches and policies more generously than their provincial constituent organizations. That is understandable. It's not the federal minister that explains why a certain procedure isn't being performed or why a certain patient is leaving the country, the ten provincial and two territorial ministers have that privilege. As Nye Bevan once said of the National Health Service in England: "If a ward nurse dropped a bed pan in a public hospital anywhere in England, the sound resonated through the Parliament of Westminster." The complaints department for the health-care system is unfortunately the provincial legislature and the daily newspaper. So, too, the leader of the national organizations are less involved in the day-to-day struggle for dollars than their provincial counterparts. Canadian health reform is a struggle of ideas at the national level and a battle of financial interests as well as ideas at the provincial and local level.

New Ways to Make Public Policy

Traditional public policy-making in Canada is failing to keep pace with needed change. The old ways of Royal Commissions, hierarchical government departments and academic institutions are unable to contend with the onslaught of television, lobbyists and public expectations of speed. How can a Royal Commission be credible after five years when all the same experts gave their identical views on television the night it was launched and again when it concluded? Particularly when five years and twenty-five million dollars have failed to deliver any new insights! How can government officials successfully advise elected leaders on the complexity of issues in a thirty second television clip?

Speed has come to dominate our channel changing, fast food, ATM, fax and cellular phone society. It cannot leave public policy unscathed. New ways of merging competing interest and obtaining intelligent advice are arising. So too, are innovative decision-making forums. How are we making public health policy in the 1990s?

Several new ways policies are being made, are delineated briefly below. They range from new approaches to provider (physician/hospital) negotiations, to devolution from provinces to regions, to greater consumer involvement. None has gained hegemony in the discussion of how to achieve transformation of our system. All are being experimented with or being implemented in various Canadian jurisdictions at this very moment.

More Interventionist Public Policy Leadership by Governments

Governments are shifting from an insurance role to a more directive managerial role. In a number of instances, governments in Canada are acting unilaterally, through legislation or policy to accomplish change. This new role is much more intrusive than governments have played in the past. As noted above, Saskatchewan, Alberta and New Brunswick have taken particular action in the case of hospital restructuring and governance. The British Columbia government legislated a cap on total payments to physicians after failing to reach a negotiated settlement, which led to further talks and eventual agreement.

Governments managing under severe fiscal constraints are taking more explicit decisions and finding, if not full public support, at least not the same degree of opposition that existed in the past. The view that hard choices will need to be made to preserve Medicare has gained considerable weight throughout the country, although there are still suspicions, largely among provider groups, that some of these actions constitute a dismantling of Medicare. In Alberta where the government is reducing funding by 17% over three years the debate is very heated.

In some instances governments have announced targets or decisions and then negotiated with providers within the limits. For example, in its 1991 Budget, the Government of Ontario proposed to reduce fees paid to private laboratories by 5% across-the-board. Instead, it reached agreement with the laboratory association to reduce fees for eighteen particular tests by a larger percentage achieving the same result.

Governments have also undertaken to publish supplementary budget documents and health action plans, which set out specific directions and allocation of resources. These documents represent the translation of health policy into the concrete reality of dollars allocated among health programmes.

Negotiations between Governments and Providers

Negotiations are taking improved forms, and diversified/alternative bargaining structures are being established. Historically, government-provider negotiations dealt almost exclusively with price of services. After several years of failure to agree on anything significant, the Government of Ontario and the physicians' organization, the Ontario Medical Association (OMA), reached a landmark Framework Agreement in the Spring of 1991. Under this agreement, a Joint Management Committee was established with representation from both the OMA and the Ministry of Health. Other features included the so-called Rand formula (a compulsory dues payment to the association) and the awarding of representation rights for all physicians in the province to the association. The scope of the agreement was also unusual in that it involved the physicians' organization in physician human resource planning, utilization and affordability. In short, it represents simultaneously the coming of age of the physicians' association as a union on one hand, and the acceptance by that organization of significant responsibility for management on the other.

It's too early to tell how well this agreement will work. It is however evident that a number of features of the agreement, including the Joint Management Committee, have been adopted by other Canadian provincial jurisdictions. As well, arbitration has been granted to Ontario physicians as a way of settling fee disputes. A third innovation in negotiations is a much greater focus not just on physician and laboratory utilization, but overall services. Rather than conducting narrow discussions focused only on price, all governments are seeking some control and management over the volume of procedures and billings.

Collective or Stakeholder Processes

There is greater interest by government and the public in consultative processes involving all stakeholders. The evolution of the discussions on better management of physician human resources provides an important example. Following the Barer-Stoddart Report, described earlier, ministers of health endorsed a national action strategy and plan. A national conference was subsequently held involving all stakeholders, and a wide array of consultations with individual provinces was conducted. This process produced a more constructive policy process, although not yet total agreement, by all of the players on what decisions are to be made.

Collective or stakeholder process does not absolve governments of their responsibilities for resource allocation. It does, however, blunt criticism and enhance understanding of the complexities of issues.

Greater Consumer Involvement in Choices

There are three important dimensions to greater consumer involvement. The first is emphasis on Total Quality Management (TQM) or Continuous Quality Improvement (CQI) techniques which involve a more consumer-centred approach to reform. The second thrust is informed consumer choice. The work of Dr. Jack Wennberg, of Dartmouth Medical School, has gained considerable interest and following in Canada. Finally, rebalancing governance and advisory structures to include more consumers and fewer providers is necessary.

As more hospitals and other health service deliverers adopt TQM or CQI techniques there will be a greater focus on the individual consumer. Early results are promising with significant reductions in waiting times, amelioration in service efficiency and, most importantly, improvements in quality of service perceived by the consumer. In 1992, Canadian health ministers adopted "a vision of quality statement" to guide intergovernmental efforts in the health care delivery system; pursue quality, through greater consumer involvement.

There is a range of methods underway to involve individual patients more directly in their care choices. An informed patient is a must. The techniques of informed patient choice are discussed at greater length below.

A third area where greater consumer involvement is needed is on the boards, commissions and other governance structures. Major re-examination of the historical appointments to citizen boards is underway. Traditionally board members have been chosen to deal with such tasks as private fund-raising for institutions, generally for capital requirements. The consumer movement is gaining considerable authority.

In many Canadian jurisdictions, a specific percentage of consumer representatives (in the 30-50% range) is now gaining prominence as a norm. With more citizens on boards historical provider dominance is offset and more balanced decisions are made.

From the consumer point of view greater involvement means greater emphasis on service. One-stop shopping, convenience and absence of waiting — features normally associated with customer service — are becoming more central in health care delivery. The era of a patient passively awaiting physician's time and accepting physician's conclusions seems to be ending rapidly. Consumers are much more informed in health and medical matters, through the media and publications, than they were in the past. Much of the "black box" technology of medicine is giving way in the face of an enlightened and informed consumer.

Restructuring of governances in several provinces is also under-way. A major Senior Citizens' Consumer Alliance played a pivotal role in altering the Government of Ontario's thinking on long-term care. The Consumer Alliance insisted on greater involvement in decision-making and a non-bureaucratic structuring of the long-term care delivery system, with much more of a community emphasis.

Each of these three dimensions of consumer involvement: board appointments, being informed, and restructuring governance, will significantly alter decisions and choices and improve the quality of the health care system.

The Canadian Consumers' Association has been active in pro-moting these changes and in participating in the national Health Action Lobby (HEAL).

Where You Can Get Involved

As a Governor
- **Board of health**
- **Boards of hospital**
- **District health councils**
- **Community health organizations**
- **Volunteer health association**
- **Research organizations**

As a Voter
- **Ask candidates about their health views**
- **Help organize community discussions on health and health reform**

- Participate in all candidate meetings and other public forums and ask questions about health and health care
- Insist on common sense about health and health care, not tired old clichés

As a Volunteer
- Volunteer nearly anywhere (there are hundreds of groups extending from local Meals on Wheels, to the Cancer Society)

As a public servant
- Provide clear, factual information to the public

Your Role — All of This Only Works If *You* Get Involved.

Where can citizens get involved? There are the traditional board structures, community health centres, hospital boards or C.L.S.C.s. There are also new local authorities, some elected and some appointed. None of these have any chance of success without your active participation. If the only people rolling up their sleeves are providers, we will not shift to a more consumer-based system. Some 30,000 Canadians already volunteer as governors of our health system as hospital trustees and members of boards of health.

More Evidence-Based Policy Making

Several Canadian provinces have opened institutes to bring together notable expertise in clinical epidemiology and related fields. This is the institutionalization of the ad hoc Royal Commission and Task Forces of the 1970s and 1980s which flourished in most Canadian jurisdictions.

The Institute for Clinical Evaluative Sciences (ICES), established under the Joint Management Committee (JMC) by the Government of Ontario and the Ontario Medical Association, will have consequential effect. The mandate of the Institute is to conduct research to assist the JMC in improving the quality and effectiveness of medical services. ICES replaces an earlier Joint Task Force on utilization, with the major differences being scale and permanence. ICES has a $4.5 million per annum budget and a permanent core staff. The Task Force was smaller and not as well financed.

The Government of Manitoba established the Manitoba Centre for Health Policy & Evaluation with university-based researchers, who function at arm's length from the government, through the Department of Community Health Sciences, at the University of Manitoba. The Centre, although small, with two career scientists and associates of the Canadian Institute of Advanced Research, is examining health expenditures, outcomes and service effectiveness. The Advisory Board of the Centre has substantial national and international expertise.

The Government of Saskatchewan founded the Saskatchewan Health Services Utilization and Research Commission with a mandate to produce information on effectiveness, efficiency and relative usefulness of various programmes, procedures and intervention. This new commission subsumes the earlier Saskatchewan Health Research Board.

The challenge for each of these centres of analysis, research and expertise will be to alter behaviour and to help us understand and react to a dynamic system. The translation of research work into clinical guidelines, decision algorithms and protocols requires new insights into physician-patient interactions. Altered behaviour requires much more than insight. It also needs incentives or disincentives.

Producing evidence of inappropriate or unnecessary procedures does not, in and of itself, determine any reduction of such activity or change its pattern. The infrastructure to reconfigure incentives is in a fledgling state. Its evolution will largely determine whether the range of newly-established institutes simply contribute to advancing knowledge or more directly influencing service delivery.

The emerging network of institutes will compile data, information and analysis. How rapidly and how successfully this is brought to bear on clinical practice remains an open question. But, compelled by fiscal pressures, governments will seek to bring about some practical applications.

One challenge for evidence from solid research is to serve as a counter balance to the "complaints department" — the daily Question Period in each Provincial and territorial assembly — nature of health care management with more diverse health goals. The aforementioned Nye Bevan's experience is common to parliamentary democracies based on the British model. Question Period is a powerful influence on health decision making. Perhaps, magnified by television and the other media, too powerful. The influence of the case is greatest when it pits the individual's human interest against the indifference of THE SYSTEM. Sometimes these individual heart-wrenching cases are symptoms of underlying and profound problems. More often they are the statistical reality of errors in a large system. The buffeting that Ministers take, shortens their effective time as Ministers; they are moved to other portfolios more rapidly than is sensible or they lose momentum. The most insidious impact of the complaints department mentality is to divert attention and resources from real problems to firefighting of media or political emergencies.

How then can we build the importance and profile of broad health goals? One reality is clear. We have no ability to diminish the complaints department. It fulfils a valuable, if distorting, role in enhancing the responsibility and accountability of the health care delivery system. Instead, we need to continue elevating debate about the real determinants of health.

One very successful device utilized in the United States has been public, high profile reports by the surgeons general. The elevation of this position to that of a senior spokesperson on health issues and health hazards has been valuable. In Canada, some medical officers have taken leadership in issuing broad policy reports as well as in tackling public education at the local level. The Chief Medical Officer in Ontario, Dr. Richard Schabas has issued three powerful reports in recent years and intends to continue.

Devolution

Another approach taken by many provinces is to create advisory bodies or consultative forums of a broad sort to provide advice, not only on *health* policy, but on *healthy* public policy. The Premier's Council on Health Strategy in Ontario expanded its focus to become The Premier's Council on Health, Well Being and Social Justice. The Alberta Roundtable on Health held in Red Deer in August, 1993, brought together 160 people to "chart a fundamentally new direction for health and health care in Alberta."[1]

As noted previously, the Province of Quebec has devolved a significant range of decisions in health and social services to local boards. This trend continues there, with further devolution, as well

1   *Alberta Roundtable Report*, Alberta Health, Government of Alberta, August, 1993, p. 6.

as democratization of local boards. In fact, Quebec is creating a new level of government for health and social services.

The most recent Quebec initiative is contained in Bill 120 — *An Act Respecting Health Services and Social Services* which set out the following key changes:

- the creation of a regional level of government responsible for the development and organization of health and social services
- the abolition of the present councils on health and social services
- to replace them, the creation of a health and social services authority in each administrative region of Quebec

The new sharing of responsibilities envisioned in Bill 120 permits a clear delegation of powers to regional authorities. The regions have 2 main responsibilities:

- to carry out the services within their jurisdiction
- to allocate to that end the available financial resources[2]

Two other provinces, Saskatchewan and New Brunswick, have combined regional or district restructuring in a devolved model. Saskatchewan describes its efforts to create new health districts and mandate them.

It is expected that the new health districts will:

- conduct health needs assessments and develop district health plans
- integrate and co-ordinate health services within the district; this will include establishing arrangements to safeguard the rights and missions of privately-owned health facilities
- manage all health services within the district
- develop 'community health centres'; these centres may take a variety of forms to be determined by the district, such as "health and social centres," co-operative health centres, "community clinics" or "wellness centres"
- ensure that all health services within the district meet specific provincial guidelines and standards
- be governed by a single health board[3]

2 *The Policy on Health and Well-Being*, Government of Quebec, Ministry of Health and Social Services, 1992.
3 Hon. Louise Simard, "A Saskatchewan Vision for Health, A Framework for Change," Minister of Health, Regina, August, 1992, p. 17.

New Brunswick has also moved recently to a legislated integration of previously independent hospitals under regional governance structures.

Advocates of devolution argue for the greater convergence of local or regional needs and resources. There has also been a view that devolution would allow provincial governments to transfer fixed "envelopes" of money for allocation by local or regional bodies. Whether this strategy will enable provincial governments to avoid demands for more funding remains to be seen. It's likely that devolution of significant management authority will lead to better integration of health and community services at the service delivery level.

The report of the Comprehensive Health System Planning Commission in Ontario proposed a fully integrated regional health planning and management authority for the southwest region with 1.4 million population.[4] It presented Ontario with a full devolution opportunity already taken up in several other Canadian provinces. To date it has not been accepted. Devolution without citizen involvement is not a solution. With your help it may be part of the answer.

Good Stuff To Read

Reports of the U.S. Surgeon General.

Reports of the Chief Medical Officer of Health, Ontario.

Tobacco and Your Health, Queen's Printer, Toronto, 1991.

The Policy on Health and Well Being, Government of Quebec, Ministry of Health and Social Services, 1992.

4   Earl Orser, ''Report of the Comprehensive Health System Commission,'' a report to the Minister of Health for Ontario, 1992.

Chapter 10
Managing Demand
for Services

Most of the activity in Canadian health care reform has been on the supply side. Although this is essential, it's not enough. Unless we also influence the demand for services, we will fail because the problems are too big to be solved purely on the supply side. Individuals seek health care for a wide variety of reasons, not just because of need. We often visit health providers — doctors and emergency rooms — because we need information. Why does this hurt? Should I apply heat or cold? With the collapse of extended families and the loss of grandmother-held-health-knowledge we have been driven into the formal health system.

Much of what we do to take control of health and health care rests with each of us as individuals. But, we need leadership and innovation from the formal health system to help us take that control. The list of ways this can be accomplished is not yet as long as the list of how we can re-engineer hospitals but is just as important. As we develop our tool kit on the demand side and learn new techniques the list will grow.

Making Costs Transparent to Providers

One of the unintended consequences of single payer, government insurance of hospital services and global budgets was the elimination of detailed accounting in hospitals in the 1950s and 1960s. With investments in information systems, hospitals are regaining their ability to track costs at the provider level. This allows managers to make known the cost of various activities to providers.

Sunnybrook Health Sciences Centre in Toronto is a leader in this trend. By making comparative resource data available to physicians, Sunnybrook is influencing behaviour. Physicians who know how their resource use compares to their peers are more willing to consider alternatives. For professionals who are trained to react to evidence, the necessary change in behaviour is best accomplished with data and evidence.

One of my younger brothers, an energetic family practitioner in a rural community, told me about a visiting expert who explained the huge cost difference between intravenous and oral antibiotics. Will this influence how my brother practices? Yes, I believe it will. Cost must not become the sole determinant in health care decisions, nor should cost information be so totally absent that there is an inability to consider it as an aspect of managing care.

Making Costs Transparent to Consumers

The flip side of the cost transparency issue is making patients and the public aware, as consumers, of the costs involved in health services. The Canadian health care system is the second most expensive in the world, exceeded only by the United States. This fact has been obscured by twenty-five years of invisible cost information and political attachment to a confusing vocabulary. Payment for services as a collective responsibility creates the erroneous conclusion that health care is free. By restoring cost information to patients, they can gain greater insight into more appropriate use of hospital services. Lest the reader draw the wrong conclusion — that this type of transparency is step one on the inexorable road to billing patients — it should be noted that billing patients is a direction I fully and vigorously oppose. I am advocating that people know exactly what they are getting and at what cost. Transparency of costs will cause a lot of very good questions and probably a few bad ones to be raised along the way. We must be careful to place this initiative of cost transparencies in the context of patient education. The goal and outcome must be to avoid scapegoating or frightening ill and elderly patients.

Sunnybrook Hospital in Toronto has developed its information system to permit it to issue full cost reports to each patient. Whether other hospitals and governments will follow remains to be seen. It would be an excellent and sobering idea for each of us to know what our activities as health consumers cost us as taxpayers.

Managing Demand for Hospital Services[1]

One area where we can learn from the United States is in managing more appropriate use of hospital services. Educating the patient in a variety of ways has been a central task of well-managed U.S. health maintenance organizations such as Kaiser Permanente. Canadian health care managers are gradually understanding the potential of actions which affect the demand side. Most of our health reform effort remains on the supply side, but more balance is needed. If we do not utilize available techniques and technologies to affect demand for health services through public and patient education, we are giving up half the leverage for necessary change. We are also perpetuating a system judged by many observers to be inappropriately dominated by providers. A few ideas on the demand side:
- nurse call lines
- video cassettes for patient education
- advertising campaigns to convince common cold sufferers to visit a pharmacy not a doctor or a hospital

Shared Decision-Making: Informed Patient Choice

Perhaps the best known advocate of this change is Dr. Jack Wennberg, from Dartmouth Medical School, who in conjunction with Sony Corporation, is making available a continuing series of video discs dealing with informed patient choice. These video discs focus on a particular procedure and are based on the view that there is no one correct course of treatment. For example, Dr. Wennberg's rather well-known work on prostate treatments indicate that there are three general courses of action. These are watchful waiting, surgery or treatment with drugs. Depending on one's tolerance for risk and one's particular circumstances, one could reasonably choose any of these three options.

1   An excellent article on demand management "Reducing Health Care Costs by Reducing the Need and Demand for Medical Services," *New England Journal of Medicine*, Vol 329, No. 5, July 29, 1993, p. 321-325. Authored by former US Surgeon General Everett Koop, Mary Jane England, The Health Project Consortium et al. It identified a number of measures to manage demand for health services and to reduce need for care.

Kaiser Permanente's work in the United States has indicated a significant reduction in the percentage of patients choosing surgery when confronted with all of the available information and evidence on their other choices. The Government of Ontario is supporting production of a video disc for cardiovascular surgery being developed by the University of Toronto. It is likely that more and more specific information will be made available to patients capable of making a choice. Of particular emphasis would be procedures which involve significant resource usage.

What is Expected from Interactive Video Disks?

The rationale for using interactive video disks is most often tied to concerns about utilization and an interest in patient utilities, quality of life, health education and the dynamics of medical decision-making. The reasons varied from place to place, but the most common were:

- CONSUMER EDUCATION — giving individuals a consistent, thorough review of treatment options is a meaningful step toward consumer empowerment. Anyone facing a surgical decision needs information about the disease and available treatments and an opportunity to balance personal preferences against probable health outcomes. Detailed information is presented in an understandable way that helps consumers ask questions and participate in the treatment decision.
- PATIENT UTILITIES — personal values and preferences of a consumer facing serious treatment decisions are not always discussed with the physician. Whether through embarrassment, timidity or lack of opportunity, consumers often keep their fears and opinions under wraps. The interactive video disk openly presents a range of considerations and preferences that can be explored.
- REDUCED UTILIZATION — inappropriate utilization is driven by physicians and consumers. Surgeons see people who were referred to them for a reason and feel an obligation to fix the problem. Consumers sometimes demand treatments that are excessive. Interactive video disks push both sides to rethink their assump-

tions. The Foundation claims that prostate surgeries decrease by up to 50% when the disks are used as part of the decision-making process.

- INFORMED CONSENT — in the litigious environment of U.S. health care, informed consent is a significant issue. After viewing a disk, the consumer receives a print-out of the interaction: the personal information that was recorded before the disk started and the material that was reviewed in the program. A signature line on the print-out turns the form into legal protection for the physician.

- OUTCOMES RESEARCH — as a research tool, the disks capture consumer demographics, disease condition, preferences and decisions. Follow-up questionnaires capture patient satisfaction with the information provided and the decisions made. The potential exists for research that establishes utilization changes, patient preferences at various points of disease progression and outcomes from various decisions.[2]

Another technology with the same objective is the decision board developed by the Centre for Health Economic Policy Analysis (CHEPA) at McMaster University in Hamilton. The CHEPA decision board tool is a portable foamcore board, easily transported to an office, home or bedside. The fundamental assumption of the board is that patients are capable of making a decision that is right for them if they have the necessary information.

How informed are the patient choices made in your hospital? How available is information for the patient and their family? Could you improve the situation?

Patient Education

If you are a parent, chances are high that at one time you have made the journey to the hospital emergency ward because your child bumped his or her head on the sidewalk, fell off a bicycle or engaged in some other regular childhood mishap. Chances are also high that

2   Colleen Savage, "A Interactive Video Disks as Shared Decision-Making Programs in Health Care," Report for the Health Strategies Office Ontario Ministry of Health, June 1993, p. 6-7.

you returned home after a long or short wait in the emergency department clutching a piece of paper labelled "head injury sheet." This valuable paper informed you of the danger signs indicative of a possible concussion. Many parents' anxieties have been diminished by simple informational tools such as cold kits or head injury sheets.

Public Education

Public education is essential to healthy public policy and management of demand for health services. Government leaders have a role in changing public attitudes and perceptions. For two decades in Canada, governments have tended to say: "Isn't our health care system wonderful: it's free, it's accessible, it's universal." The reality has been that it is not free. It's the second most expensive health care system in the world and the public has been encouraged in a belief that everything is solvable, that death can not only be postponed but may be eliminated altogether if only enough treatments are applied. Moreover, the public has not been given much help as consumers in how to appropriately use the system.

A good analogy is energy conservation. People were not told, "Stop using energy. Turn off the heat and freeze to death in your houses." They were told that they could adjust how they used energy and how to have a more affordable situation which was equally good in quality terms. We are starting nationally, in Ontario, and in other jurisdictions, to look at how health ministries talk to the public. Is the public informed about self-limiting illnesses? About appropriate use of emergency rooms? Are people given guidance to better manage the system? There is a lot of distance to be made up here. We need the health equivalent of a dimmer switch to replace the on-off mechanism.

The physicians have been put in the middle of an unpleasant sandwich by being told on the one hand, "People can come to your office and if they are not really sick, by the time you determine that, you have already invested your professional time in that determination." On the other hand, governments get upset and say "Why is the single biggest expense in physician services in Ontario the common cold? Why is that the major reason for office visits?"

One of the major reasons is that the public has not been told, through public education, that visiting the physician for a common cold is not going to get them much benefit in the process. Nor has much investment been made, until recently, in getting an informed and knowledgeable patient.

Health care providers have not been extraordinarily forthcoming about everything involved in treatment either. Contrast that with choosing a place to go to for a ski holiday. Making this choice, thanks to the marketing efforts of a number of very aggressive American resorts, you can sit for an evening watching videos from half a dozen American ski resorts and choose the one you like. Having in a sense pre-skied the major runs, one can make a more intelligent choice. Through various technologies, care providers can create, as allies, consumers who are informed participants. This education is going to require active involvement at the workplace and community levels. The public will need to be educated where they live and work. Health care professionals are going to have to manage better and more openly.

The success of the health care system will be determined by the ability to marry very difficult contending objectives. We will succeed because none of us wants to look our grandchildren in the eye a few years hence, admit we had a health care system envied all over the planet, one that we let get away from us. We are already on track, but there will be roads we venture down that are in the wrong direction. We will have to be honest enough, on all sides, to admit that seemed like a good idea at the time but it wasn't. We may have to step back and find another way of achieving the objective. The objective is clear: we want a quality system and one we can afford. Those are two non-contending and achievable goals.

Chapter 11
Community and Public Health Services

People died while public health authorities and the political leaders who guided them refused to take the tough measures necessary to curb the epidemic's spread, opting for political expediency over the public health.... In those early years, the federal government [US] viewed AIDS as a budget problem, local public health leaders saw it as a political problem, gay leaders considered AIDS a public relations problem, and the news media regarded it as a homosexual problem that wouldn't interest anybody else. Consequently, few confronted AIDS for what it was, a profoundly threatening medical crisis.... It is a tale that bears telling, so that it will never happen again, to any people, anywhere.[1]

Randy Shilts, 1987

No single event in matters of health during our lifetime has captured the public interest and attention as thoroughly as the AIDS epidemic. It is a pervasive reality of life in the 1990s and is likely to remain so, well into the next century. In a series of blows to an evolving human mastery over disease or at least over plagues, the AIDS pandemic has revealed our inability to prevent premature death. It has shaken our faith in many health institutions. In many industrialized countries public fear about AIDS related blood safety has

1   Randy Shilts, *And The Band Played On* (New York: St. Martin's Press, 1987), p. xxiii.

become a central issue. In France senior health officials are in jail for their negligence and inaction in the face of the AIDS prevalence. In the United States, the Federal Drug Administration had the American Red Cross blood activities placed under court administration due to safety concerns. The Krever Commission provides a daily forum for the debate of safety issues pertaining to Canada's blood system, past, present and future. As we sort our path through the HIV/AIDS issue, we rediscover the roots of public health.

Public Health

Three key public health issues: tobacco, AIDS, and vaccines and immunization are critical to our success in achieving and maintaining a healthy nation. We have lessons to learn from our experiences in each case, from both successes and failures.

Tobacco

Tobacco is a key public health issue. The World Bank estimates that tobacco related deaths will increase from two million per annum at present to twelve million per annum by 2050 if present consumption trends continue.

Prominent public health officials do not primarily advocate for more treatment services in health. For example, the 1991 report in Ontario by the Chief Medical Officer of Health stated:

...we must prevent our children from becoming tobacco users. We must help current smokers quit. And we must protect non-smokers from exposure to tobacco smoke.[2]

Legislation introduced by the Ontario Health Minister in November, 1993, was created to reduce children's access to cigarettes. The Federal Government is considering a generic packaging requirement which would further hinder marketing efforts by the tobacco industry. Yet, despite all we know about tobacco as the number one preventable killer of Canadians, the Federal government, for a host of dreadful reasons, collapsed on tobacco taxation in 1994. It seems that knowing the facts is insufficient.

2   Dr. Richard Schabas, *Tobacco and Your Health*, Report of the Chief Medical Officer of Health, Ontario, 1993, p. 7.

World Bank Policy on Tobacco

In 1992, in recognition of the adverse effects of tobacco consumption on health, the World Bank articulated a formal policy on tobacco. The policy contains five main points.

- The World Bank's activities in the health sector — including sector work, policy dialogue, and lending — discourage the use of tobacco products.

- The World Bank does not lend directly for, invest in, or guarantee investments or loans for tobacco production, processing, or marketing. However, in the few countries that are heavily dependent on tobacco as a source of income and of foreign exchange earnings (for example, those where tobacco accounts for more than 10% of exports) and especially as a source of income for poor farmers and farmworkers, the World Bank treats the subject within the context of responding most effectively to these countries' development requirements. The World Bank seeks to help these countries diversify away from tobacco.

- To the extent practicable, the World Bank does not lend indirectly for tobacco production activities, although some indirect support of the tobacco economy may occur as an inseparable part of a project that has a broader set of objectives and outcomes (for example, rural roads).

- Unmanufactured and manufactured tobacco, tobacco-processing machinery and equipment, and related services are included on the negative list of imports in loan agreements and so cannot be included among imports financed under loans.

- Tobacco and tobacco-related producer or consumer imports may be exempt from borrowers' agreements with the Bank to liberalize trade and reduce tariff levels.[3]

3   World Bank Development Report, "Investing in Health," World Bank, New York, July 1993, p. 89.

Canadian governments and banks should consider following the World Bank's approach to tobacco as well. Instead the Government of Canada lead a shameful retreat on the tobacco taxation issue, causing a significant increase in tobacco consumption with the attendant future deaths.

AIDS

Much has been written about AIDS and much more will be written. No recent tragedy captures more fully the apparent helplessness in the face of the unknown. What is particularly depressing about the pandemic is how little action in public health measures we took in the early stages against the spread of the disease. In a failure there are always a myriad of villains upon whom some blame falls. Randy Shilts captures the breadth of the failure in his books and others have recount it in articles and television documentaries. Our challenge is to learn from our experiences with HIV/AIDS both so that we can improve present actions and to prevent a replication of this tragedy in the future.

The fundamental lesson to be learned is that the basic public health principles that we have painfully learned over the past one hundred years should not be abandoned for any reason. Although the advocacy for protection of AIDS patients and the gay community from discrimination was powerful in the early stages of the AIDS situation, it should not have eclipsed, as it did, proper public health. We need to take steps to limit infectious diseases not on the basis of which community, or individual is infected but on the basis of protecting others and limiting the spread of the disease. This notion has been central to public health since its inception.

The classic public health story is the tale of the removal of the pump handle and saving countless thousands from water borne disease. There is a clear parallel to the AIDS story. Action was eventually taken in regards to HIV/AIDS to treat the blood supply, to close bath houses and to properly warn the whole population as well as those in high risk groups. But these actions lagged far behind the certain knowledge of the deadliness of the disease.

Even now, the pendulum seems to have swung too far. Instead of directing our efforts to those at risk we may be spreading our energy too widely. Public education, programmes of testing and the tightening of all preventive measures took a very long time to come to pass in Canada. There are further steps to be taken: needle exchange programmes and distribution of condoms in prison. No one likes to admit the realities behind these necessities. Even if inaction is jeopardizing human lives, there are still some who don't want to believe that drugs are present in prisons or that risky sexual practices go on behind bars. Our only option is to ensure all preventive efforts are taken.

If we are prepared to learn about the AIDS tragedy there are some positive lessons. We have seen the community as a group of consumers bringing great advocacy and thoughtfulness to bear on the pandemic. This dialogue between health consumers and providers has been at times an extreme and aggravating one, but it has taught providers some general lessons about the need to involve consumers more directly. As well, options for palliative care, hospices and other less acute care settings than the hospital have sprung up to provide options for those dying of AIDS. Among these options is important leadership in terms of the evolution of palliative care for many others with incurable or untreatable conditions. There are also lessons about the appropriateness of different types of care.

Not all of the lessons are positive. It may come to pass that we learn that rushing untested or not fully tested drugs through into general use has produced harmful consequences and side effects. It may also emerge that, with all the advocacy in the world, scientific discovery may not be rapid enough or successful enough to solve the problem. We may have to come to terms with a pace at which dollars can be invested in worthwhile AIDS research. I take no position on our current level of investment but, it does seem possible that we invested too little in the early stages and may be in danger of overloading the research capacity in response. We need better tracking of emerging threats to public health. We need to act on them early and in a comprehensive fashion.

Evolution of the
HIV-AIDS Epidemic

Region	HIV incidence (millions) 1990	HIV incidence (millions) 2000[a]	HIV prevalence (millions) 1990	HIV prevalence (millions) 2000[b]	AIDS-related (millions) 1990	AIDS-related (millions) 2000[c]
Demographically developing group	1.6	2.5	7.4	25	0.3	1.7
Sub-Saharan Africa	1.1	1.0	5.8	12	0.3	0.9
Asia	0.3	1.3	0.4	9	*	0.6
EME and FSE[d]	0.1	*	1.4	1	0.1	0.1

* Less than 0.05 million
Note: Incidence refers to new infections in a given year, prevalence refers to the total number of persons infected.
a. Conservative estimates
b. The countries of the demographic regions Sub-Saharan Africa, India, China, Other Asia and islands, Latin America and the Caribbean, and Middle Eastern crescent.
c. India, China, and the demographic region Other Asia and islands.
d. EME, established market economies; FSE, formerly socialist economies of Europe.
Source: World Health Organization data.[4]

As the AIDS epidemic decimates the poorer nations we must be careful to learn the important lessons that public health has to teach us.

Vaccines and Immunization

Investments in vaccines and immunization are easily our best health care and health status bargain, in terms of preventive medicine. Immunization programmes based on vaccines have been the most cost-effective intervention. Our progress against particular diseases has been based very much on the availability of vaccines and immunization.

4   Ibid., p. 95.

Shortly after I joined the Ministry of Health in 1991 I was approached by Dr. Richard Schabas, Chief Medical Officer of Health in Ontario. He set out to convince me that we should add the vaccine for haemophilias B to our programme. We could not obtain new funds to pay for this vaccine. However, Dr. Schabas and I agreed that he could squeeze the money out of his existing operation and proceed with the vaccine.

In 1994, a few months after leaving the ministry I spoke to the meeting of the Ontario Campaign for Action on Tobacco. At the end of the lecture Dr. Schabas approached me to disclose the very impressive results that adding this new vaccine had achieved. The table below details those results.

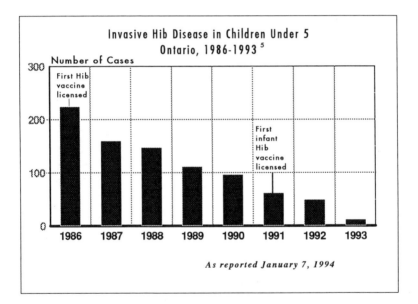

In Ontario, the Ministry of Health budget totals over $17 billion per annum. Of this amount, total spending on the public health system was about $230 million, or about 1.5%. Within public health, vaccines accounted for only about $25 million of spending, although the cost of implementing vaccine programmes adds to that. Still, it is worth considering that our single best public investment in the future health of Ontario children and adults was drawing only .15% of the

5   Provided by Dr. Richard Schabas, Chief Medical Officer of Health in Ontario, 1994.

Ministry budget. Or, simplified, only one dollar out of every $680 was being spent by the Ministry on vaccinations. By contrast, the Ontario Medical Association estimated that we were spending $200 million on the common cold paying physicians for office visits by cold sufferers.[6]

Imunization with vaccines are key determinants of the state of public health on a global basis. The World Bank notes, "Vaccines to prevent tuberculosis, measles, diphtheria, pertussis, tetanus and polio have revolutionized preventive medicine over the past two decades. Costs are less than $10 per DALY[7] immunization and less than $25 for polio plus diphtheria and tetanus."[8] The Expanded Programme on Immunization (EPI) pursued by the World Health Organization now reaches about 80% of children in developing companies. It is estimated that this programme alone averts an estimated 3.2 million deaths per year. An increase in immunization in developing countries from 5% in 1977 to 30% by 1985 and 90% for all children by 1990 has been achieved. Estimates are that if this massive improvement in vaccination levels had occurred, preventable disease would total 23% of the global burden of disease among children. The table below illustrates the scope geographically.

The World Health Organization projects that polio will be eradicated by the year 2000. The World Bank argues for the extension of the Expanded Programme in Immunization (EPI) in two directions. First, coverage should be moved up from 85 to 95% of all children born. The total cost would be between $500 and $750 million a year but the gains would dramatically outweigh the cost. The second direction is adding additional items to the package, hepatitis B and yellow fever vaccines for selected countries, micro nutrients in regions where deficiencies are highly prevalent. These additions would improve health substantially.

The following table from the World Bank Report indicates that fifty-five million disability-adjusted life years (DALYS) could be saved by the recommended EPI expansion. The total annual costs of less than 2% are a fraction of the amount that is spent on public health in the developing countries. While we have made great progress we have a way to go to achieve the 95% level. Within the

6   Ontario Medical Association unpublished work by Darrel Weinkauf, 1991.
7   What the heck is a DALY? A DALY is a Disability Adjusted Life Year—or a year of healthy life added. DALYs are the best measure of bang-for-the-buck in health investment.
8   "Investing in Health," World Bank, New York 1993, p. 72.

developed countries, maintaining, or, in the case of the United States, achieving the 95% immunization level will continue to be a challenge.

Burden of Childhood Diseases Preventable by the Expanded Programme on Immunization (EPI) by Demographic Region, 1990

	share of the total burden in children under age 5 BURDEN		burden per 1,000 children under age 5
	(millions of DALYs per year)	(percent)	(DALYs)
Region			
Sub-Saharan Africa	23	15	242
India	16	12	137
China	1	3	8
Other Asia and Islands	7	10	81
Latin America and the Caribbean	1	3	18
Middle Eastern Crescent	7	10	86
Formerly Socialist Economies of Europe	*	*	1
Established Market Economies	*	*	1
World	55	10	87

* Less than 1.

Note: The EPI includes immunizations for pertussis, polio, diphtheria, measles, tetanus, and tuberculosis. These estimates exclude the burden from tuberculosis because most of it falls on adults.[9]

Source: Calculated from Murray and Lopez, background paper.

Connaught, one of the world's major producers of vaccines, is introducing multiple vaccines. At the time of writing, Connaught is working on a pentavalant vaccine which would combine polio with four other major vaccines in a single injection. The advantages of this, both in cost-effectiveness and health terms, are significant. Research that combines vaccines into single applications will improve the cost-effectiveness and the health outcome of the World Health Organization's Extended Immunization Programme and similar projects.

9 Ibid., p. 73.

Canada should not be smug or complacent. Although we have reached near universality in vaccination programmes, we face risks in two areas. Immigration to Canada from countries without similar vaccination programmes means new arrivals to Canada could be in a risk situation. We need to provide vaccination to these people as part of their settlement process. Second, we have difficulties reaching all those in the First Nations communities. This will require developing a full partnership with First Nations governments to ensure that all Aboriginal children in Canada are also protected against the diseases we hope to eradicate from the world.

Research investments, which will be discussed further in a subsequent section, have enormous application to vaccines and immunization. We need progress not only on vaccines themselves, but also on more cost effective and safe means of delivering them. As the Provincial Auditor of Ontario recently pointed out, there has been significant wastage in the vaccine distribution system in Ontario. Total quality management in each Canadian jurisdiction would help direct money to the most cost-effective distribution mechanism. In some parts of the country, we may be relying too much on physician-based delivery systems when broader public health approaches, such as school vaccinations delivered by nurses, are more appropriate. This should turn on the age at which the vaccine is necessarily given. As well, it should take into account the cost-effectiveness of the various delivery methods.

In terms of disease, we are truly becoming a global village. We need to direct our attention to the immunization and vaccination of all those who dwell in the village. The United States has the worst track record of any developed nation in immunization and vaccination. This is a policy area which will receive significant attention from the Clinton health reforms. The rapid movement of the world's population among countries, whether for a short or long stay for immigration, whether as refugees or for holidays in warmer climates, gives us all a stake in the health of the world's population, a stake that our own humanity dramatically underscores. Drug resistant strains of tuberculosis are appearing with increasing frequency not only in New York City but also in Toronto. It is also evident in the history of the transmission of HIV/AIDS that travel had a large role in the spread of the disease.

Mandatory Public Health Programmes – The Ontario Experience

An interesting revitalization of public health services has been prompted by the introduction of the Mandatory Health Programs and Service Guidelines in 1989 by the Ontario Health Ministry. The document[10] which set out the new approach, identified four health goals and twenty specific programs. The goals included: development, community level health promotion, communicable disease reduction and environmental health. The programs covered a broad range from Tobacco Use Prevention to Sexual Health, from Healthy Children to Healthy Elderly. The legislative authority for the Mandatory Programs was under the *Health Protection and Promotion Act*, funded 100% by provincial government sources. This provided an incentive to the municipal public health system which is generally in a cost-sharing relationship with the province.

The roots of this approach are in broad population health. Dr. Schabas, Chief Medical Officer of Health in Ontario notes the following key issues around development of the mandatory programs.

1. The entire process was health goals based. The first thing we did was to establish health goals and objectives. Program discussions were then based on whether or not the programs actually addressed a health goal and whether they did it in an effective way. This approach forced us to address issues that had previously received insufficient attention. It also called into question many traditional public health programs.

2. The health goals, and therefore the entire process, was population health focused. Looking at health outcomes and health behaviours on a population-wide basis invited us to consider both high risk interventions and population-wide interventions. Perhaps the most important shift represented in the mandatory programs was the recognition that the latter approach, population-wide strategies, are critically important in addressing our health goals.

3. The entire process of developing the Mandatory

10 *Mandatory Health Programs and Services Guidelines*, Ministry of Health Ontario, Queen's Printer, April, 1989.

Programs was highly consultative. This meant that the membership on all of the committees that put together the health goals as well as the program guidelines was overwhelmingly non-ministry. The role of the ministry was to provide coordination for the process.[11]

The introduction of this new, strengthened and health goal linked approach represents progress in revitalizing public health. Evaluation of the Ontario effort will provide important lessons for that province and the rest of the country.

Community Health

In all provinces except Quebec, community health in Canada is a collection of disparate and remarkable organizations epitomised by community health clinics. In Quebec the organized CLSC system[12] operates. In a recent paper former Quebec Health Minister Claude Forget and Monique Jerome-Forget, the head of the Institute for Research on Public Policy (IRPP), capture the difficulties Quebec has experienced in endeavouring to implement the CLSCs as the mainstream health care mechanism.

In 1971, Quebec introduced the concept of the CLSC (or local community service centre), drawing inspiration from Swedish and Czechoslovakian models and incorporating a full range of medical and social services, with salaried medical staff, thereby creating a primary care gateway to the whole system. The Quebec government found itself unable to implement the changes in the form desired. In retrospect, the reason for that failure are apparent — the neglect of preexisting institutional arrangements. Quebec physicians had, at the time, little experience of, and even less appetite for, group practice. The general public, as well as the medical profession, had little understanding of the complementarity between primary medical care and a host of social services. Finally, while CLSCs were promoted in parallel with the introduction of medicare (instead of being able to bank on its existence and a medical profession familiarity with it), the notion of a salary for physicians was

---

11 Dr. Richard Schabas letter to the author, May 9, 1994.
12 The CLSCs are community health and social services organizations.

widely seen (not just by physicians) as a tactic to reduce medical income levels under a new publicly financed system.[13]

CLSCs remain a key element of Quebec's health reform strategy. We should consider for a moment some of the examples of community health activities in other parts of Canada before contemplating what sort of framework into which they could be amalgamated or organized. In particular it is essential to understand that community health centres have grown from community activism and the crusading leadership of individuals. They have not been sparked by external forces, nor could a successful community based organization evolve without strong community support.

Among the examples are the approximately fifty community health centres in Ontario, including the South Riverdale Community Health Centre, the long-standing Group Health Centre in Sault Ste. Marie, which is heading towards a role as a comprehensive health organization, and Mount Carmel Klinic in Winnipeg, Manitoba. Like hospitals before them, many of these community health initiatives have sprung up with governance from the community and, more recently, funding from government. In many cases, government funding has gradually displaced voluntary charitable funding for these organizations. Most frequently a dynamic individual or a community-based organization provided the spark, determination and drive. Anne Ross lead the Mount Carmel Clinic against all odds for decades in Winnipeg's north end. The United Steelworkers Union supported the creation of the Group Health Centre in Sault Ste. Marie and remain its defenders and protectors. While governments can encourage the development of community health centres, the experience of Quebec CLSCs and community health centres elsewhere suggest that grassroots community support is essential for success.

Health in the Workplace

Shortly before I left my position as Deputy Minister of Health for the Province of Ontario in November of 1993, I had a visit from Mr. Frank Stronach, the dynamic founder and Chair of the Board of Magna. Mr. Stronach has built and rebuilt a huge and successful autoparts manufacturing concern which employs roughly 11,000

---

13 Monique Jerome-Forget and Claude Forget, "Too Smug for Comfort?," IRPP/Brookings International Conference, Montreal, May 15-16, 1994, p. 6.

Canadian workers and will produce upwards of $3 billion worth of products this year. Why would he seek to meet the government's Senior Health Official? His concern was the health and well being of his employees. Accompanied by Dr. Arif Bhimji, his progressive chief medical advisor, Mr. Stronach was very keen on exploring a Comprehensive Health Organization (CHO) model for Magna employees and the communities in which they live. His unique Magna Employee's Charter contains a commitment to a safe and healthful workplace. The objectives for a Magna CHO are:

- set an example for others in industry to follow
- shift the emphasis in health care to health promotion and disease prevention
- establish a partnership between providers and consumers
- change the focus to preventive health practice from institutional care
- allow for effective and appropriate use of allied health personnel
- permit the best use of resources and institutions
- improve health outcomes and the health status of all consumers involved.[14]

Mr. Stronach told a personal story about his early days as a young factory labourer, in either Austria or Canada, I can't recall. The essence of it was that he had drilled a sizable hole in his finger with the drill due to carelessness. Rather than seek medical help and forfeit a starting position on the soccer team, the young Stronach stuck his finger in a bottle of iodine, wrapped it in a bandage and went off to play. Today a workplace accident of this sort would trigger an orgy of forms, investigations and medical treatment.

Neither Mr. Stronach nor I would advocate the return to the "good-old" days before improvements to workplace health and safety laws and regulations. We did find common ground, however, on the subject of greater workplace education and more individual responsibility. Neither of us were expressing simple altruism in the exchange.

Mr. Stronach's competitive company depends on healthy, productive workers. The economic survival of any health ministry and Medicare depends on convincing employers and individuals to focus on wellness rather than generating, either passively or actively, more business for the care delivery system. Mr. Stronach and I had a strong

---

14 Proposal by Magna for a Comprehensive Health Organization, October, 1993.

shared interest. Employers in Canada have a key role to play in employee health and wellness.

Two very important avenues for engaging Canadians in achieving greater wellness and health status are healthier communities and healthier workplaces. They are by no means mutually exclusive for there would be little point in creating healthier communities if the people who lived in them went off each day to work in unsafe or unhealthy working environments. Similarly, the safest and healthiest working environment will not compensate for a violent, dangerous and unhealthy community. We must work on both if we are truly to achieve progress.

Healthy Communities Movement

One of the most innovative aspects of revitalized public health is the rediscovery of the powers of local governments to improve the environment and health of cities. While our senior levels of government debate health care, as a federal or provincial problem, our cities are moving forward on health issues at the local level. Toronto has been a leader in the Healthy Cities Movement as the following material demonstrates. Other Canadian cities have much to learn from Toronto in this regard.

Excerpts from Healthy Toronto 2000

Many would be surprised to learn that the greatest contribution to the health of the nation over the past 150 years was made, not by doctors and hospitals, but by local government.

Dr. Jessie Parfit
The Health of a City:
Oxford 1770 to 1974

To make Toronto the healthiest city possible, we must ensure that health is a principal concern on everyone's agenda and that the health impacts of our decisions are recognized and taken into account. This is the central message of Health Toronto 2000.

Some Fundamental Concepts and Values

We see health as a resource for everyday life. People wish to be healthy in order to lead rich and fulfilling lives, and to attain their maximum potential. In this context, health is more than just physical health—we have to pay much more attention to mental and social well-being.

We recognize that the level of health of our community is a reflection of the quality of our community and that a high level of health for all in our community must be our aspiration. Therefore the basic prerequisites for health must be available to everyone.

Health is a complex phenomenon involving physical, mental and social well-being and is determined by many factors. We therefore need a sophisticated understanding of health, one which illuminates the complex interactions and the holistic nature of the determinants of health and can guide us in our actions.

We have come to recognize certain fundamental public health values. These include:
- Promotion of health and prevention of disease are better than cure.
- Social interventions to enhance the common health of the community are appropriate and may take precedence over individual concerns.
- Inequalities in health must be reduced and their roots in social inequities must be addressed.
- We must treat our natural ecosystem with respect, both for our own benefit and for the benefit of future, generations and we must provide for them a clean, green, quiet, healthy and sustainable environment.
- Our community must be human-centred and human scale, a caring, sharing, cooperative and supportive community that places people above material things.
- Each individual in society needs a meaningful role and the ability and the opportunity to participate actively in the community and in decisions affecting their health.

A Health Promotion Strategy

The five strategies of the Ottawa Charter should be used as the basis for developing the Healthy City Initiative.

Thus, as a City and as a Department we must:
- establish public policies that support health;

- create or help in the creation of environments supportive of health;
- strengthen and facilitate community action for health;
- develop or aid in the development of personal skills for health;
- reorient health services towards health promotion and a community-based health services system.

Health Goals for the City

The following broad health goals, which correspond to proposed health goals for Ontario, are not primarily the responsibility of the Department of Public Health; they require the commitment of City Government as a whole.

1. Reduce inequities in health opportunities in Toronto.
2. Create physical environments supportive of health.
3. Create social environments supportive of health.
4. Advocate for a community-based health services system.[15]

Does your city or community have healthy community policies? What could you do to spark change? How could the Ottawa Charter improve the health of your community?

Workplace Wellness: a Proposal

Healthier communities and workplaces can move us towards better health as a nation. If employers take a keen interest in the health of their employees much benefit can be shared by all.

Workplaces are sources of injury and ill health as well as a major positive part of giving our lives and relationships meaning. Our images of which workplaces as hazardous to health are often dated. The images of filthy factories and unsafe construction sites need to make room for a few realities for those who work in the health care sector. Accidents and injuries in hospitals and nursing homes are frequent.

Most provinces are now collecting an employer payroll tax or levy on the basis that employers should contribute to health care

---

15 Excerpts from "Healthy Toronto 2000," City of Toronto.

costs of Medicare. Perhaps it is time to base the levy on employers willingness to take steps to improve employee wellness. A charter of workplace wellness drafted collaboratively by health experts, employers, bargaining agents and governments might serve as a foundation to a new initiative. A discount in the levy or employer health tax for employers willing to abide by such a charter is a worthwhile idea.

Good Stuff To Read

And the Band Played On — Politics, People and the AIDS Epidemic by Randy Shilts, St. Martin's Press 1987, or Penguin paperback 1988. As a journalist, Randy Shilts covered the plague from its initial days. If there can be such a creation as a wonderful book describing one of the great and preventable tragedies of our era — this is it. The Shilts' chronicle of the failure of both will and systems is a gripping unfolding of tragedy. A must-read for all of those who want to ensure that it is never allowed to happen again. Public health must be vigilant and unmoved by the politics of the moment if it is to protect us all.

The Memoirs of America's Family Doctor, by Dr. Everett Koop, the former U.S. Surgeon General, Random House, New York, N.Y., 1991. An interesting, quite personal memoir which provides a glimpse behind the scenes at health policy making and lack thereof in the Reagan era in Washington. Dr. Koop played a major role in the smoking and AIDS issues. A useful read for those intrigued by the politics of health policy. Dr. Koop's case histories of his surgery on babies and young children are also fascinating.

Tobacco and Your Health, Report of the Chief Medical Officer, Ministry of Health, 1991. A short, easy to read, presentation of the grisly facts on tobacco as the major preventable cause of illness and death. Good graphics add to the impact of the numbers.

Part 4

World Health
Economic Development
in the Global Village

The short-hand story, then, is that despite their diversity, health care systems in every society have all evolved without mechanisms to assure accountability for effectiveness, efficiency, and appropriateness of care provided. The response of providers to every issue, every problem, every question, has been, 'We must meet needs — Give us more.'[1]

Robert Evans, 1993

Health is an essential human desire. The activity of seeking health and providing health care represent a major economic endeavour for our species.

In health and health care, the global village presents Canada with opportunities for learning and prospering. Two developments in 1993 on the global scene are worthy of special attention. The unprecedented commitment of an American President, Bill Clinton, to health and health care for all Americans is noteworthy; the United States is the last major industrial nation to make this commitment. The publication of the World Bank Development Report, "Investing In Health," entirely devoted to health issues, is also unprecedented. With these two events, health and health care have moved to the global centre stage. Confronted simultaneously with twin realizations that much progress has been accomplished and we know how to achieve much more, it is time for an important reformation of health and health care on a global basis. Ideas about reform may vary from country to country but they are taking hold in many, many systems.

Health economic development is the link between health care endeavour as nations, the care of ourselves and our neighbours, and business opportunities and research which all add enormous value to our health and economy.

For Canada, health economic development can be a strong support to Medicare and to our economic well-being, if directed properly, or it can be the leading edge of a misguided privatization and eventual destruction of our Canadian success. The public administra-

1   Robert Evans, "Our Bill of Health," *Alberta Health*, 1993, p. 17.

tion and not-for-profit nature of Canadian Medicare is one of its essential and necessary qualities. It must be maintained. However, we need the continuing creative energy of the Canadian private sector in several important ways. These do not include insurance of basic, necessary health care services or ownership and management of health care delivery. These should remain not-for-profit and publicly administered.

As Canadians, we need to focus on three aspects of health economic development that support our ability-to-benefit approach. Increasing our exports of health goods and services, increasing research in Canada and expanding the Canadian production of more affordable goods and services which supply our health care delivery system. These endeavours are inter-related. Strengthening our exports provides larger markets and revenues to support domestic research. Efficiencies achieved through greater volumes will assist affordability of products in Canada. Most importantly, because our wealth as a nation is a direct result of our health as a nation, our health economic development side will have direct health benefits in reduced unemployment and increased income for Canadians.

Learning from other nations is essential for our progress. We contribute to world progress in health by teaching others what we know. If we are to benefit fully, our role in the global village must be as both student and teacher.

Chapter 12
We Have Much to Learn from Each Other

> Among the six countries surveyed Canada's health care services get the best overall marks from its citizens. Canadians are especially satisfied with the quality, personal control, not having to wait too long to see a doctor and minimizing personal costs of care.[1]

Canada has much to teach and much to learn. We need only to look at the experiences of our neighbours on the planet, both those with whom we share a border and those with whom we share values and historical roots. A cautionary note on ideas from elsewhere: two approaches should to be avoided. The first is a winner-take-all or "Stanley Cup" notion of comparative health care systems where we argue about who has the best system and then everyone else copies the winner.[2] This approach is fatally flawed. Health care systems are rooted in national histories and are not simply transportable. The other extreme view is just as wrong, that we can learn nothing from other places because everything is unique and different here. Lessons can cross national borders, but we must think critically about which

---

1   "An International Comparison of Health Care Systems," Harvard Community Health Plan, Annual Report, 1990, p. 6.
2   I am grateful to Ted Marmor of Yale University for this idea which he effectively presented. In Professor Marmor's formulation the World Series was referenced, but since Toronto seems to win the World Series frequently I needed a more appropriate example!

are general and which are only country-specific. Bad ideas travel just as easily as good ones.

Canada and the United States

After twenty-five years of relative stability, Canadian Medicare is facing twin challenges posed by the demand from our nation's bankers and taxpayers of affordability and a parallel consumer demand for quality. President Clinton has embarked upon the most ambitious re-engineering of health care delivery in many decades, perhaps even in the history of the United States.

There is much mythology about these two countries approaches to health care. Many of the advocates in one nation believe the grass is greener on the other side of the longest undefended border in the world. Often the debate stirs more negative aspects.

Dispelling Some Myths About Canadian Medicine

Myth No. 1:

Canadian doctors are employees of a socialist state which tells them how to practise medicine and ration care.

Reality:

Canadian doctors are overwhelmingly (90%+) self-employed, fee for service practitioners. The ten provincial health plans pay for medically necessary services on a fee schedule negotiated annually between the government and the professional association. In comparison to the United States we have little to no utilization management or prior approvals. Doctors are able to bill separately on a fee schedule they get for non-essential, largely cosmetic, procedures, for treating non-Canadians and for third party services (insurance medicals and the like).

Canadian doctors have far less intrusion into their medical practice than U.S. doctors. (Some believe too little intrusion, but that is a separate issue.) No Canadian doctor needs to discuss ability to pay with a patient. Nor do they face bad debts from patients or expensive malpractice insurance. Many doctors find this appealing.

Myth No. 2:

Canadian doctors are migrating to the United States to escape socialized medicine.

Reality:

Out of a total physician population of about 22,000, Ontario loses about one hundred doctors a year to the United States (or .5%). Of those one hundred doctors, about half return to Canada within five years.

Canada is a middle country in medical migration. We recruit in Commonwealth countries such as the U.K., Australia, New Zealand, Hong Kong. We do lose some of our best and brightest to the United States, but Canada remains a very good place to be a doctor.

Myth No.3:

Waiting lists characterize the Canadian health care system and provide proof of rationing.

Reality:

Judged on the basis of number of major procedures to population, Ontario compares to either California or New York. We do as many or more by-passes, gall bladders, etc. We have waiting lists for some procedures as a means of better organizing our system. For example, in cardiac surgery, Ontario has a provincial registry and network. A patient can decide to either wait for their surgeon or to be on the registry and take the first available one.

A recent study concluded that mortality rates on the Ontario waiting list were at the same level as mortality rates during surgery in New York State. Often patients wish to have surgery scheduled sometime in the future. We have the same global shortage of radiation oncologists as other countries.

Myth No. 4:

Canada has the same affordability problems and financial pressures as the United States.

Reality:

Affordability — Comparing Costs

How has a single-payer publicly-insured system affected affordability? If we use health spending as a percentage of GNP as our measure, the following data is revealing.

Pre-Medicare Period:

1960   **U.S.**   **5.5%**
        Canada **5.5%**

1970   **U.S.**   **7.3%**
        Canada **7.0%**

For the pre-Medicare period, health spending grew from the same level and at the same rate in both countries as a share of GNP. In both, the share increased from 5.5% to a little over 7%. In the nearly twenty-five years of Canadian Medicare (1968-93) the rate of growth has sharply diverged. U.S. spending has risen from a little over 7% of GNP to almost 14%. This doubling of the GNP share in the U.S. compares to a much more modest growth in Canada from 7% to about 10% in the same period.

Medicare Period:

1993   **U.S.**   **From 7% to about 14%**

        Canada   **From 7% to about 10%**

Canada's system has achieved a greater containment of costs. While we face a continuing affordability challenge, it is on a slower growth path.

Myth No. 5:

The United States achieves a better health status by spending 40% more on health care services.

What does spending 40% more of its GNP on health care yield the United States?

210 Healing Medicare

Reality:

Better Outcomes

According to the Harvard Community Health Plan International Comparison carried out by the Louis Harris Co.:

	Canada	U.S.
Life Expectancy	79.2 years	75.6 years
Infant Mortality	7.3 deaths per 1000 live births under 1 year	10.4 deaths per 1000 live births under 1 year
Satisfaction	No. 1 – Canadians satisfied with quality, personal control, not waiting too long and minimizing personal costs of care	No. 2 – Americans satisfied with access to advanced tests, drugs and not waiting too long
Dissatisfaction	Canadians dissatisfied with access to high technology, Medicare and elective surgery. Although less dissatisfied than other nations.	Americans dissatisfied with quality, cost and equal care.

In summary Canadians have somewhat better health status than Americans. It is important to note that social and policy determinants such as poverty and frequent violent acts such as shootings cause the U.S. result. The important point is that spending more on health care services does not offset these social determinants. Harvard's study concludes that Americans rank the opportunity to receive top quality care, regardless of income, as first in importance, last in satisfaction.[3]

---

3   Michael Decter, ''We Have Much to Learn from Each Other,'' 18th Annual Garland Lecture, Boston Medical Library, November, 1993.

Shared Lessons

Health systems are rooted in culture, values shaped by history, and not wholly or simply shipped across national borders. The United States needs a "made-in-the-U.S.A." health care system. President Clinton and Congress are embarked on creating, or remaking such a system. In Canada as a nation we have a constitution based on the concept "peace, order and good government." Our starting point in health is ability-to-benefit. The United States Declaration of Independence has as its principles life, liberty and the pursuit of happiness. The American starting point in health has been ability-to-pay.

Nevertheless, much can be learned from comparative health studies. In all countries, citizens would rather see resources going to support services than overheads. The human body is not a fundamentally different entity in Toronto than in Buffalo. And so the great challenge — what can the United States learn from Canada about the operation of a health care system at a macro level? Conversely what knowledge can Canada acquire from the United States about the operation of a health care system at the micro level?

Some Lessons from Canada

Canada is a very good teacher. It *IS* possible to provide health care for *ALL*. It is not easy nor will it be achieved without conflict, but it is possible.

Watch Those Overhead Costs: lean is better in health administration. If competing insurers means creating significant overhead, a single payer approach has cost advantages. Canadian provinces manage care for anywhere from 100,000 to 10.8 million "lives" to use the American insurance lingo. The efficiencies of both scale and simplicity are significant. Some of these scale efficiencies are captured by large U.S. health maintenance organizations such as Kaiser Permanente and California Blue Cross. The U.S. General Accounting Office (GAO) has studied overhead costs. Its conclusion is that the U.S. could find the funds to pay for health care for the thirty-five million uninsured by achieving the Canadian level of administrative efficiencies. Some aspects of the proposed Clinton health reform would improve efficiencies in the American health care system, but as long as there are over one thousand different health plans in place, that complexity imposes a very high administrative cost.

There are deals to be had through bargaining and bulk purchasing: one of the strengths of the Canadian approach is the "bulk" purchase by government of most services offered by the physicians. Negotiations with doctors can be noisy and contentious. They also produce savings.

Litigation Can Be Avoided: Canada has a very modest amount of litigation in health care. Perhaps the United States should consider a compensation-based approach rather than a litigation-based means of settling malpractice claims. Canada considered this approach, however, the anticipated increase in Canadian medical litigation has not occurred. Defensive medicine, with over-testing, does impose a cost burden in both countries, albeit a higher burden in the United States.

Generic Drugs Offer Significant Room in Affordability of Drug Plans: by legislating the principle of interchangeability Canadian provincial governments saved themselves and their taxpayers billions of dollars. At both the state and private insurer level, Americans could learn some aspects of cost-containment in the drug area from Canadians.

Some Lessons from the U.S.

Micro efficiencies are possible at the delivery level: put dramatically, if Canada could achieve the same efficiency in the use of hospital beds as the United States, we could close up to 30% to 40% of our existing hospital beds and shift resources to day surgery, outpatient and community care.

Larger Physician Practices: the Kaiser Permanente Health maintenance organization has some five thousand physicians employed in its organization. In Canada, most doctors are still in solo practice. Group practice offers many advantages in terms of quality of care, peer learning, as well as efficiencies. Canadian clinical resource management techniques and technologies are areas to be improved as well.

Broader definition of insured services: Canada set artificial distinctions when it locked "medical services" into various legislation. We need to broaden our definition of health services and embrace a larger range of health providers on a more level playing field. Outcomes should be the guiding light. A good example is the psychiatry/psychology distinction, vast in Canada, but much less so south of the border.

Alternate Site Delivery: the American system has made great

advances in technology, shifting services to the community and the home. Canada needs to invest in technology to enable more care to be unbundled from the hospital setting.

Strategies for Learning

How can Canada and the United States learn from each other? First, we need to acknowledge that both countries have problems and solutions. The winner-take-all mentality needs to give way to a willingness to share lessons and learning. Second, Canadians need to become more aggressive about marketing our expertise in health to the American market. The American corporate health sector is already very active in selling expertise and products to Canada.

Lessons from other Nations

The Finance Ministry, the most powerful arm of Government, operates a near monopoly in the production and sale of cigarettes in one of the world's largest and most lucrative tobacco markets. The Government-owned company, Japan Tobacco Inc., generates a cascade of taxes — $15 billion last year — making it the largest corporate taxpayer in Japan.[4]

There are lessons for Canada to be aware of from the experiences of other nations. In Japan, the profitability of a government tobacco monopoly has distorted public policy to such a degree that, in the words of Dr. Hirayama, director of the Institute of Preventive Oncology, "Eventually, this is going to create a catastrophe in the health care system."[5] This is an excellent example of what not to do.

We have set out our stall in terms of promises to the public in the Patient's Charter. We intend to cut down waiting times, develop a more responsive service, treat people as customers, provide a more personal service, measure the public reaction to see how we are doing and measure the hard bits, the waiting times and so on. Then to publish those, show who is doing well and give an account to the public on services.[6]

4   *New York Times*, October 17, 1993.
5   Ibid.
6   Interview with Sir Duncan Nicholl, CEO, National Health Service, U.K. *Management Today* , October, 1993, p. 40.

On the more positive side of the international learning curve, the example of the British National Health Service, long regarded as unresponsive and bureaucratic, becoming more consumer-centred, points to important issues for Canada. The measurement of quality must become a more public affair. We must move from the complaints department approach to true measurement of consumer reaction and satisfaction or dissatisfaction.

Early in December, 1993, I attended an international symposium on "Managing Health System Change at the District Level." Dr. Vic Neufeld of McMaster University, a leader in health care education who served as theme chairman, put forward the following thoughts on this topic.

This theme is driven by the realization that innovative restructuring of the design, delivery and financing of human services is needed at the community level, in order to maintain and improve our quality of life. The focus is on the health system and its interaction with and impact on other human services. Several assumptions underlie our exploration of this theme:

- the Canadian health system is highly valued by its citizens
- the current system is threatened by factors such as the prolonged economic recession; entrenched thinking; and unawareness of rapid global change
- new ideas are needed for managing health system change, to contain costs, while maintaining satisfactory services, and ultimately enhancing the quality of life of Canadian citizens. Creative solutions are needed at a community (district/regional) level, as well as other levels
- innovative models, and other knowledge and experience is available in Canada, and elsewhere around the world; this includes countries in "the South" where much can be learned about "how to do more with less[7]

One of the participants in the symposium came from the Benin Republic in Western Africa, one of the poorest nations on earth. Sourou Gbangbade described an award winning community health

---

7   Dr. Vic Neufeld, presentation to Health System Change Symposium, McMaster University, Hamilton, December, 1993.

and development project, CREDESA,[8] in his country. The CRE-
DESA approach uses health as a starting point for engaging communities on wider development issues.

The CREDESA approach is a holistic development model with
an integrated view of community development at its core. This
method has significant potential ramifications for smaller Canadian
rural and northern communities as well as for First Nation communities.

The Credesa Approach

Key aspects of the approach include:

VILLAGE HEALTH	- Development committee
WORKERS	- Village meeting
ADULT EDUCATION	
COMMUNITY	
PARTICIPATION	
HEALTH ACTIVITIES	- Health workers
COMMUNITY	- Curative care
ACTIVITIES	- Preventive care
INTERSECTORAL	
FINANCING AND	
DEVELOPMENT	
DIRECT ACTIVITIES	
FOOD SECURITY AND	- Supervision
INCOME GENERATING	- Training
ACTIVITIES	- Planning
DEVELOPMENT	- Monitoring
WORKERS	
COMMUNITY BANK	
EDUCATION	
SUPPORT ACTIVITIES	

CREDESA represents an integrated grass-roots development
process with health as the jumping off point. There is an arrogance
to our first world notion that international development is a one way

---

8   Eusebe Alihonou, Sourou Gbangbade, ''Improving Health of the Community at
    District Level — An Experience from Credesa in Benin, Republic (Western
    Africa),'' Centre Regional Pour le Developpement et La Sante, (CREDEA).

street with Canada and the other industrialized nations sharing expertise with the less developed nations. In fact, Canada has much to learn from the less developed nations; CREDESA is but one small example of where we might start our learning.

Chapter 13
Exporting Our
Health Expertise

In recent years, vast amounts of money have been spent on health services worldwide, and this situation is likely to continue. Many developing countries are in need of basic health systems and other aspects of care. Like other developed countries Canada — and the province of Ontario — have the expertise to satisfy the demands of these countries.[1]

Canada is a nation of twenty-seven million people struggling to preserve a very high standard of living in an increasingly difficult and competitive world economy. There are five billion other people with whom we share the planet, or for each Canadian there are two hundred other people. To sustain our wealthy and healthy nation, we need to offer something of value to the rest of the world's people.

For the first 125 years of Canada's existence, and before that as a colony, we sold natural resources. We began with fish and furs and advanced through wheat, minerals, timber, and oil and gas. The world economy has changed dramatically. Raw resources no longer command high prices. We must sell our knowledge as product and as services. Health care services and commodities products can provide a powerful, new economic driver.

Looking at health as a global market, our position is favourable:

1 *Strategies for Managing Export Opportunities in Ontario Health Industries,* "Outward Bound," Report of the Advisory Committee to the Ontario Minister of Health, 1993.

1. Canada's health care system and expertise is much admired by other nations.
2. All peoples and nations, as they gain income and wealth, invest in their own health and their nation's health.
3. Canada spends about 10% of its total gross national product (GNP) on health care, over 750,000 Canadians work in health care or health care related activities.
4. The world economy expends about 8% of its GNP on health care. A 1% share of the world market in health care products and services translates to $17 billion of income and 300,000 jobs for Canadians. Even 0.1% could support 30,000 jobs in Canada.

We have a number of obstacles to overcome in pursuing international markets for our expertise and products. The opportunity is enormous, but so are the challenges. A history of selling commodities has left us with a price-takers attitude and lacking in aggressive sales tactics. We have historically emphasized expertise in mining or drilling in the production end rather than in the selling. Other obstacles include:

- Lack of health care goods production. We do not make many of the products our health care system uses. About 80% of the health care products (everything from bedpans to syringes to drugs) we use are directly imported from the U.S. We do, however, make some very high quality products in fields as diverse as diagnostic imaging and generic drugs and have the capacity to produce many more.
- Absence of marketing expertise for services. Because our health care delivery system operates on a not-for-profit, publicly-administered basis, marketing expertise has not been developed. We do hire consultants, among others as intermediaries.
- Companies are not geared to export. Many of our companies, in health care products or related fields, are small and not yet focused on exporting goods.

Whether these obstacles are too profound or fundamental to be overcome is an important question. The evidence suggests otherwise. Two key realities underscore our ability to jump the barriers. The first, and most important, is the outstanding progress of several

Canadian firms active both in Canada and internationally in the health products and services field. Three Canadian success stories range from a small Canadian-owned private company, RMC, to a large, diverse Canadian-owned public company, MDS, to a large subsidiary of a major health multinational corporation, Connaught. Each can teach Canadians about export.

RMC

RMC: Resource Management Consultants is a dynamic Canadian consulting firm founded in 1967 and led by Walter Kudryk. RMC has consulting projects across Canada in health care and other sectors. Despite this, corporate headquarters is a modest brick building in a residential part of Toronto.

RMC's expanding role and possible opportunities are most evident in Poland where they have an important role in a major World Bank Project. That country is struggling to evolve an affordable health care system. RMC is providing advisory services to the Ministry of Health in policy formulation and strategic planning. Through RMC $200 U.S. million is being invested by the World Bank with the Polish Ministry of Health benefitting from Canadian expertise. The next phase of the work in Poland is likely to be an examination of National Health Insurance.

RMC has undertaken work in a range of other countries including The Bahamas and Uganda, work that has followed some twenty-five years of Canadian consulting experience in health care and other fields. It is important to note that scale is not an absolutely essential ingredient. Through expertise and quality work, RMC has succeeded internationally, in competition with much larger firms. Canada's reputation for quality in health care has also assisted. Our financial participation in world development organizations such as the United Nations, the World Health Organization and the World Bank is another advantage.

The important lesson for Canadian consulting and health service firms is that size is only one factor in international success. Persistence and active marketing are equally as critical. RMC and a growing number of other Canadian consulting firms are successfully transporting our health expertise to other markets around the world.

MDS Health Group

The MDS Health Group is the largest for-profit health care business in Canada, which employs more than six thousand people in its diversified endeavours.

Canadian-owned, its employees own a significant share of the company. Other Canadians, such as police officers, fire fighters, teachers and office workers are investors in MDS through their pension funds. The Ontario Municipal Employees Retirement System (OMERS) is also a major shareholder group. While known primarily for laboratory operations, MDS exports to over one hundred countries. Its Nordion subsidiary is a major international supplier of isotope products.

In 1993, MDS decided to actively pursue the export of its lab management expertise through a new company. Success in the form of a major American contract was not long in coming.

Mayo Clinic Orders Robotic System

TORONTO, ONTARIO — MDS Health Group Limited and MDS Health Ventures announced today that it has signed an order to provide the world renowned Mayo Clinic with an Automated Specimen Handling System ("ASHS"). The Mayo Clinic conducted an extensive evaluation of more than nineteen companies in North America and Asia. It selected a system developed in Toronto at MDS Health Group facilities in partnership with AutoMed Inc., wholly owned by MDS Health Group Limited and MDS Health Ventures.

The Mayo Clinic anticipates that the implementation of this system will lower overall costs to its patients. MDS sees its system as a contribution from the private sector while responding to the need to decrease health care costs in hospitals and commercial laboratories.

The ASHS, a fully automated system, allows laboratories to triple productivity in specimen handling while virtually eliminating sorting errors. It addresses health and safety issues for technologists by eliminating risks of breakage, spillage of blood tubes and resulting contamination.[2]

---

2   MDS Health Group, press release, Friday, April 30, 1993, p. 1-2.

MDS anticipates growth of its new AUTOLAB venture within a $500 million dollar market segment and expects up to five hundred Canadian jobs will be created through this enterprise.

Connaught

As ownership consolidates on a global basis, to achieve scale and efficiencies in distribution, the interests of individual nations will be affected. Connaught's recent history provides an excellent example of the current trend toward ownership consolidation in the global economy. In 1989, Institut Merieux, a French vaccine maker, purchased Connaught with assistance from Rhone-Poulenc, a larger French pharmaceutical company. In 1993, Rhone-Poulenc consolidated its ownership in Institut Merieux by increasing its shareholding from 51% to 100%. Will Connaught, now French-owned, remain a good corporate citizen of Canada? With links between Connaught and the Canadian research community, as well as a continued securing of world product mandates by Connaught from its parent company, the answer can be a strong yes. If Canada and Ontario pay insufficient attention to forging partnerships with Connaught in research and development and in marketing vaccines, then there are long-term risks to Connaught's contribution to Canada. As with other multinationals, the issues will be strategic alliances and world product mandates. The world vaccine manufacturing industry has consolidated into four major areas. Yet, there are still opportunities for Canada. We should continue to regard Connaught as a Canadian-based, if not Canadian-owned, manufacturer.

In December, 1993, Connaught announced a contract with Merck under which Connaught will manufacture Hepatitis A vaccine for purchase worldwide. Sales of $16 million per year are forecast, once the vaccine is introduced in 1995/96. This approach links Merck's research, development and marketing ability to Connaught's manufacturing expertise. Michael Trainow, president of Merck Frost, Merck's Canadian subsidiary, commented: "The men and women of Connaught do what they do better than anybody in the world. Canadians can and will compete given the chance."[3]

This comment underscores precisely the reality of Canadian expertise and the opportunities we must pursue to realize our health economic development.

3   *Toronto Star*, December 11, 1993.

Despite the large scale of numerous, global pharmaceutical companies, there is enormous scope for a consolidation of the world pharmaceutical industry. Merck, the largest firm, has, in total, only 4% of the world market. The three next biggest firms share less than 10% of the world market. There are thousands of active companies in the pharmaceutical industry. In a speech to the 1993 *Financial Post* Conference, Dr. Martin Barkin, Chief Executive Officer of Deprenyl Research presented the following data:

Country	Number of Active Pharmaceutical Companies
Japan	1500
Germany	1000
U.S.A.	800
France	350

As cost containment in the pharmaceutical sector takes hold in the United States, there is accelerated pressure for global consolidation of the pharmaceutical industry. American policy changes, proposed by the Clinton administration, will impact upon the United States. Because the United States is the largest single country market it will shape the evolution of the global industry. As noted previously, the shift of investment from new products to delivery systems, evident in the Merck acquisition of Medco, points to a new reality.

Canada has, through its experience with Connaught, an insight into emerging world-wide trends. As part of a strategy of increasing Canadian health exports, we will need to actively pursue international product mandates for subsidiaries of multi-national corporations housed in Canada. From MDS and its experience with Autolab we gain a glimpse of the export potential of expertise; from RMC we learn that persistence succeeds in distant markets. Global consolidation presents both threats and opportunities to Canada in the health care sector. We will need to be strategic in what we pursue, and nimble in that pursuit, to succeed.

Firms on the Health Care Export Horizon

RMC, MDS and Connaught, the three firms described above, are each leaders. There are many others with export activity or potential. Among the most interesting are:

- Diagnostic Chemicals Ltd., a PEI-based company supplies diagnostic testing kit chemicals. Sales to twenty countries generate 70% of the $7 million in sales.
- Alellix is developing biotechnology products.
- EFOS exports most of its production of light-activated dental equipment.
- ISG is a world leader in computer graphics to assist complicated surgery.
- LacMac is a manufacturer of hospital gowns and linens to world markets.
- Medtronic is developing low cost, reliable pacemakers.
- The Ottawa Heart Institute, lead by Dr. Wilbert Keon, is best known for its excellence in cardiac surgery and research. Now, the Ottawa Heart Institute is developing an artificial heart with CAE and CME.
- Sherritt, originally Sherritt Gordon, a Canadian mining company, has evolved into a technology leader through its Westaim operation in Alberta. The company is developing anti-microbial systems to prevent infections utilizing advanced industrial materials. Sherritt presents an interesting rebirth of a company rooted in the old economy of resources emerging into the new economy of knowledge-based production.
- Torcan is developing fine chemical processes for major international pharmaceutical companies.
- Vascath supplys cardiovascular devices to world markets.

As the brief profiles of these firms illustrate, there are great opportunities for Canadian expertise in the larger world market. And these openings are not confined to the for-profit sector. Another important reality is Canada's commitment to international development, both through the efforts of the Canadian International Development Agency and hundreds of volunteer organizations. Canada has been a constructive advocate of international development and cooperation among nations. We needn't choose between continuing our humanitarian efforts or becoming more active on a commercial basis. We must do both.

Our approach to marketing Canadian expertise must be in response to different nations' needs for our goods and services. The following chart illustrates the differing requirements.

Nations' Needs — Opportunities

Countries & Annual Income Levels	Health Care Market Opportunities
Lowest income countries with less than $500 GNP per capita - Asia - Africa	preventive programmes public health health promotion sector planning/ management basic infrastructure
Lower income countries with from $500 to $1,500 GNP per capita	preventive programmes public health health promotion sector planning/ management basic infrastructure training primary care
Middle income countries with more than $1,500 GNP per capita	hospital management services laboratory services health policy
Highest income countries with more than $15,000 GNP per capita - Western Europe - U.S. - Japan - Australia	cost containment technologies long-term care facilities large-scale health system management high technology

The emphasis of the World Bank and other international financial institutions is on financing preventive and health promotion programmes in developing nations. Canada has proficiency in health promotion, prevention programmes and public health. Most of this is lodged in public health units, departments of health and universities. To successfully export this expertise, we need new partnerships and joint ventures between the public and private sectors.

Canadian International Development Agency (CIDA)

CIDA's role is not only development aid and education, it also provides a very important potential entry point for Canadian enterprise. I spent five weeks during the summer of 1990 touring China, conducting an evaluation of the Open Cities Project which CIDA had sponsored with the Federation of Canadian Municipalities and the Special Economic Zones Office of the Government of China. As one of its initiatives, the project had brought very senior Chinese civic officials mayors and vice-mayors of the largest cities in China to Canada.[4] The Chinese leaders were not only extremely impressed by our cities and how we manage them, but they also expected Canadians to return to China and sell them some good old Canadian know-how. Instead Americans, whose cities have many difficult problems, have been selling the good old Yankee know-how at very handsome prices. Why? We had not been back to follow up CIDA's good work. Less developed countries want fair trade, quality health and health care for their citizens, as much as they want aid. We can contribute enormously, without exploitation, by establishing and expanding trade and selling our health products and services to the developing countries of the world.

Efforts are already underway in Canada to increase our international activities. Can we compete with the best? Yes, we can if we are determined.

The Manitoba Health Industry Initiatives

My earliest acquaintance with health economic development and the

---

4   A note on Chinese government and business structures. Chinese city governments appoint the managers of most of the enterprises within their boundaries. The Mayor of Shanghai is the Canadian equivalent of the Mayor of Toronto, Premier of Ontario and the top 100 business managers in Ontario all rolled into one. And, Shanghai has about 1 million more residents than the Toronto Metropolitan area.

ability of government to make a difference arose during the period from 1981 to 1986. I served as Cabinet Secretary in the Manitoba government as well as Deputy Minister for Intergovernmental Relations at that time. A good portion of this job was trying to pry federal dollars from Ottawa. During the period when Lloyd Axworthy was the Manitoba Minister, we enjoyed a great deal of success. Mr. Axworthy was a determined regional minister and the only prominent elected Liberal between the Manitoba-Ontario border and the Pacific Ocean. With his help, Manitoba was able to secure Canada's first Economic Regional Development Agreement (ERDA). It not only covered funds for traditional expenditures like physical infrastructure — roads in the north, water and sewer — but it created opportunities in Mr. Axworthy's transportation portfolio to benefit the province (and the country) economically. In 1984, when the Government of Canada changed, Jake Epp became Minister of Health and Welfare and also the regional minister for Manitoba. Our challenge was to figure out how Mr. Epp could be helpful to Manitoba, even though he had strongly and publicly opposed Mr. Axworthy's largesse to the province. On the health side of Mr. Epp's portfolio, there were significant allotments for issues such as research. The Manitoba government decided to attempt to construct a partnership between the two levels of government, to expand the health sector in Manitoba.

Our starting point was that Manitoba was blessed, as is much of Canada, with formidable resources in health. Winnipeg had the University of Manitoba with a faculty of medicine, two teaching hospitals — the Health Sciences Centre and St. Boniface — as well as some industry related to health care. What began then as a voyage of discovery has continued since as a strong initiative of the Manitoba government: public investment in the form of actual monies to research laboratories. Private sector investment has meant drug and device manufacturers have set up in Manitoba, largely because Manitoba has the right ingredients to support them: a hard working and skilled labour force with research skills, relatively low cost for land and business operations, and a first-class health infrastructure. The focus that the Manitoba health industries initiative brought was important to the overall success of investment in that province. Those active in health care in Manitoba became aware of business with implications for jobs and technology.

Manitoba's success was not because of unwarranted federal or provincial government spending. It succeeded because of a focus on the public sector investment and strong ties forged to the private sector. The Canadian landscape is littered with badly conceived regional development efforts that attempted to fly in the face of the real economy: heavy water plants, and car manufacturing plants, in the Atlantic region; white elephants in all areas of the country. What fundamentally distinguished Manitoba's health initiatives from misguided attempts was that they built on strengths already present in the Manitoba economy.

Companies subsidized by government rarely succeed. Michael Porter argues persuasively and with a massive weight of empirical evidence in his book, *The Competitive Advantage of Nations*. Nations succeed because industries succeed. Governments can play a role in the success of particular industries and sectors, as long as they avoid the ruinous activity of trying to select individual corporate winners. The public sector can make a difference by reinforcing the infrastructure of a particular industry or sector. Reinforcing health infrastructure, whether in support of research or in other ways, has strengthened the health sector in Manitoba. This in turn led to the creation of jobs and greater economic health and activity.

The Quebec Sector Strategy Approach

Quebec uses a cluster approach in their industrial economic strategy. The province draws very heavily on the work of Michael Porter and others, who in turn follow A.O. Hirschman and Vasily Leontief. Harvard Professor Hirschman developed theories of forward and backward linkages; Vasily Leontief won the Nobel Prize for his work on input/output tables. Their work, refined further by Michael Porter, goes to the heart of how economies function and grow, recognizing the existent connections among various industries.

The Quebec strategy has focused heavily on the pharmaceutical industry and on biotechnology. Through tax policies and the management of its drug formulary, Quebec has managed to attract significant pharmaceutical industry investment into the Montreal region. Some of this may have been at the expense of other regions of the country, and, these investments might have taken place in an absence of subsidy, at the expense of federal and Quebec taxpayers. A difficult one to fully assess. What is clear is that Quebec's concentration on particular clusters has allowed linkages to develop between the plants attracted and Quebec suppliers. Quebec's view of the relationship between biotechnology and pharmaceuticals is that it connects to the rest of the Quebec economy which is deepening and strengthening.

Ontario's Health Industry Initiatives

When I became Deputy Minister of Health for Ontario in 1991 I began working on how the Ontario Health Ministry might contribute to the renewal of the Ontario economy. The Ontario economy had undergone a dramatic job loss over the previous two years. Some 300,000 jobs vanished, many of them in the manufacturing sector.

The Free Trade Agreement and the accompanying recession accelerated the pace of an economic restructuring driven by Canada's need to be globally competitive in a more open world. Economic renewal was essential to Ontario.

What contribution could the health sector make? On the delivery of care side, it was clear, from 1991 on, that the care delivery system, as it restructured for effectiveness and survival, would shed some employment. And it could not be counted on for additional jobs. That left the supply side of the equation: companies supplying input to health care and the export market. Ontario had a rich array of health resources, including a number of major companies and a myriad of consulting firms selling health expertise. Some of these were architectural and engineering firms capable of designing and building health facilities. Others were consultants active in the evaluation of health policy. Mr. Graham Scott, a lawyer and public servant who served in the early 1980s as Deputy Minister of Health, was asked to chair a committee which, in an excellent report, *Outward Bound*, recommended the creation of Interhealth.

Interhealth is a consortium approach to marketing, both Ontario, and Canadian expertise, outside the country. During the writing of this book I remained involved with Interhealth, chairing an implementation committee. As of this writing, the basic direction has been established on the basis of the Interhealth recommendations and accepted by the Government of Ontario. The Government has pledged an investment of $3.5 million to be matched by the private sector. A committee of twenty is working on the corporate structure, financing and policies. The committee will turn the full responsibility over to a Board of Directors and Chief Executive for Interhealth.

Other aspects of Ontario's health initiatives include a Health Industry Advisory Committee (HIAC) chaired by Mr. Bill Blundell, the retired chief executive officer of General Electric Canada. The enthusiasm with which individual companies are active, for a short or a long period of time, in international markets greet a more organized approach to these markets is encouraging. It will be essential for Canada to present a united front internationally; other nations have already taken this approach. For many international projects there is a French or a German national bid. We need structure and organization in order to succeed. Many disparate proposals for the same work will not go forward. In the international market, some of which is heavily shaped by the decisions of the World Bank, Canada must have, in addition to its good reputation, a strong organized approach to obtaining business.

Interhealth Canada Limited Proposal

It is proposed that Ontario health companies and public sector organizations in the health field join to spearhead a renewed competitive thrust in the export market. The committee is unanimous in its belief in and its commitment to a joint endeavour, tentatively named Interhealth Canada Limited ("Interhealth"). It is conceived as an Ontario corporation with shareholders, drawn from firms across the health private sector and from health organizations in the Ontario public sector. Membership would provide individual firms, associations and universities with an added degree of strength, which they would not have on their own. It would also enhance their reputations and standing in those markets they seek to penetrate.

Mission

Interhealth is committed to a disciplined, flexible, multidimensional approach that seeks to maximize profitable opportunities for Canadian companies engaged in health goods and services consulting activities in key markets worldwide.

Value Statement

Interhealth will seek to promote, encourage and sustain the quality of life through the delivery of efficient, culturally-appropriate quality health services in all countries where international projects are undertaken.

Role and Function

As the primary focus for Ontario's health export initiative, the company would have a variety of roles and functions as follows:

- Market intelligence gathering/international networking. Responsibility for gathering, evaluating and acting on current market intelligence to develop a competitive position in overseas markets. Linkages would be formed and maintained with existing organizations, such as the Ontario International Corporation, Ontario Ministry of Health, Health Canada, Industry, Science and Technology Canada, External Affairs and other provincial governments to allow the company to exploit fully this existing intelligence network.
- Project management. When projects are awarded to the company, it would have both the legal authority and the lead role for managing them from beginning to end. There should be a management structure in place to ensure that each project is given full attention and the best combination of expertise the membership has to offer. Clearly, the role of the project manager is critical, as he or she will be responsible for all the major decisions of the undertaking.

The establishment of project teams, preparation of bids and submissions, securing and managing contracts, and arranging export financing must reflect the best the company has to offer. As a result, this may often call for secondment of individuals from shareholder companies.

In addition, one of Interhealth's strengths would be the combination of health products and services. As Interhealth bids on major international health consulting projects, it could offer a full range of products to support the front-end consulting work.

- Marketing opportunities. The company would be responsible for a variety of activities in support of securing international projects. These may involve the development of an infrastructure in the local markets to encourage effective client liaison, including language translation, background on business habits and cultural assessment and understanding.
- Administrative support. There are also numerous administrative functions to be carried out, including the provision of member and shareholder services, public and investor relations and public education, financial management, and general office administration [5]

Earning Our Way

Canadians have the talent to work anywhere in the world. We have a rich, internationally-linked multicultural talent bank from which to draw. In addition to our health skills, we have, within our borders, almost every language spoken on earth. We are becoming organized to tackle these markets in a thoughtful and successful manner. If we are to reach beyond our historic role of exporting our resources, to a twenty-first century role of marketing our expertise, the health sector has a huge role to play. Governments will need to provide leadership and use their international connections. The Government of Canada, in particular, will need to use its High Commissions and Embassies around the world in a cooperative way to support the efforts of individual provinces and the private sector to market Canadian endeavours.

We must also reinforce the infrastructure within Canada. Our health services must be of the highest quality and that we can demonstrate their effectiveness. This is necessary, first of all, to ensure that Canadians are getting excellent health care and good value for their tax dollar. We also need quality insurance to meet the test of the world marketplace in convincing our customers that what they buy is truly the best.

Many of the investments needed in Canada to create necessary infrastructure will support both making more products here and exporting them. The amalgamation of capital to support innovation

5   Outward Bound Report, Strategies for Maximizing Export Opportunities in the Ontario Health Industries, a report to the Ontario Minister of Health, 1993, p. 9-10.

will also support expansion of marketing activities beyond Canada's border. Investments by government, in research and particularly in ways of commercializing research, will enhance our production and exports. Finally, a focus by the health industry sector, on recognizing itself as a sector, sharing information and opportunities within that sector will allow much stronger linkages and more powerful marketing to global markets.

The sheer scale of the global market for health care and the success to date of some of our firms are sound reasons for optimism. Much effort will be required to realise our full potential in exporting Canadian health expertise to the rest of the world.

Good Stuff to Read

The Competitive Advantage of Nations by Michael Porter. The most powerful recent analysis of what drives competitive advantage among nations and industries. Harvard Professor Michael Porter's Studies reveal that industries with strong pressures in their local markets and competition become strong initiated competitors — the Japanese car industry and Italian tiles are excellent examples.

Outward Bound — Strategies For Maximizing Export Opportunities in the Ontario Health Industry. Available from the Health Economic Development Office, Ontario Ministry of Health, 56 Wellesley Street West, Toronto, Ontario M5S 2S3. Fax: (416) 314-5916.

Chapter 14
Canadian Health Economic Development

Increasing Canadian exports is only one challenge to be taken up in the health economic development field. Creating more health products and services in Canada and increasing our research are also vital. We need to combine the ingredients of research, production and marketing. Our health economic development has enormous potential to create jobs and economic activity of a long-term sustainable nature.

Making More Stuff Here

Healthy & Wealthy,[1] the Health Industries Advisory Committee (HIAC) report to the Ontario Government provided an interesting profile on health industries. The gap of $2 billion per annum, between Canada's $5 billion production of health care products and our consumption of $7 billion, provides one target for making more health products here. So, too, is the 40,000 jobs which the report estimates could be created in this field.

The relationship between public policy and health economic development opportunity is well illustrated by an examination of the origins of two of Canada's most successful health-related companies, Novopharm and Apotex. In 1974, the Ontario government established the Ontario Drug Benefit Programme (ODB). The legislation

---

1   "Healthy & Wealthy — a Growth Prescription for Ontario's Health Industries," *The Report of the Health Industries Advisory Committee to the Minister of Health*, March 1994, p. 12.

which created the ODB contained the legal principle of interchangeability. Simply stated, interchangeability meant that the pharmacist was required to dispense the lower cost generic drug in place of the more expensive "brand name" drug where the two drugs were of the same chemical compound. In addition to saving the government tens of millions of dollars on ODB, interchangeability, coupled with the Federal government policy of compulsory licensing, created a rapidly growing market for Apotex and Novopharm, both manufacturers of generic drugs. Both of these companies have grown to be significant employers and exporters. They are described below.

Apotex

In September, 1992, *Profit Magazine* named Dr. Barry Sherman as one of Canada's Top 10 Entrepreneurs of the Decade. They described him as "The Robin Hood of Pharmaceuticals" and noted the growth of Apotex Inc. from a 1974 start-up to a conglomerate with revenues of $500 million per year. Some 40% of revenues are still from generic drugs, despite strong diversification. The Apotex Healthcare Group of companies has diversified into development, manufacturing and distribution of non-prescription medicines, vitamins, diagnostic products, laboratory equipment and supplies, disposable plastic products for medical use, and hospital waste management systems.

From its two-employee, 5,000 square foot birth, the company has grown to employ 2,000 people in research, development and manufacturing. Canadian operations now occupy over 800,000 square feet in Toronto, Montreal, Winnipeg and Vancouver. Apotex produces more than one hundred generic pharmaceuticals which, in Canada, are used to fill almost fifteen million prescriptions a year.

Dr. Sherman has been an aggressive litigator defending and expanding markets for his products. He has also been a spectacularly successful Canadian businessman. Apotex exports to over 80 countries around the globe with export markets representing an ever-growing portion of the total sales. Apotex has also established a presence through subsidiaries, joint ventures or licensing agreements, in Morocco, France, the Czech and Slovak Republics, Mexico, Peru, Costa Rica, New Zealand, Australia and Russia.

Novopharm

It's difficult to find a contrast in personalities and business styles greater than those between Novopharm founder and Chief Executive Leslie Dan and Apotex founder Barry Sherman. Although their generic drug manufacturing firms have grown side by side, Barry Sherman's litigation-oriented, aggressive style is the antithesis of Leslie Dan's calm, quiet approach.

Leslie Dan is a Hungarian by birth. Driven from his native country by war and prejudice, he, like millions of others, settled in Canada. Through decades of toil and investment, Mr. Dan has built Novopharm into a huge generic drug manufacturer with sales of several hundred million dollars per year.

In January, 1994, Novopharm announced it had acquired a large minority position in the Hungarian state-owned pharmaceutical manufacturer Human Serum and Pharmaceutical Co. of Godallo. Human Serum employees 950 people and its business includes injectable pharmaceuticals, vaccines, insulin and blood-derivative products. Through this acquisition, Canadian expertise will allow Novopharm to expand Human Serum's business in Eastern Europe.

Why did the Hungarian government approach Leslie Dan as a partner/purchaser of their state company? For the previous two years Novopharm and Human Serum had successfully operated Human-pharma Ltd., a joint venture manufacturing pills and tablets. Trust and a well-earned reputation for putting quality first were the attributes which convinced the Hungarian government to build their partnership with Novopharm.

The success stories of Apotex and Novopharm, Canada's two largest generic drug manufacturers, illustrate the benefits of increasing Canadian production of inputs to our own health system. Canada has gained two world class and globally competitive companies with their homebase and ownership in Canada. We *can* "home-grow" new firms to produce new products. But, home-growing firms with public policy support is only one means of furthering health economic development. Canadian governments can also encourage existing health-related businesses to expand their product lines by entering new product markets. Canadian businesses, not currently involved in the health products sector, can expand by entering into it. Canadian governments can encourage multi-national firms to establish production facilities here, and to grant world product mandates to their Canadian subsidiaries, so they may export, as well as sell in

Canada. These approaches are not mutually exclusive. All four activities can be combined into a strategy. But, to succeed this strategy needs fuel in the form of private investment dollars to finance research, product development and marketing. Such financing is not always easy to obtain in Canada. The business and labour communities, and the health sector, will need to advocate and support this effort.

Financing Health Ideas

Fraser Mustard is one of Canada's leading thinkers and advocates on matters of health and wealth. As one of the founders, and the driving force behind the Canadian Institute for Advanced Research (CIAR), he has pushed Canadian political and business leaders, as well as policy-makers, to confront realities beyond the conventional wisdom upon which much flawed policy is based. One of his recent crusades is that Canadian financial institutions, particularly our chartered banks, should lend money for ideas, as well as for bricks and mortar. Dr. Mustard points out that the rise of Japan has been accomplished with significant lending and investment inside the Japanese business organizations — Keritsu — which combine finance and ideas.

Dr. Mustard's dominant concern has been that a decline in our country's wealth would also erode our standard of health. In every study health-wealth are fundamentally married. He is also certain that future Canadian prosperity does not rest on the resource-based economy which generated Canada's initial wealth as a nation. A financial sector heavily-oriented to lending against hard, tangible assets, rather than against the more ethereal intellectual property of ideas, is a legacy of Canada's pioneer economy. What if our chartered banks had shifted a few billion dollars of lending away from the red hot Toronto property market in the late 1980s and into small, idea-driven enterprises? Perhaps we would have had less carnage in the real estate market and more dynamism in the economy.

We are a nation well-supplied, perhaps over-supplied, with shopping centres and office towers. While this may be admirable, investment in the world of intellectual property will allow us to continue a high standard of living through a high valued-added economy. Our financial community, particularly the banks, must expand their understanding and support small business, in general, and small knowledge-based businesses above all others.

There are encouraging signs. Some modest pools of capital have formed, specifically to invest in health economic development. As well, a number of venture capital companies consider health-related investments among their priorities. Interesting examples are the MDS Health Ventures and the BioCapital Biotechnology Investment Fund. Other similar health investments include Vencap Equities in Alberta, which has an informal target of investing 20% of its total portfolio in the health sector. But what types of companies do these pools of capital seek? What are their investments for the future?

A few examples are helpful in understanding the range and diversity of the investments.

MDS Health Investments

Diagnostic Products and Other Services

ADI Diagnostics Inc. is a manufacturer of rapid human diagnostic kits for the major screening markets: reference laboratories, blood banks and public health institutions.

CME Telemetrix Inc. is involved in the development of a proprietary non-invasive instrument for the measurement of blood analyses including glucose, cholesterol, lactates and alcohol.

Tokos Medical of Canada Inc. is investigating the availability of government funding which will enable it to sell products and services to the women's health care market in Canada that Tokos Inc. markets in the United States. Tokos Inc.'s principal product is used in the assessment and treatment of pregnant women at home for symptoms associated with pre-term labour.

Pharmaceutical and Biotechnology Products and Services

Allelix Biopharmaceuticals Inc., a publicly-traded company is involved in the discovery and development of novel biopharmaceutical products for tissue repair and inflammation.

Ethical Pharmaceuticals Ltd. (U.K.) is the parent company of a specialized group of pharmaceutical development companies offering products, technologies and services with a special emphasis on delivery systems.

Ethical Pharmaceuticals North America Inc. is a 15/85

joint venture between Ethical Pharmaceuticals (UK) and MDS Ventures. They have rights to develop, manufacture and sell, in Canada, all products and technologies owned by Ethical Pharmaceuticals (UK). In addition, Ethical Pharmaceuticals North America retains certain royalty rights on sales of products and technologies of Ethical Pharmaceuticals (UK) in the United States.

Hemosol Inc. is actively engaged in the development of a human blood substitute based on hemoglobin.

Rehabilitation Products and Other Services

3c Rehabilitation Technologies is involved in developing pain relief treatment devices and services.

Columbia Health Group Inc. is developing a network of acute and chronic care clinics in Canada and the United States.

Medical Information and Robotics

Andronic Devices Ltd. is developing automated products for the laboratory and operating room both to facilitate surgical procedures and to assist in automating the manual aspects of the laboratory and the operating room.

AutoMed Associates is a partnership between AutoMed Inc. and Automated Specimen Handling, Inc. which is developing a series of modules for automation of the specimen handling aspect of a laboratory. Automated Specimen Handling, Inc. is 50% owned by MDS Health Group Inc., a U.S. subsidiary of MDS, and MDS Ventures.

I.S.G. Technologies Inc. is a publicly-traded company which designs, manufactures and markets full-solution medical-imaging workstations to construct three-dimensional images of patient anatomy from Computerized Tomography ("CT") Scan and Magnetic Resonance Imager (MRI) data.

Access Health Marketing Inc. is a health care marketing services company that designs, markets, implements and supports information based marketing and telemarketing programmes in the health care industry.

Homecare Products and Other Services

Disys Corporation, formerly Dicon Systems Limited, is a publicly-traded company and a leading manufacturer and marketer of equipment for the detection of smoke, gas and intrusion in the home.

Thompson & Nielsen Electronics Ltd. is a manufacturer of instruments for radiation protection in medical, environmental and industrial fields.[2]

The BioCapital Biotechnology Investment Fund

In May 1990, Balthazard, Coupal et Associés inc. (BC et Associés), in collaboration with the Fonds de solidarité des travailleurs du Québec (FTQ), created a focused investment fund called the Fonds d'investissement en biotechnologie BioCapital. The goal of this fund is to support the growth of this sector, mainly in Quebec, by establishing close cooperation between companies and the financial and scientific communities. BioCapital highlights the innovative potential of the many research teams working in the industrial, academic and hospital environments.

Since its creation, the Fund has received more than 200 projects, including about 100 from Quebec. Up to now, BioCapital has invested in 12 companies in the biotechnology sector, providing them with the support necessary for the scientific comprehension of their projects and the development of their operations. Investments by the Fund totalled $6.6 million as of April 30, 1992.

BioCapital is a venture capital fund specializing in biotechnology and managed by a company held by BC et Associés. This fund has $10.5 million (Cdn.) in capital, subscribed mainly by the Fonds de solidarité des travailleurs du Québec (FTQ), the Société d'investissement de la Province de Namur (S.I.B.S.), The Generics Group plc and by Gestion BioCapital Inc.

The fund invests in innovative companies offering

2 MDS Health Ventures, Corporate Material, 1993.

high growth potential and operating in strategic fields related to biotechnology.

1.   Aggressive Investment and Action

BioCapital is a fund committed to making profits from venture capital investments. BioCapital relies on methodology supplied by a well-established network of expertise which offers the best possibilities for success.

Selection of Innovative Firms
- Identification and devaluation of companies by committees of national and international experts in science, technology and business;
- Selection of 15 to 20 companies in the start-up or development stages; specializing in biotechnology;
- Technical and management support for companies;
- Ongoing supervision of companies;
- Geographical distribution (70% in Quebec).

2.   A Diversified Portfolio of Companies Specializing in Biotechnology

BioCapital offers fund sponsors a diversified portfolio of innovative companies featuring high growth potential.

Holding Companies
- Lipopharm
- Médi-Force
- Biomatrix Médical Canada
- Quantum Biotechnologies
- Polychol
- IBS
- Diagnostics Biovet
- Serrener
- UniSyn Technologies
- Bio-Systèmes Biosys
- Haemacure Biotech
- Ventana Growth Fund II

3.	**Tax Advantages that Favour Technological Development in Quebec**

BC et Associés has developed, with BioCapital, the expertise necessary to take advantage of government financial vehicles and programmes aimed at facilitating the financing of biotechnology R & D projects. These assistance programmes substantially reduce the sponsors' investment risks.

4.	**A National and International Network of Expertise**
	BioCapital has access to a national and international network of expertise which includes the Fonds de solidarité des travailleurs de Québec (FTQ); The Generics Group plc of London, England; the Ventana Growth Fund II of San Diego, California; S.I.B.S. de Namur of Belgium; Biosurvey s.a. of Belgium, as well as members of the consultative committees.[3]

Capital linked to ideas also changes the role of our research institutes. The institute must strengthen the bridges to intermediate structures with a capacity for commercialization. More output here will require more investment in health economic development. Our dilemma is joining our research to commercial ventures. In Ontario, alone, there are eighty research institutes and associations in the health care field; most are affiliated with a hospital, a university or both. Others are connected to a particular disease or condition. Together they constitute a key resource and powerful engine for the production of valuable intellectual property. A major challenge, which investment pools are helping to address, is harnessing this engine to the creation of high value-added jobs and exports.

Building on Our Research Strength

"Research is essential to any strategy to improve health."[4]

"The major challenge for both developing and developed nations

---

3 BioCapital Corporation Material, 1993.
4 *Health of the Nation*, U.K. Government, 1992.

is how to strike the correct balance between basic medical research, with the longer term perspective that this entails, and research into our more immediate requirements in the provision of health care. While the latter is less newsworthy, recent advances in epidemiology and statistical methods have given it the potential to be of enormous benefit to our patients.[5]

Canada has developed a varied and rapidly growing array of research institutions. We also have elaborate structures in place through which funding flows to research institutions, and a formidable collection of fundraising organizations. Our overall research enterprise as a nation is a complex and valuable endeavour. In a world where knowledge and information command premiums which once accrued by natural resources, Canada badly needs a new economic engine. In the health sector, research can be a powerful lever for enhanced efficiency of our own health delivery systems. As well, research can underpin an important export effort, directed to sharing our advances in both health products and services, with other nations.

All of the companies described in the previous two chapters require sustained investment in research and development simply to survive. Success will require luck, proficient marketing and skilful management. Without research the prospects are dismal. Canada is rapidly expanding a talented network of researchers, as noted in Chapter 9, this network includes a cluster of new health services or applied clinical epidemiology research organizations.

As hospital duties unbundle to the outpatient and community setting, hospital space often becomes available for other purposes. One potential use for this real estate is conversion to research. The success of a research enterprise requires it to have separate and identifiable leadership from a hospital in which it resides or is associated.

Health is a technology and knowledge based endeavour. We need to devote a greater share of our national health resources to research. Many successful companies producing knowledge intensive products or services devote 10% or more of their annual *revenues* to R & D. Canadian health care devotes only about 1–2% of total expenditures to R & D in aggregate. This is far too little.

---

5   Sir David Weatherall, Editorial, *Science and Public Affairs*, University of Oxford, Autumn, 1993, p.5.

One of the most compelling arguments for strengthening our research base is the need to retain talented young Canadians. Our education system, through the university graduate level produces bright, well-educated researchers. These people constitute our future health intelligence capacity. We need to employ, nurture and develop their skills to solve the problems we face.

There are good reasons for favouring a balanced Canadian research programme with more resources, both human and financial. Health systems and biomedical research are both vital ingredients in healing Medicare. We need vaccines against new diseases, new medicines and new surgical techniques. Science tools deployed against medical problems will give us real progress. We also need better techniques for promoting health.

Many of our successes in building health research excellence have been achieved by pioneers motivated by dreams of finding a better way to tackle health problems. Three examples are located in St. Boniface, Manitoba, on the grounds of the Sunnybrook Health Sciences Centre and on University Avenue in downtown Toronto.

St. Boniface Hospital Research Centre

Today, a modern research building, standing on the bank of the Red River which divides Winnipeg and St. Boniface, provides a home for the St. Boniface General Hospital Research Centre. A decade ago, the research centre was a dream, and a remote one at that. Realizing this vision required a remarkable voyage with a varied and talented cast of characters drawn from all over the world. One key player was the long-time Manitoba Minister of Health, Larry Desjardins. As Minister for Lotteries, Mr. Desjardins allowed the Research Foundation to sell break-open lottery tickets and to operate a major annual lottery. Mr. Desjardins boosted the Foundation's efforts. The International Award and Dinners, organized by the Foundation, have brought major world figures, from Andre Sakharov to Christian Barnard to the St. Boniface General Hospital. The Award and Dinners focused the entire enterprise of the Research Foundation and Centre on excellence in the world context. In travelling to Moscow to arrange for Dr. Sakharov to visit, St. Boniface leaders were determined to secure a visa for Dr. Sakharov and his wife Yelenna Bonner. They conquered the formidable Soviet bureaucracy to bring their guest to Canada.

The profile and stature of the Research Foundation has also been elevated by the quality and international stature of Award recipients. The late Sam Cohen, who, along with Cam MacLean was one of the key leaders of the St. Boniface Foundation. The former wagered with a wealthy member of the Bronfman family that a St. Boniface researcher would win a Nobel Prize for medical research before the Montreal Expo's won a World Series. Having left Winnipeg I lost track of the St Boniface Research Centre until I arrived back in Winnipeg for Christmas, 1993. The front page of *The Winnipeg Free Press*, prominently featuring Dr. Naranjan Dhalla, head of the cardiovascular science research team at the St. Boniface Research Centre, rapidly brought me up to date. The article noted, "In what is one of the largest medical research teams in the world — and the only one in Canada concentrating on heart research — more than 80 faculty, students and staff from 28 countries are working together to understand the causes of heart disease."[6] It also mentioned an exceptionally large grant — $5.2 million — from the Medical Research Council of Canada.

From 50 cent break open Nevada tickets and the vision of a handful of remarkable Canadians, a research endeavour now flourishes on the banks of the Red River. Whether a Nobel Prize eventually honours work at the Centre or not, Sam Cohen's bet is well won. A legacy of excellence is deeply entrenched.

Institute for Clinical Evaluative Sciences

The Institute for Clinical Evaluative Sciences, also known as ICES, was a dream of Dr. Adam Linton, an exceptional medical leader in Ontario. ICES came into being shortly after Dr. Linton's premature death in 1991. As president of the Ontario Medical Association, Dr. Linton convinced his profession that partnership with government was preferable to confrontation. He also insisted that evaluation of medical practice outcomes and development of guidelines should be insulated from government and from the profession's direct control. His vision was ICES, an independent body pursuing very practical research with dedicated and adequate financial resources.

The reality is that a well-run ICES will, on different issues, antagonize either the medical profession or government, or both. The public is the constituency that should defend ICES. Health care

---

6   *Winnipeg Free Press*, December 22, 1993, p.1.

consumers only stand to gain from improving our knowledge of what works and, how well it works.

Today, ICES is a reality. A $4.5 million per year research enterprise with bright, research and practice minds. Under the determined leadership of Dr. David Naylor, ICES has produced an impressive stream of very practical studies which will profoundly influence the way medicine is practised and health care services delivered. At Sunnybrook Health Sciences Centre, where ICES is located there is a powerful mix of excellence in delivery and in research about clinical outcomes.

With six career scientists supported by external peer reviewed awards ICES is successfully developing its core funding to expand its activities.

Reshaping University Avenue

The largest concentration of health care resources in Canada is on University Avenue in downtown Toronto. Major hospitals, such as the Hospital for Sick Children, Mt. Sinai Hospital, The Toronto Hospital and the new Princess Margaret Hospital stand cheek by jowl on the broad avenue leading from the business district to Queen's Park. Long known for health care excellence, University Avenue and the University of Toronto are changing with the times, placing greater emphasis on research.

Dr. Louis Siminovitch is the gentle but determined giant of health research on University Avenue. As the Geneticist in Chief at the Research Centre at the Hospital for Sick Children and, more recently, as Director of the Samuel Lunenfeld Research Institute at Mt. Sinai Hospital Research, Dr. Lou has been a leader, mentor and instigator of health research.

The strengthening between researchers and patients and researchers and funders are among Dr. Siminovitch's innovative contributions. At the Hospital for Sick Children, he stressed the need for researchers to meet patients and to be motivated by real medical problems, not just theory.

Dr. Tak Mak is proof that research dollars are drawn to talent. Amgen, a major U.S. biotechnology company has invested $10 million per year for ten years, a total of $100 million, in Dr. Mak's team at the Ontario Cancer Institute/Princess Margaret Hospital. With world leadership in research on the immune system, Dr. Mak is another Canadian bright light. He has received the largest investment in Canadian research ever made by a biopharmaceutical company. The Amgen Institute, dedicated to study of the immune system, will be located immediately adjacent to the new Princess Margaret Hospital on University Avenue.

The work of Dr. Siminovitch, Dr. Mak and hundreds of others is reshaping the activities on University Avenue. With luck and determination, this one street alone will continue to transform itself into a research collaboration with dynamism.

Redirecting the Medical Research Council of Canada

Improving management of health services in Canada will require a greater investment in health services research. This necessity has recently been recognized by the Medical Research Council of Canada (MRC) our major national medical research institution in its new strategic plan. Research councils in many countries including the United Kingdom, Australia and South Africa have already recognized the need to balance their overall health research agenda. Historic emphasis on biomedical research is being equalized by investments in health services research.

In 1992, the MRC and its sixty-five staff distributed some $250 million. This supports a network of 2,200 researchers, 1,500 research trainees and 4,000 technical staff. Yet total MRC spending across Canada is about the same annual amount as the budget of one large, urban teaching hospital. MRC spends less than 0.4% of our total Canadian health budget. This is too little for the challenges ahead.

Over the past two years, the Medical Research Council, undertook a sweeping reappraisal of its role. Broad consultation and development of a new strategic plan assisted the MRC in planning its future.

Three areas emerged from the planning exercise for new attention and focus by MRC:
- a broadened vision encompassing all areas of health research
- building greater excellence in existing activities
- evaluating more thoroughly the outcomes of MRC activities

Implementing this new and expanded vision will be a phenomenal challenge for the MRC. The organization will need to reach beyond its roots in the biomedical research community and embrace a broad spectrum of health research, including disciplines such as economics, political science and sociology. With a more comprehensive approach, the MRC can assist in healing Medicare by enhancing quality and affordability in health service delivery. It must not, however, abandon the essential core of biomedical research for which it will remain the key funder.

QED

Canada is a wonderful place in which to undertake research. We have a solid base of scientific talent, an excellent data base for population health studies and a diverse multicultural population. We need to expand our health research sector.

Others have forcefully stated the reasons for investing in research, include jobs and knowledge benefits. These views understate the full rationale. Consider the sentiments expressed by Professor Doolittle of Dalhousie University: "A good theory about the nature of the physical or biological world is as valuable a product of our culture as a ballet or painting. It should not, any more than art, have to justify itself only in terms of new products and job creation."[7] The stress should be on the "only." Research has many virtues and values.

Surely we want it all, within the limits of our resources. We want to dream and have our curiosity supported for its own merit. We want our ideas to translate into jobs and real progress for our fellow Canadians and, more importantly, for our fellow human beings. Balance can be struck between competing research demands. We must also find clever, creative and entertaining ways to secure necessary resources, to dramatically expand the research enterprise in Canada. National leadership from the Medical Research Council of Canada and others is paramount. So, too, is grassroots energy in the spirit of the St. Boniface Research Foundation.

Good Stuff to Read

The Next Canadian Economy by Kristin Shannon and Dian Cohen. Although nearly ten years old, it is still very relevant. It captured the main themes of the new economy early and with insight.

Shifting Gears: Thriving in the New Economy, by Nuala Beck, Harper Collins, 1992. A provocative and insightful look at the new

7   Professor Doolittle, *Globe and Mail*, December 15, 1993, p. 21.

economy. The strong focus on how to measure the new economy is refreshing with a key analysis of knowledge workers.

Healthy & Wealthy — A Growth Prescription for Ontario's Health Industries. The Report of the Health Industries Advisory Committee to the Ontario Minister of Health, March, 1994. Queen's Printer for Ontario, IBSN 0-7778-2558-9. This is the report of the Committee chaired by Bill Blundell. The report notes Canada's major trade deficit in health care products and proposes a strategy to create jobs, industry and exports in the health industries sector.

Investing in Canada's Health, A Strategic Plan for the Medical Research Council of Canada, Minister of Supply and Services, Ottawa. Available from the Medical Research Council of Canada, Holland Cross, Tower B, 5th Floor, 1600 Scott Street, Ottawa, Ontario, K1A OW9.

Annual Reports of the following Canadian health research organizations as well as their publication lists are well worth obtaining:
- Mt. Sinai (Samuel Lunenfeld Research Institute)
- St. Boniface Research Institute
- Hospital for Sick Children
- Medical Research Council of Canada
- Centre for Health Economic Policy Analysis (CHEPA). Although older than many of the other health policy centres, CHEPA has the wisdom and maturity of its rich history of contributing to better thinking about health policy. Located at McMaster University it retains the pioneering spirit of the McMaster Medical School.

Towards the Next Canadian Health Care System

Learning disabilities are tragic in children, but they are fatal in organizations. Because of them, few corporations live even half as long as a person — most die before they reach the age of forty.[1]

Canadian Medicare is twenty-five years old. Will it see a fortieth birthday? Will it celebrate it in good health? Can we heal and nurture Medicare to a full and continuing vigour?

What lies ahead is a tremendous amount of difficult but crucial work in reforming Canadian health care delivery. The stakes are high, not only for Canadians, but for nations looking to Canada as a model and a guide.

A marriage of technology to the challenges of re-engineering is one clear trend. Affordability and quality are being added as the sixth and seventh principles of the Canada Health Act, in practice, if not in law. All our new ways of making choices are the result of provincial governments seeking simultaneously to improve the quality of the health care delivery system and its affordability. As well, governments are also adopting a population health, or determinants of health, perspective.

We are in the early days of Canadian health care reform. Most of the improvements, excluding Quebec, have only been underway for months or a few years, not decades. The real results will be seen through the 1990s, as Canadian governments and other stakeholders in the health care system grapple with the problems. Some early evidence is encouraging. Expenditure growth rates within the health care delivery system have shrunk dramatically from levels of 10% per annum or more through the 1970s and 1980s, to levels in the minus 3% per annum in the early 1990s. There has been no significant proof of adverse health outcomes. Nor is there evidence of

1   Senge, op. cit., p. 17.

adverse outcomes for individual political leaders and elected governments. There is an increasing sophistication in the Canadian media with emphasis shifting from stories of financial crisis and waiting lists, to management of the health care delivery system. There is a profound sense of innovation at the level of individual hospitals as they introduce utilization measurement and better information systems.

The introduction of user fees in Canada has been debated. Most Canadians believe that an accessible health care system is one of the most consequential achievements of the Canadian nation. Most individuals involved in health care in Canada — managers, providers or consumers — have confidence that with a managed re-engineering of the delivery system and greater emphasis on the determinants of health, Canadian health care is sustainable and affordable. Quality improvement is a reasonable expectation. A significant minority of Canadian physicians, and some others however, view Canadian Medicare as financially unsustainable. They favour movement to a two-tiered system with patient co-payments, premiums or user fees. By the late 1990s, it should be evident whether health reform has achieved preservation of the principles of Medicare within a restructured delivery system or whether a fundamental privatization of the system is underway.

My conclusion is that reform is underway but must be accelerated in some parts of the country. Transforming so many aspects of the delivery system is a huge challenge but — on the evidence to date — we are equal to that challenge. More leadership is needed from within health provider groups. Resistance to change is counterproductive. It needs to be replaced by constructive advocacy for reform which improve *both* quality and affordability.

Policies and initiatives of various Canadian provinces illustrate the evolution of differing choice options. Saskatchewan and New Brunswick provide evidence of the consequences of a devolution approach. Ontario will prove an interesting area for examining innovative negotiated outcomes with providers, as well as clinical epidemiology research efforts. We'll look to Manitoba for both interventionist public policy and health policy research approaches.

What will the next Canadian health care system look like? How will it operate? Here are a few thoughts about and hopes for the Canadian health care system in the year 2000:

- Canada's over 900 hospitals have been consolidated into about 200 large health systems. In several provinces, these systems are regionally-based, with an integration of health and social services at the district level. In several other provinces, health systems focus on acute care and have been brought about by merging and networking around key hospitals.

- At each academic health science centre, specific population health agreements are in place between the local health system, the academic university-linked teaching unit, and various local health delivery authorities.
- The role of ministries of health is to set a broad policy framework based on population health, with the responsibility of funding the health systems. Most funding flows on a per capita basis adjusted for local health needs. Dollars flow to real health concerns, not to the pattern of history and politics.
- From a consumer standpoint, the system is dramatically altered. All Canadian citizens now carry health cards with smart card technology. Embedded in each card is a small chip with each person's personal identification number, their entire health history, the health histories of their immediate families, parents, grandparents (where available), record of immunizations, and record of all encounters with health systems and health providers. Individuals are able to read their health records on their television screens in their homes. All providers are able to review card records at the point of service. All consumers have access by telephone, interactive television and computer networks to health advice and information.
- Health providers work in teams. Health-system based teams are either physician-led or nurse-led. The nurse-led teams operate independently of physician's direction, but often have a consulting physician. Physician-led teams are comprised of a range of health professionals. Very few conditions require a lengthy hospital stay.
- Many births take place either in out-of-hospital free standing birthing centres or in-hospital birthing centres. Home births have regained some importance. Infant mortality has been significantly reduced through the decade.
- The previous public health system has evolved into healthy community action units. These units are accountable to both local and provincial governments, and are intensively involved in community education programmes for the education system, particularly through interactive cable television programming.

- Research infrastructure in Canada, for health services research and biomedical research has been strengthened and expanded. More than $1 billion per year has been redirected from inappropriate care to research.
- Canadian health consultants are active in a number of countries designing and installing health systems — the Canadian way! Notable involvements are in Eastern Europe, China, India and parts of the emerging African continent.
- Canadian health products and services have gained a worldwide reputation for their quality and affordability.

Our ability to re-engineer care, learn new skills and take control of our own health and health care will all be critical determinants of success. We must balance our efforts to better manage the supply of health services against new challenges. We must also invest in the wider facets of health. Necessary change will not happen by itself. We must make it happen.

Will we succeed? Are we going to take the pains to struggle for the reform of Medicare, its evolution and future success? I believe so. Canadians care deeply about health and health care. Medicare is a vital barometer of our capacity as a nation. To abandon the struggle would be to abandon our values. We will succeed.

The early evidence suggests we are on the path to healthy reform. Through their leadership, their work and their compassion, tens of thousands of Canadians involved in health and health care will determine the future. Our experience with reform is rich with lessons. We are living and making our own history. Our efforts will show us the sane road forward. We shall succeed.

Afterword & Acknowledgements

On a very personal note this book has been a transition from my public sector management role as Deputy Minister of Health for Ontario to new adventures as a writer, teacher, consultant, private sector manager and continuing advocate of progressive change. It has been a joyful and painful struggle to assemble thoughts in a fashion which endeavours to assist the continuing task of managing health system change with technology and compassion.

Our struggle for Canadian Medicare will not end with any measurable victory. We will pass the torch and the obligation to continue the struggle to our children and they to theirs. We are accountable to them and to our consciences for the quality and sustainability of what we leave as a health care legacy.

There is a significant but immeasurable risk that I will write further on the subject of health and health care. The ideas and possibilities continue to haunt me. For every health policy issue addressed there were a dozen important issues left unexplored. For every good story there are a hundred stories omitted.

My obligations are significant. While not a large work, *Healing Medicare* had many helpers. My deep gratitude to all those extremely busy friends and colleagues who took time to encourage, comment, edit and critique. Thank you.

My six months as Senior Research Scholar at the Centre for Bioethics, University of Toronto, provided the window of opportunity to write. University President Rob Prichard, Dr. Fred Lowy, Director of the Centre, Professor Peggy Leatt, Head, Department of Health Administration and Dr. Carol Nash were all responsible for this sanctuary. The Centre is a remarkable coming together of disciplines and people. I wish all of them well. Dr. Peter Singer and Dr. Eric Meslin were both influential during my all too brief sojourn.

Early inspiration to write on matters of health policy and management came from Dr. Robert Maxwell of King Edward's Hospital Fund in London, England. My inclusion as a Fellow of the King's Fund International Seminar brought me in contact with leaders in health care from the United Kingdom, the United States, Australia and New Zealand as well as Canada.

Three ministers of health with whom I have worked were powerful influences on my understanding of the art of the possible in health politics. Larry Desjardins, Frances Lankin and Ruth Grier were all excellent teachers. Several deputy ministers of health have provided inspiration to me in my career. K.O. Mackenzie and Reg Edwards in Manitoba, Tom Campbell, Graham Scott and Martin Barkin in Ontario have my respect and gratitude for their wise counsel.

Six colleagues were brave enough to read the early manuscript and provide comments. The efforts of Brad Graham, Dr. Eugene Le Blanc, Dr. David Naylor, Marilyn Knox, Lisa Priest and L.A. (Tony) Quaglia were insightful and critically important.

The journey from raw ideas to a published book was only possible with the unrelenting confidence and support of my publisher and editor, Ann Decter. The manuscript also benefited significantly from the work of Angela Hryniuk as copy editor. Gwen North, as she has for many years, aided and abetted the translation into print.

My family, Lucille, Riel and Geneviève bore the brunt of absences and frustrations. They were patient and supportive throughout.

No endeavour is as humbling as the creation of a book. All of its flaws and shortcoming are my own. Where it occasionally rises to the challenge presented by its subject, the credit must accrue to my many mentors and teachers.

Index

MICHAEL B. DECTER

Michael Decter is a health care manager, consultant and now author. He served most recently as Deputy Minister of Health for the Province of Ontario. Previously, he served as Cabinet Secretary and Clerk of the Executive Council in Manitoba. Private sector positions have included Partner, Peat Marwick Consulting Group; Chair, Shawinigan Energy; and President, Vista Strategic Information Management. Mr. Decter received his training in economics at Harvard University. He has also been Senior Research Scholar at the Centre for Bioethics, University of Toronto. He is also active in consulting with clients in Canada, the United Kingdom and the United States and is Director-Canada for APM Inc., North America's leading health care consulting firm. He lives in the Beach area of Toronto with his wife Lucille and children Geneviève and Riel.